"The Nose"
A Stylistic and Critical Companion to Nikolai Gogol's Story

Companions to Russian Literature

Series Editor
Thomas Seifrid (University of Southern California, Los Angeles)

"The Nose"

A Stylistic and Critical Companion to Nikolai Gogol's Story

....

KSANA BLANK

BOSTON
2021

Library of Congress Cataloging-in-Publication Data

Names: Blank, Ksana, author. | 880-01 Gogol', Nikolaĭ Vasil'evich, 1809-1852. Nos.
Title: "The Nose": a stylistic and critical companion to Nikolai Gogol's story / Ksana Blank.
Other titles: Companions to Russian literature.
Description: Boston: Academic Studies Press, 2021. | Series: Companions to Russian literature | Includes bibliographical references and index.
Identifiers: LCCN 2020049545 (print) | LCCN 2020049546 (ebook) | 9781644695197 (hardback) | 9781644695203 (paperback) | 9781644695210 (adobe PDF) | 9781644695227 (epub)
Subjects: LCSH: Gogol', Nikolaĭ Vasil'evich, 1809-1852. Nos. | Gogol', Nikolaĭ Vasil'evich, 1809-1852—Language. | Gogol', Nikolaĭ Vasil'evich, 1809-1852—Aesthetics.
Classification: LCC PG3332.N63 B53 2021 (print) | LCC PG3332.N63 (ebook) | DDC 891.73/3--dc23
LC record available at https://lccn.loc.gov/2020049545
LC ebook record available at https://lccn.loc.gov/2020049546

Copyright © 2021, Academic Studies Press
All rights reserved.

Illustrations to Gogol's "The Nose" by Julia Belomlinsky, 2018. Reproduced by the author's permission.

Cover design by Ivan Grave

Cover illustration by Julia Belomlinsky

Book design by Tatiana Vernikov

Published by Academic Studies Press
1577 Beacon Street
Brookline, MA 02446, USA

press@academicstudiespress.com
www.academicstudiespress.com

Contents

Note on Translation and Transliteration 6
Introduction 7

Part One. How "The Nose" Is Made

Н. В. Гоголь «Нос» 13
Annotations to the Russian Text 49
    I 51
    II 63
    III 82
Language Game as the Engine of the Plot 85

Part Two. Interpretations

1. Joke, Farce, Anecdote 112
2. Social Satire 125
3. Mockery of the Demonic and of the Sacred 133
4. Chronicle of Folk Superstitions 149
5. A Case of Castration Anxiety 161
6. An Echo of German Romanticism 168
7. Perfect Nonsense 179
8. Shostakovich's Opera *The Nose* 191
9. A Play with Reality: "The Nose," Kafka, and Dalí 207

Instead of a Conclusion 219
Selected Bibliography 220
Index 232
Acknowledgements 236

Note on Translation and Transliteration

Unless otherwise indicated, all translations from the Russian are mine. Russian names in the text are spelled in the form most familiar to English readers. For all other Russian words I have followed the Library of Congress transliteration system.

Introduction

A great number of books and scholarly articles have been devoted to Gogol's artistic language, but just a few of them are dedicated specifically to the language and style of Gogol's "The Nose"—the story about a collegiate assessor, Platon Kuzmich Kovalev, who awakes on the morning of March 25 to discover that his nose is missing.[1] The reason for this absence may very well be the story's uniqueness, as "The Nose" differs significantly from all other works by Gogol. Unlike many of them, it does not contain archaic bookish vocabulary or metaphors of early romanticism. In contrast with Gogol's Ukrainian short stories and his novel *Dead Souls*, there are very few litotes and hyperboles in the work, and it has no lyrical digressions. "The Nose" also differs from the stories of his Petersburg cycle.

For example, unlike "The Overcoat," with its protagonist's famous emotional complaint "Why do you insult me?," "The Nose" does not contain sentimental passages. In comparison with

---

[1] The most notable studies on Gogol's artistic language and style include I. E. Mandel'shtam, *O kharaktere gogolevskogo stilia: Glava iz istorii russkogo literaturnogo iazyka* (Gel'singfors: Novaia tip. Guvudstadsbladet, 1902). See also works by Viktor Vinogradov, such as *Gogol' i natural'naia shkola* (Leningrad: Obrazovanie, 1925) (English edition: V. V. Vinogradov, *Gogol and the Natural School*, trans. Debra K. Erickson and Ray Parrott, introd. by Debra K. Erikson [Ann Arbor, MI: Ardis, 1987]); "Etiudy o stile Gogolia," in *Poetika russkoi literatury: Izbrannye trudy* (Moscow: Nauka, 1976), 228–66; *K istorii leksiki russkogo literaturnogo iazyka*, ed. L. V. Shcherba (Leningrad: Academia, 1927), *Ocherki po istorii russkogo literaturnogo iazyka XVII–XIX vv.* (Moscow: Gos. uchebno-ped. izd-vo, 1934); "Iazyk Gogolia i ego znachenie v istorii russkogo iazyka," in *Iazyk i stil' russkikh pisatelei: Ot Gogolia do Akhmatovoi; Izbrannye trudy*, ed. A. P. Chudakov (Moscow: Nauka, 2003), 54–96. Another important work is Andrei Belyi, *Masterstvo Gogolia: Issledovanie*, foreword by L. Kamenev (Moscow: Gosudarstvennoe izdatel'stvo khudozhestvennoi literatury, 1934) (English edition: Andrei Bely, *Gogol's Artistry*, trans. and introd. by Christopher Colbath, foreword by Vyacheslav Ivanov [Evanston, IL.: Northwestern University Press, 2009]).

Introduction

"The Notes of a Madman," it has fewer expressions derived from bureaucratic jargon. In contrast with "Nevsky Prospect" and its famous claim about the city's main artery—"It lies all the time, this Nevsky Prospect, but most of all at the time when night heaves is dense mass upon it . . . when the whole city turns into a rumbling and brilliance, myriads of carriages tumble from the bridges . . . and the devil himself lights the lamps only so as to show everything not as it really looks"—there are no exaggerations in the description of the city in "The Nose."[2] In other words, the question of what constitutes the specific stylistic and lexical features of this story is still open.

In the annotations to the Russian text in the first part of this book, I intend to demonstrate that the originality of the story owes a great deal to Gogol's wordplay on idiomatic expressions, which are abundant in the work, specifically to the technique of "literalizing" Russian idioms. To be sure, the prime example of such literalization is Gogol's play with the idiom остаться с носом ("to be fooled"; lit. "to be left with a nose"); this idiom has been noted in Gogol studies on many occasions. In its inverted form it serves as the engine of the plot: the story of how Major Kovalev was left *without* his nose. The annotations demonstrate that there are dozens of other examples in Gogol challenging the stability of lexical components in set phrases. This device is used for a variety of purposes: to create a comical effect, a biting satire of Russian society, an ironic mode, and a sense of absurdity.

These twisted and turned idioms often remain unnoticeable to English readers. Walter Redfern, a renowned scholar of French literature, rightfully observes, "Idioms are the hardest part of a language for a foreigner to use or understand appositely. As their root suggests they are the most autarkic area of speech and writing. The segments that make them up frequently create something different as a totality."[3]

---

[2] Nikolai Gogol, "Nevsky Prospect," in *The Collected Tales of Nikolai Gogol*, trans. Richard Pevear and Larissa Volokhonsky (New York: Pantheon Books, 1998), 278.

[3] Walter Redfern, *Clichés and Coinages* (Oxford: Basil Blackwell, 1989), 126.

Introduction

The purpose of my annotations is to facilitate the reading of this little masterpiece. The annotations also focus on confusing stylistic details, oddly formed sentences, as well as many other obscure remarks the narrator makes in his witty banter with the reader. Gogol's descriptions of everyday life in St. Petersburg would have been familiar to his contemporaries and fellow citizens but are hidden from the modern reader, therefore they require commentaries as well. To make the use of annotations more convenient, the book opens with the Russian text of the story.[4]

In the section titled "How 'The Nose' is Made: Language Game as the Engine of the Plot," I state that the main protagonist of the story is the Russian language. There I also formulate the role and functions of Gogol's narrative manner and point out that Gogol's play on idiomatic expressions in "The Nose" creates a form of *skaz*—a type of narrative recounted by a person whose manner of speech is different from the style of the author. In other words, the development of the plot in "The Nose" is propelled by the narrator's masterful language game with the reader.

The second part of the book is devoted to the story's interpretations. In 1859, the literary critic Apollon Grigoryev, who referred to his own style of criticism as "organic" (in contrast with the socially oriented critics Vissarion Belinsky, Nikolai Chernyshevsky, and Nikolai Dobrolyubov), commented on "The Nose" with a subtle

---

[4] There are three editions of "The Nose"—the 1835 version sent to the *Moscow Observer*; the 1836 version published in Pushkin's *The Contemporary* (*Sovremennik*), and the 1842 version as part of Gogol's first collected works. Because of his censors' criticism, Gogol was forced to alter some details in the second and third versions. The second one is more concise than the first and has a different ending. The scene in Kazan Cathedral was criticized by censors, so Gogol replaced Kazan Cathedral with Gostiny Dvor (a vast department store in Saint Petersburg). Gogol also removed the suggestion that the "incredible incident" happened in the dream and added an ironic afterword, a parody of a review in the conservative newspaper *The Northern Bee*. In the third version, Gogol again revised and expanded the ending of the story, turning it into a third chapter. See N. L. Stepanov's commentary in N. Gogol', *Polnoe sobranie sochinenii*, 14 vols. (Moscow: Izdatel'stvo AN SSSR, 1937–1952), vol. 3, ed. N. L. Meshcheriakov, 649–60. The third version is now considered canonical.

warning against excessive interpretations of this story: "The most original and bizarre work, where everything is fantastic and at the same time everything is extremely poetic truth, where everything is clear without an explanation and where any explanation would kill poetry."[5] The next four decades were a period of silence, but at the turn of the twentieth century Gogol's work, including "The Nose," became the focus of attention for many Russian writers and critics, who approached it from different perspectives. In his essay "Gogol" (1909), Andrey Bely wrote, "I don't know who Gogol is: a realist, symbolist, romantic or classicist . . . . Gogol is a genius whom you cannot approach at all with a scholastic definition. I have a penchant for symbolism; consequently, it is easier for me to see the features of Gogol's symbolism; a romantic will see a romantic in him; a realist will see a realist."[6]

As short as it is, the story inspired scholars belonging to different branches of literary studies to search for very different motivations for the disappearance of the nose from Major Kovalev's face, and to view the story from sociological, formalist, psychoanalytic, folk, religious, intertextual, mythological, and philosophical perspectives. Scholars have debated the meaning of the story, some of them claiming that it has none. Funny, fantastic, and original, in the course of the past 185 years, "The Nose" has been approached from a great variety of perspectives; it was viewed as a mere joke and as a satire of Russian society; as Gogol's mystical insight and as an expression of his anticlerical feelings; as a case of castration anxiety and as pure nonsense.

The second part provides an overview of a broad spectrum of such perspectives and of a wide range of interpretations, which are often oppositional and contrasting, but not mutually exclusive. Despite Apollon Grigoryev's warning, the interpretations given by Gogol's first critics, the ideas voiced by the scholars in the twentieth

---

[5] Apollon Grigor'ev, *Literaturnaia kritika* (Moscow: Khudozhestvennaia literatura, 1967), 194.

[6] Andreiy Belyi, "Gogol'," in *Gogol' v russkoi kritike: Antologiia*, ed. S. G. Bocharov (Moscow: Fortuna, 2008), 268–69.

Introduction

century, as well as some more recent insightful studies published both in Russia and in the West, coexist and do not kill the poetic truth of "The Nose." Instead, they give evidence of its versatility.

Part One

How "The Nose" Is Made

Николай Гоголь

Нос

I

1. Марта 25 числа случилось в Петербурге необыкновенно странное происшествие. Цирюльник Иван Яковлевич, живущий на Вознесенском проспекте (фамилия его утрачена, и даже на вывеске его — где изображен господин с намыленною щекою и надписью: «И кровь отворяют» — не выставлено ничего более), цирюльник Иван Яковлевич проснулся довольно рано и услышал запах горячего хлеба. Приподнявшись немного на кровати, он увидел, что супруга его, довольно почтенная дама, очень любившая пить кофий, вынимала из печи только что испеченные хлебы.

2. — Сегодня я, Прасковья Осиповна, не буду пить кофию, — сказал Иван Яковлевич, — а вместо того хочется мне съесть горячего хлебца с луком.

3. (То есть Иван Яковлевич хотел бы и того и другого, но знал, что было совершенно невозможно требовать двух вещей разом, ибо Прасковья Осиповна очень не любила таких прихотей.) «Пусть дурак ест хлеб; мне же лучше, — подумала про себя супруга, — останется кофию лишняя порция». И бросила один хлеб на стол.

4. Иван Яковлевич для приличия надел сверх рубашки фрак и, усевшись перед столом, насыпал соль, приготовил две головки луку, взял в руки нож и, сделавши значительную мину, принялся резать хлеб. Разрезавши хлеб на две половины, он поглядел в середину и, к удивлению своему, увидел что-то белевшееся. Иван Яковлевич ковырнул осторожно ножом и пощупал пальцем. «Плотное! — сказал он сам про себя, — что бы это такое было?»

5   Он засунул пальцы и вытащил — нос!.. Иван Яковлевич и руки опустил; стал протирать глаза и щупать: нос, точно нос! и еще, казалось, как будто чей-то знакомый. Ужас изобразился в лице Ивана Яковлевича. Но этот ужас был ничто против негодования, которое овладело его супругою.

6   — Где это ты, зверь, отрезал нос? — закричала она с гневом. — Мошенник! пьяница! Я сама на тебя донесу полиции. Разбойник какой! Вот уж я от трех человек слышала, что ты во время бритья так теребишь за носы, что еле держатся.

7   Но Иван Яковлевич был ни жив ни мертв. Он узнал, что этот нос был не чей другой, как коллежского асессора Ковалева, которого он брил каждую середу и воскресенье.

8   — Стой, Прасковья Осиповна! Я положу его, завернувши в тряпку, в уголок; пусть там маленечко полежит, а после его вынесу.

9   — И слушать не хочу! Чтобы я позволила у себя в комнате лежать отрезанному носу?.. Сухарь поджаристый! Знай умеет только бритвой возить по ремню, а долга своего скоро совсем не в состоянии будет исполнять, потаскушка, негодяй! Чтобы я стала за тебя отвечать полиции?.. Ах ты, пачкун, бревно глупое! Вон его! вон! неси куда хочешь! чтобы я духу его не слыхала!

10 Иван Яковлевич стоял совершенно как убитый. Он думал, думал — и не знал, что подумать.

11 — Черт его знает, как это сделалось, — сказал он наконец, почесав рукою за ухом. — Пьян ли я вчера возвратился или нет, уж наверное сказать не могу. А по всем приметам должно быть происшествие

несбыточное: ибо хлеб — дело печеное, а нос совсем не то. Ничего не разберу!..

12 Иван Яковлевич замолчал. Мысль о том, что полицейские отыщут у него нос и обвинят его, привела его в совершенное беспамятство. Уже ему мерещился алый воротник, красиво вышитый серебром, шпага... и он дрожал всем телом. Наконец достал он свое исподнее платье и сапоги, натащил на себя всю эту дрянь и, сопровождаемый нелегкими увещаниями Прасковьи Осиповны, завернул нос в тряпку и вышел на улицу.

13 Он хотел его куда-нибудь подсунуть: или в тумбу под воротами, или так как-нибудь нечаянно выронить, да и повернуть в переулок. Но, на беду, ему попадался какой-нибудь знакомый человек, который начинал тотчас запросом: «Куда идешь?», или: «Кого так рано собрался брить?» — так что Иван Яковлевич никак не мог улучить минуты. В другой раз он уже совсем уронил его, но будочник еще издали указал ему алебардою, примолвив: «Подыми! вон ты что-то уронил!» И Иван Яковлевич должен был поднять нос и спрятать его в карман. Отчаяние овладело им, тем более что народ беспрестанно умножался на улице, по мере того так начали отпираться магазины и лавочки.

14 Он решился идти к Исакиевскому мосту: не удастся ли как-нибудь швырнуть его в Неву?.. Но я несколько виноват, что до сих пор не сказал ничего об Иване Яковлевиче, человеке почтенном во многих отношениях.

15 Иван Яковлевич, как всякий порядочный русский мастеровой, был пьяница страшный. И хотя каждый день брил чужие подбородки, но его собственный был

у него вечно небрит. Фрак у Ивана Яковлевича (Иван Яковлевич никогда не ходил в сюртуке) был пегий; то есть он был черный, но весь в коричнево-желтых и серых яблоках; воротник лоснился, а вместо трех пуговиц висели одни только ниточки. Иван Яковлевич был большой циник, и когда коллежский асессор Ковалев обыкновенно говорил ему во время бритья: «У тебя, Иван Яковлевич, вечно воняют руки!» — то Иван Яковлевич отвечал на это вопросом: «Отчего ж бы им вонять?» — «Не знаю, братец, только воняют», — говорил коллежский асессор, и Иван Яковлевич, понюхавши табаку, мылил ему за это и на щеке, и под носом, и за ухом, и под бородою — одним словом, где только ему была охота.

Этот почтенный гражданин находился уже на Исакиевском мосту. Он прежде всего осмотрелся; потом нагнулся на перила, будто бы посмотреть под мост: много ли рыбы бегает, и швырнул потихоньку тряпку с носом. Он почувствовал, как будто бы с него разом свалилось десять пуд; Иван Яковлевич даже усмехнулся. Вместо того чтобы идти брить чиновничьи подбородки, он отправился в заведение с надписью «Кушанье и чай» спросить стакан пуншу, как вдруг заметил в конце моста квартального надзирателя благородной наружности, с широкими бакенбардами, в треугольной шляпе, со шпагою. Он обмер; а между тем квартальный кивал ему пальцем и говорил:

— А подойди сюда, любезный!

Иван Яковлевич, зная форму, снял издали еще картуз и, подошедши проворно, сказал:

— Желаю здравия вашему благородию!

20 — Нет, нет, братец, не благородию; скажи-ка, что ты там делал, стоя на мосту?

21 — Ей-Богу, сударь, ходил брить, да посмотрел только, шибко ли река идет.

22 — Врешь, врешь! Этим не отделаешься. Изволь-ка отвечать!

23 — Я вашу милость два раза в неделю, или даже три, готов брить без всякого прекословия, — отвечал Иван Яковлевич.

24 — Нет, приятель, это пустяки! Меня три цирюльника бреют, да еще и за большую честь почитают. А вот изволь-ка рассказать, что ты там делал?

25 Иван Яковлевич побледнел... Но здесь происшествие совершенно закрывается туманом, и что далее произошло, решительно ничего не известно.

II

26 Коллежский асессор Ковалев проснулся довольно рано и сделал губами: «брр...» — что всегда он делал, когда просыпался, хотя сам не мог растолковать, по какой причине. Ковалев потянулся, приказал себе подать небольшое стоявшее на столе зеркало. Он хотел взглянуть на прыщик, который вчерашнего вечера вскочил у него на носу; но, к величайшему изумлению, увидел, что у него вместо носа совершенно гладкое место! Испугавшись, Ковалев велел подать воды и протер полотенцем глаза: точно, нет носа! Он начал щупать рукою, чтобы узнать: не спит ли он? кажется, не спит. Коллежский асессор Ковалев вскочил с кровати, встряхнулся: нет носа!.. Он велел тотчас подать себе одеться и полетел прямо к обер-полицмейстеру.

27 Но между тем необходимо сказать что-нибудь о Ковалеве, чтобы читатель мог видеть, какого рода был этот коллежский асессор. Коллежских асессоров, которые получают это звание с помощью ученых аттестатов, никак нельзя сравнивать с теми коллежскими асессорами, которые делались на Кавказе. Это два совершенно особенные рода. Ученые коллежские асессоры... Но Россия такая чудная земля, что если скажешь об одном коллежском асессоре, то все коллежские асессоры, от Риги до Камчатки, непременно примут на свой счет. То же разумей и о всех званиях и чинах. Ковалев был кавказский коллежский асессор. Он два года только еще состоял в этом звании и потому ни на минуту не мог его позабыть; а чтобы более придать себе благородства и веса, он никогда не называл себя коллежским асессором, но всегда майором. «Послушай, голубушка, — говорил он обыкновенно, встретивши на улице бабу, продававшую манишки, — ты приходи ко мне на дом; квартира моя в Садовой; спроси только: здесь ли живет майор Ковалев? — тебе всякий покажет». Если же встречал какую-нибудь смазливенькую, то давал ей сверх того секретное приказание, прибавляя: «Ты спроси, душенька, квартиру майора Ковалева». По этому-то самому и мы будем вперед этого коллежского асессора называть майором.

28 Майор Ковалев имел обыкновение каждый день прохаживаться по Невскому проспекту. Воротничок его манишки был всегда чрезвычайно чист и накрахмален. Бакенбарды у него были такого рода, какие и теперь еще можно видеть у губернских и уездных землемеров, у архитекторов и полковых докторов,

также у отправляющих разные полицейские обязанности и вообще у всех тех мужей, которые имеют полные, румяные щеки и очень хорошо играют в бостон: эти бакенбарды идут по самой средине щеки и прямехонько доходят до носа. Майор Ковалев носил множество печаток сердоликовых и с гербами, и таких, на которых было вырезано: середа, четверг, понедельник и проч. Майор Ковалев приехал в Петербург по надобности, а именно искать приличного своему званию места: если удастся, то вице-губернаторского, а не то — экзекуторского в каком-нибудь видном департаменте. Майор Ковалев был не прочь и жениться, но только в таком случае, когда за невестою случится двести тысяч капиталу. И потому читатель теперь может судить сам, каково было положение этого майора, когда он увидел вместо довольно недурного и умеренного носа преглупое, ровное и гладкое место.

Как на беду, ни один извозчик не показывался на улице, и он должен был идти пешком, закутавшись в свой плащ и закрывши платком лицо, показывая вид, как будто у него шла кровь. «Но авось-либо мне так представилось: не может быть, чтобы нос пропал сдуру», — подумал он и зашел в кондитерскую нарочно с тем, чтобы посмотреться в зеркало. К счастию, в кондитерской никого не было; мальчишки мели комнаты и расставляли стулья; некоторые с сонными глазами выносили на подносах горячие пирожки; на столах и стульях валялись залитые кофеем вчерашние газеты. «Ну, слава Богу, никого нет, — произнес он, — теперь можно поглядеть». Он робко подошел к зеркалу и взглянул. «Черт знает что, какая дрянь! — произнес он, плюнувши. — Хотя бы уже что-нибудь было вместо носа, а то ничего!..»

30 С досадою закусив губы, вышел он из кондитерской и решился, против своего обыкновения, не глядеть ни на кого и никому не улыбаться. Вдруг он стал как вкопанный у дверей одного дома; в глазах его произошло явление неизъяснимое: перед подъездом остановилась карета; дверцы отворились; выпрыгнул, согнувшись, господин в мундире и побежал вверх по лестнице. Каков же был ужас и вместе изумление Ковалева, когда он узнал, что это был собственный его нос! При этом необыкновенном зрелище, казалось ему, все переворотилось у него в глазах; он чувствовал, что едва мог стоять; но решился во что бы то ни стало ожидать его возвращения в карету, весь дрожа, как в лихорадке. Чрез две минуты нос действительно вышел. Он был в мундире, шитом золотом, с большим стоячим воротником; на нем были замшевые панталоны; при боку шпага. По шляпе с плюмажем можно было заключить, что он считался в ранге статского советника. По всему заметно было, что он ехал куда-нибудь с визитом. Он поглядел на обе стороны, закричал кучеру: «Подавай!» — сел и уехал.

31 Бедный Ковалев чуть не сошел с ума. Он не знал, как и подумать о таком странном происшествии. Как же можно, в самом деле, чтобы нос, который еще вчера был у него на лице, не мог ездить и ходить, — был в мундире! Он побежал за каретою, которая, к счастию, проехала недалеко и остановилась перед Казанским собором.

32 Он поспешил в собор, пробрался сквозь ряд нищих старух с завязанными лицами и двумя отверстиями для

глаз, над которыми он прежде так смеялся, и вошел в церковь. Молельщиков внутри церкви было немного; они все стояли только при входе в двери. Ковалев чувствовал себя в таком расстроенном состоянии, что никак не в силах был молиться, и искал глазами этого господина по всем углам. Наконец увидел его стоявшего в стороне. Нос спрятал совершенно лицо свое в большой стоячий воротник и с выражением величайшей набожности молился.

33 «Как подойти к нему? – думал Ковалев. – По всему, по мундиру, по шляпе видно, что он статский советник. Черт его знает, как это сделать!»

34 Он начал около него покашливать; но нос ни на минуту не оставлял набожного своего положения и отвешивал поклоны.

35 — Милостивый государь... — сказал Ковалев, внутренно принуждая себя ободриться, — милостивый государь...

36 — Что вам угодно? — отвечал нос, оборотившись.

37 — Мне странно, милостивый государь... мне кажется... вы должны знать свое место. И вдруг я вас нахожу, и где же? — в церкви. Согласитесь...

38 — Извините меня, я не могу взять в толк, о чем вы изволите говорить... Объяснитесь...

39 «Как мне ему объяснить?» — подумал Ковалев и, собравшись с духом, начал:

40 — Конечно, я... впрочем, я майор. Мне ходить без носа, согласитесь, это неприлично. Какой-нибудь торговке, которая продает на Воскресенском мосту очищенные апельсины, можно сидеть без носа; но, имея в виду получить... притом будучи во многих домах знаком с дамами: Чехтарева, статская советница, и другие...

Вы посудите сами... я не знаю, милостивый государь. (При этом майор Ковалев пожал плечами.) Извините... если на это смотреть сообразно с правилами долга и чести... вы сами можете понять...

41 — Ничего решительно не понимаю, — отвечал нос. — Изъяснитесь удовлетворительнее.

42 — Милостивый государь... — сказал Ковалев с чувством собственного достоинства, — я не знаю, как понимать слова ваши... Здесь все дело, кажется, совершенно очевидно... Или вы хотите... Ведь вы мой собственный нос!

43 Нос посмотрел на майора, и брови его несколько нахмурились.

44 — Вы ошибаетесь, милостивый государь. Я сам по себе. Притом между нами не может быть никаких тесных отношений. Судя по пуговицам вашего вицмундира, вы должны служить по другому ведомству.

45 Сказавши это, нос отвернулся и продолжал молиться.

46 Ковалев совершенно смешался, не зная, что делать и что даже подумать. В это время послышался приятный шум дамского платья; подошла пожилая дама, вся убранная кружевами, и с нею тоненькая, в белом платье, очень мило рисовавшемся на ее стройной талии, в палевой шляпке, легкой, как пирожное. За ними остановился и открыл табакерку высокий гайдук с большими бакенбардами и целой дюжиной воротников.

47 Ковалев подступил поближе, высунул батистовый воротничок манишки, поправил висевшие на золотой цепочке свои печатки и, улыбаясь по сторонам, обратил внимание на легонькую даму, которая, как весенний

цветочек, слегка наклонялась и подносила ко лбу свою беленькую ручку с полупрозрачными пальцами. Улыбка на лице Ковалева раздвинулась еще далее, когда он увидел из-под шляпки ее кругленький, яркой белизны подбородок и часть щеки, осененной цветом первой весенней розы. Но вдруг он отскочил, как будто бы обжегшись. Он вспомнил, что у него вместо носа совершенно нет ничего, и слезы выдавились из глаз его. Он оборотился с тем, чтобы напрямик сказать господину в мундире, что он только прикинулся статским советником, что он плут и подлец и что он больше ничего, как только его собственный нос... Но носа уже не было; он успел ускакать, вероятно опять к кому-нибудь с визитом.

Это повергло Ковалева в отчаяние. Он пошел назад и остановился с минуту под колоннадою, тщательно смотря во все стороны, не попадется ли где нос. Он очень хорошо помнил, что шляпа на нем была с плюмажем и мундир с золотым шитьем; но шинель не заметил, ни цвета его кареты, ни лошадей, ни даже того, был ли у него сзади какой-нибудь лакей и в какой ливрее. Притом карет неслось такое множество взад и вперед и с такою быстротою, что трудно было даже приметить; но если бы и приметил он какую-нибудь из них, то не имел бы никаких средств остановить. День был прекрасный и солнечный. На Невском народу была тьма; дам целый цветочный водопад сыпался по всему тротуару, начиная от Полицейского до Аничкина моста. Вон и знакомый ему надворный советник идет, которого он называл подполковником, особливо ежели то случалось при посторонних. Вон и Ярыгин, столоначальник в сенате, большой приятель, который вечно в бостоне обремизивался, когда играл восемь. Вон и другой майор, получивший на Кавказе асессорство, махает рукой, чтобы шел к нему...

49 — А, черт возьми! — сказал Ковалев. — Эй, извозчик, вези прямо к обер-полицмейстеру!

50 Ковалев сел в дрожки и только покрикивал извозчику: «Валяй во всю ивановскую!»

51 — У себя обер-полицмейстер? — вскричал он, зашедши в сени.

52 — Никак нет, — отвечал привратник, — только что уехал.

53 — Вот тебе раз!

54 — Да, — прибавил привратник, — оно и не так давно, но уехал. Минуточкой бы пришли раньше, то, может, застали бы дома.

55 Ковалев, не отнимая платка от лица, сел на извозчика и закричал отчаянным голосом:

56 — Пошел!

57 — Куда? — сказал извозчик.

58 — Пошел прямо!

59 — Как прямо? тут поворот: направо или налево?

60 Этот вопрос остановил Ковалева и заставил его опять подумать. В его положении следовало ему прежде всего отнестись в Управу благочиния, не потому, что оно имело прямое отношение к полиции, но потому, что ее распоряжения могли быть гораздо быстрее, чем в других местах; искать же удовлетворения по начальству того места, при котором нос объявил себя служащим, было бы безрассудно, потому что из собственных ответов носа уже можно было видеть, что для этого человека ничего не было священного и он мог так же солгать и в этом случае, как солгал, уверяя,

что он никогда не видался с ним. Итак, Ковалев уже хотел было приказать ехать в Управу благочиния, как опять пришла мысль ему, что этот плут и мошенник, который поступил уже при первой встрече таким бессовестным образом, мог опять удобно, пользуясь временем, как-нибудь улизнуть из города, — и тогда все искания будут тщетны или могут продолжиться, чего Боже сохрани, на целый месяц. Наконец, казалось, само Небо вразумило его. Он решился отнестись прямо в газетную экспедицию и заблаговременно сделать публикацию с обстоятельным описанием всех качеств, дабы всякий, встретивший его, мог в ту же минуту его представить к нему или, по крайней мере, дать знать о месте пребывания. Итак, он, решив на этом, велел извозчику ехать в газетную экспедицию и во всю дорогу не переставал его тузить кулаком в спину, приговаривая: «Скорей, подлец! скорей, мошенник!» — «Эх, барин!» — говорил извозчик, потряхивая головой и стегая вожжой свою лошадь, на которой шерсть была длинная, как на болонке. Дрожки наконец остановились, и Ковалев, запыхавшись, вбежал в небольшую приемную комнату, где седой чиновник, в старом фраке и очках, сидел за столом и, взявши в зубы перо, считал принесенные медные деньги.

61 — Кто здесь принимает объявления? — закричал Ковалев. — А, здравствуйте!

62 — Мое почтение, — сказал седой чиновник, поднявши на минуту глаза и опустивши их снова на разложенные кучи денег.

63 — Я желаю припечатать...

64 — Позвольте. Прошу немножко повременить, — произнес чиновник, ставя одною рукою цифру на

бумаге и передвигая пальцами левой руки два очка на счетах.

65 Лакей с галунами и наружностию, показывавшею пребывание его в аристократическом доме, стоял возле стола, с запискою в руках, и почел приличным показать свою общежительность:

66 — Поверите ли, сударь, что собачонка не стоит восьми гривен, то есть я не дал бы за нее и восьми грошей; а графиня любит, ей-Богу, любит, — и вот тому, кто ее отыщет, сто рублей! Если сказать по приличию, то вот так, как мы теперь с вами, вкусы людей совсем не совместны: уж когда охотник, то держи легавую собаку или пуделя; не пожалей пятисот, тысячу дай, но зато уж чтоб была собака хорошая.

67 Почтенный чиновник слушал это с значительною миною и в то же время занимался сметою: сколько букв в принесенной записке. По сторонам стояло множество старух, купеческих сидельцев и дворников с записками. В одной значилось, что отпускается в услужение кучер трезвого поведения; в другой — малоподержанная коляска, вывезенная в 1814 году из Парижа; там отпускалась дворовая девка девятнадцати лет, упражнявшаяся в прачечном деле, годная и для других работ; прочные дрожки без одной рессоры; молодая горячая лошадь в серых яблоках, семнадцати лет от роду; новые, полученные из Лондона, семена репы и редиса; дача со всеми угодьями: двумя стойлами для лошадей и местом, на котором можно развести превосходный березовый или еловый сад; там же находился вызов желающих купить старые подошвы, с приглашением явиться к переторжке каждый день от восьми до трех часов утра. Комната, в которой

местилось все это общество, была маленькая, и воздух в ней был чрезвычайно густ; но коллежский асессор Ковалев не мог слышать запаха, потому что закрылся платком и потому что самый нос его находился Бог знает в каких местах.

68 — Милостивый государь, позвольте вас попросить... Мне очень нужно, — сказал он наконец с нетерпением.

69 — Сейчас, сейчас! Два рубля сорок три копейки! Сию минуту! Рубль шестьдесят четыре копейки! — говорил седовласый господин, бросая старухам и дворникам записки в глаза. — Вам что угодно? — наконец сказал он, обратившись к Ковалеву.

70 — Я прошу... — сказал Ковалев, — случилось мошенничество или плутовство, я до сих пор не могу никак узнать. Я прошу только припечатать, что тот, кто ко мне этого подлеца представит, получит достаточное вознаграждение.

71 — Позвольте узнать, как ваша фамилия?

72 — Нет, зачем же фамилию? Мне нельзя сказать ее. У меня много знакомых: Чехтарева, статская советница, Палагея Григорьевна Подточина, штаб-офицерша... Вдруг узнают, Боже сохрани! Вы можете просто написать: коллежский асессор, или, еще лучше, состоящий в майорском чине.

73 — А сбежавший был ваш дворовый человек?

74 — Какое дворовый человек? Это бы еще не такое большое мошенничество! Сбежал от меня... нос...

75 — Гм! какая странная фамилия! И на большую сумму этот господин Носов обокрал вас?

76 — Нос то есть... вы не то думаете! Нос, мой собственный нос пропал неизвестно куда. Черт хотел подшутить надо мною!

77 — Да каким же образом пропал? Я что-то не могу хорошенько понять.

78 — Да я не могу вам сказать, каким образом; но главное то, что он разъезжает теперь по городу и называет себя статским советником. И потому я вас прошу объявить, чтобы поймавший представил его немедленно ко мне в самом скорейшем времени. Вы посудите, в самом деле, как же мне быть без такой заметной части тела? Это не то, что какой-нибудь мизинный палец на ноге, которую я в сапог — и никто не увидит, если его нет. Я бываю по четвергам у статской советницы Чехтаревой; Подточина Палагея Григорьевна, штаб-офицерша, и у ней дочка очень хорошенькая, тоже очень хорошие знакомые, и вы посудите сами, как же мне теперь... Мне теперь к ним нельзя явиться.

79 Чиновник задумался, что означали крепко сжавшиеся его губы.

80 — Нет, я не могу поместить такого объявления в газетах, — сказал он наконец после долгого молчания.

81 — Как? отчего?

82 — Так. Газета может потерять репутацию. Если всякий начнет писать, что у него сбежал нос, то... И так уже говорят, что печатается много несообразностей и ложных слухов.

83 — Да чем же это дело несообразное? Тут, кажется, ничего нет такого.

84 — Это вам так кажется, что нет. А вот на прошлой неделе такой же был случай. Пришел чиновник таким же образом, как вы теперь пришли, принес записку, денег по расчету пришлось два рубля семьдесят три копейки, и все объявление состояло в том, что сбежал пудель черной шерсти. Кажется, что бы тут такое?

А вышел пасквиль: пудель-то этот был казначей, не помню какого-то заведения.

85 — Да ведь я вам не о пуделе делаю объявление, а о собственном моем носе: стало быть, почти то же, что о самом себе.

86 — Нет, такого объявления я никак не могу поместить.

87 — Да когда у меня точно пропал нос!

88 — Если пропал, то это дело медика. Говорят, что есть такие люди, которые могут приставить какой угодно нос. Но, впрочем, я замечаю, что вы должны быть человек веселого нрава и любите в обществе пошутить.

89 — Клянусь вам, вот как Бог свят! Пожалуй, уж если до того дошло, то я покажу вам.

90 — Зачем беспокоиться! — продолжал чиновник, нюхая табак. — Впрочем, если не в беспокойство, — прибавил он с движением любопытства, — то желательно бы взглянуть.

91 Коллежский асессор отнял от лица платок.

92 — В самом деле, чрезвычайно странно! — сказал чиновник, — место совершенно гладкое, как будто бы только что выпеченный блин. Да, до невероятности ровное!

93 — Ну, вы и теперь будете спорить? Вы видите сами, что нельзя не напечатать. Я вам буду особенно благодарен; и очень рад, что этот случай доставил мне удовольствие с вами познакомиться...

94 Майор, как видно из этого, решился на сей раз немного поподличать.

95 — Напечатать-то, конечно, дело небольшое, — сказал чиновник, — только я не предвижу в этом никакой для

вас выгоды. Если уже хотите, то отдайте тому, кто имеет искусное перо, описать это как редкое произведение натуры и напечатать эту статейку в «Северной пчеле» (тут он понюхал еще раз табаку) для пользы юношества (тут он утер нос) или так, для общего любопытства.

96 Коллежский асессор был совершенно обеznадежен. Он опустил глаза в низ газеты, где было извещение о спектаклях; уже лицо его было готово улыбнуться, встретив имя актрисы, хорошенькой собою, и рука взялась за карман: есть ли при нем синяя ассигнация, потому что штаб-офицеры, по мнению Ковалева, должны сидеть в креслах, — но мысль о носе все испортила!

97 Сам чиновник, казалось, был тронут затруднительным положением Ковалева. Желая сколько-нибудь облегчить его горесть, он почел приличным выразить участие свое в нескольких словах:

98 — Мне, право, очень прискорбно, что с вами случился такой анекдот. Не угодно ли вам понюхать табачку? это разбивает головные боли и печальные расположения; даже в отношении к геморроидам это хорошо.

99 Говоря это, чиновник поднес Ковалеву табакерку, довольно ловко повернув под нее крышку с портретом какой-то дамы в шляпке.

100 Этот неумышленный поступок вывел из терпения Ковалева.

101 — Я не понимаю, как вы находите место шуткам, — сказал он с сердцем, — разве вы не видите, что у меня именно нет того, чем бы я мог понюхать? Чтоб черт

побрал ваш табак! Я теперь не могу смотреть на него, и не только на скверный ваш березинский, но хоть бы вы поднесли мне самого рапе.

102 Сказавши это, он вышел, глубоко раздосадованный, из газетной экспедиции и отправился к частному приставу, чрезвычайному охотнику до сахару. На дому его вся передняя, она же и столовая, была установлена сахарными головами, которые нанесли к нему из дружбы купцы. Кухарка в это время скидала с частного пристава казенные ботфорты; шпага и все военные доспехи уже мирно развесились по углам, и грозную треугольную шляпу уже затрогивал трехлетний сынок его; и он, после боевой, бранной жизни готовился вкусить удовольствия мира.

103 Ковалев вошел к нему в то время, когда он потянулся, крякнул и сказал: «Эх, славно засну два часика!» И потому можно было предвидеть, что приход коллежского асессора был совершенно не вовремя; и не знаю, хотя бы он даже принес ему в то время несколько фунтов чаю или сукна, он бы не был принят слишком радушно. Частный был большой поощритель всех искусств и мануфактурностей, но государственную ассигнацию предпочитал всему. «Это вещь, — обыкновенно говорил он, — уж нет ничего лучше этой вещи: есть не просит, места займет немного, в кармане всегда поместится, уронишь — не расшибется».

104 Частный принял довольно сухо Ковалева и сказал, что после обеда не то время, чтобы производить следствие, что сама натура назначила, чтобы, наевшись, немного отдохнуть (из этого коллежский асессор мог видеть, что частному приставу были

небезызвестны изречения древних мудрецов), что у порядочного человека не оторвут носа и что много есть на свете всяких майоров, которые не имеют даже и исподнего в приличном состоянии и таскаются по всяким непристойным местам.

105 То есть не в бровь, а прямо в глаз! Нужно заметить, что Ковалев был чрезвычайно обидчивый человек. Он мог простить все, что ни говорили о нем самом, но никак не извинял, если это относилось к чину или званию. Он даже полагал, что в театральных пьесах можно пропускать все, что относится к обер-офицерам, но на штаб-офицеров никак не должно нападать. Прием частного так его сконфузил, что он тряхнул головою и сказал с чувством достоинства, немного расставив свои руки: «Признаюсь, после этаких обидных с вашей стороны замечаний я ничего не могу прибавить...» — и вышел.

106 Он приехал домой, едва слыша под собою ноги. Были уже сумерки. Печальною или чрезвычайно гадкою показалась ему квартира после всех этих неудачных исканий. Взошедши в переднюю, увидел он на кожаном запачканном диване лакея своего Ивана, который, лежа на спине, плевал в потолок и попадал довольно удачно в одно и то же место. Такое равнодушие человека взбесило его; он ударил его шляпою по лбу, примолвив: «Ты, свинья, всегда глупостями занимаешься!»

107 Иван вскочил вдруг с своего места и бросился со всех ног снимать с него плащ.

108 Вошедший в свою комнату, майор, усталый и печальный, бросился в кресла и наконец после нескольких вздохов сказал:

109 — Боже мой! Боже мой! За что это такое несчастие? Будь я без руки или без ноги — все бы это лучше; будь я без ушей — скверно, однако ж все сноснее; но без носа человек — черт знает что: птица не птица, гражданин не гражданин, — просто возьми да и вышвырни за окошко! И пусть бы уже на войне отрубили или на дуэли, или я сам был причиною; но ведь пропал ни за что ни про что, пропал даром, ни за грош!.. Только нет, не может быть, — прибавил он, немного подумав. — Невероятно, чтобы нос пропал; никаким образом невероятно. Это, верно, или во сне снится, или просто грезится; может быть, я как-нибудь ошибкою выпил вместо воды водку, которою вытираю после бритья себе бороду. Иван, дурак, не принял, и я, верно, хватил ее.

110 Чтобы действительно увериться, что он не пьян, майор ущипнул себя так больно, что сам вскрикнул. Эта боль совершенно уверила его, что он действует и живет наяву. Он потихоньку приблизился к зеркалу и сначала зажмурил глаза с тою мыслию, что авось-либо нос покажется на своем месте; но в ту же минуту отскочил назад, сказавши:

111 — Экой пасквильный вид!

112 Это было, точно, непонятно. Если бы пропала пуговица, серебряная ложка, часы или что-нибудь подобное; но пропасть, и кому же пропасть? и притом еще на собственной квартире!.. Майор Ковалев, сообразя все обстоятельства, предполагал едва ли не ближе всего к истине, что виною этого должен быть не кто другой, как штаб-офицерша Подточина, которая желала, чтобы он женился на ее дочери. Он и сам любил за нею приволокнуться, но избегал

окончательной разделки. Когда же штаб-офицерша объявила ему напрямик, что она хочет выдать ее за него, он потихоньку отчалил с своими комплиментами, сказавши, что еще молод, что нужно ему прослужить лет пяток, чтобы уже ровно было сорок два года. И потому штаб-офицерша, верно из мщения, решилась его испортить и наняла для этого каких-нибудь колдовок-баб, потому что никаким образом нельзя было предположить, чтобы нос был отрезан: никто не входил к нему в комнату; цирюльник же Иван Яковлевич брил его еще в среду, а в продолжение всей среды и даже во весь четверток нос у него был цел — это он помнил и знал очень хорошо; притом была бы им чувствуема боль, и, без сомнения, рана не могла бы так скоро зажить и быть гладкою, как блин. Он строил в голове планы: звать ли штаб-офицершу формальным порядком в суд или явиться к ней самому и уличить ее. Размышления его прерваны были светом, блеснувшим сквозь все скважины дверей, который дал знать, что свеча в передней уже зажжена Иваном. Скоро показался и сам Иван, неся ее перед собою и озаряя ярко всю комнату. Первым движением Ковалева было схватить платок и закрыть то место, где вчера еще был нос, чтобы в самом деле глупый человек не зазевался, увидя у барина такую странность.

113   Не успел Иван уйти в конуру свою, как послышался в передней незнакомый голос, произнесший:

114   — Здесь ли живет коллежский асессор Ковалев?

115   — Войдите. Майор Ковалев здесь, — сказал Ковалев, вскочивши поспешно и отворяя дверь.

116   Вошел полицейский чиновник красивой наружности, с бакенбардами не слишком светлыми

и не темными, с довольно полными щеками, тот самый, который в начале повести стоял в конце Исакиевского моста.

117 — Вы изволили затерять нос свой?

118 — Так точно.

119 — Он теперь найден.

120 — Что вы говорите? — закричал майор Ковалев. Радость отняла у него язык. Он глядел в оба на стоявшего перед ним квартального, на полных губах и щеках которого ярко мелькал трепетный свет свечи. — Каким образом?

121 — Странным случаем: его перехватили почти на дороге. Он уже садился в дилижанс и хотел уехать в Ригу. И пашпорт давно был написан на имя одного чиновника. И странно то, что я сам принял его сначала за господина. Но, к счастию, были со мной очки, и я тот же час увидел, что это был нос. Ведь я близорук, и если вы станете передо мною, то я вижу только, что у вас лицо, но ни носа, ни бороды, ничего не замечу. Моя теща, то есть мать жены моей, тоже ничего не видит.

122 Ковалев был вне себя.

123 — Где же он? Где? Я сейчас побегу.

124 — Не беспокойтесь. Я, зная, что он вам нужен, принес его с собою. И странно то, что главный участник в этом деле есть мошенник цирюльник на Вознесенской улице, который сидит теперь на съезжей. Я давно подозревал его в пьянстве и воровстве, и еще третьего дня стащил он в одной лавочке бортище пуговиц. Нос ваш совершенно таков, как был.

125 При этом квартальный полез в карман и вытащил оттуда завернутый в бумажке нос.

126 — Так, он! — закричал Ковалев. — Точно, он! Выкушайте сегодня со мною чашечку чаю.

127 — Почел бы за большую приятность, но никак не могу: мне нужно заехать отсюда в смирительный дом... Очень большая поднялась дороговизна на все припасы... У меня в доме живет и теща, то есть мать моей жены, и дети; старший особенно подает большие надежды: очень умный мальчишка, но средств для воспитания совершенно нет никаких...

128 Ковалев догадался и, схватив со стола красную ассигнацию, сунул в руки надзирателю, который, расшаркавшись, вышел за дверь, и в ту же почти минуту Ковалев слышал уже голос его на улице, где он увещевал по зубам одного глупого мужика, наехавшего с своею телегою как раз на бульвар.

129 Коллежский асессор по уходе квартального несколько минут оставался в каком-то неопределенном состоянии и едва через несколько минут пришел в возможность видеть и чувствовать: в такое беспамятство повергла его неожиданная радость. Он взял бережливо найденный нос в обе руки, сложенные горстью, и еще раз рассмотрел его внимательно.

130 — Так, он, точно он! — говорил майор Ковалев. — Вот и прыщик на левой стороне, вскочивший вчерашнего дня.

131 Майор чуть не засмеялся от радости.

132 Но на свете нет ничего долговременного, а потому и радость в следующую минуту за первою уже не так жива; в третью минуту она становится еще слабее и наконец незаметно сливается с обыкновенным положением души, как на воде круг, рожденный падением камешка, наконец сливается с гладкою

поверхностью. Ковалев начал размышлять и смекнул, что дело еще не кончено: нос найден, но ведь нужно же его приставить, поместить на свое место.

133 — А что, если он не пристанет?

134 При таком вопросе, сделанном самому себе, майор побледнел.

135 С чувством неизъяснимого страха бросился он к столу, придвинул зеркало, чтобы как-нибудь не поставить нос криво. Руки его дрожали. Осторожно и осмотрительно наложил он его на прежнее место. О ужас! Нос не приклеивался!.. Он поднес его ко рту, нагрел его слегка своим дыханием и опять поднес к гладкому месту, находившемуся между двух щек; но нос никаким образом не держался.

136 — Ну! ну же! полезай, дурак! — говорил он ему. Но нос был как деревянный и падал на стол с таким странным звуком, как будто бы пробка. Лицо майора судорожно скривилось. — Неужели он не прирастет? — говорил он в испуге. Но сколько раз ни подносил он его на его же собственное место, старание было по-прежнему неуспешно.

137 Он кликнул Ивана и послал его за доктором, который занимал в том же самом доме лучшую квартиру в бельэтаже. Доктор этот был видный из себя мужчина, имел прекрасные смолистые бакенбарды, свежую, здоровую докторшу, ел поутру свежие яблоки и держал рот в необыкновенной чистоте, полоща его каждое утро почти три четверти часа и шлифуя зубы пятью разных родов щеточками. Доктор явился в ту же минуту. Спросивши, как давно случилось несчастие, он поднял майора Ковалева за подбородок и дал ему большим пальцем щелчка в то самое место, где прежде

был нос, так что майор должен был откинуть свою голову назад с такою силою, что ударился затылком в стену. Медик сказал, что это ничего, и, посоветовавши отодвинуться немного от стены, велел ему перегнуть голову сначала на правую сторону и, пощупавши то место, где прежде был нос, сказал: «Гм!» Потом велел ему перегнуть голову на левую сторону и сказал: «Гм!» — и в заключение дал опять ему большим пальцем щелчка, так что майор Ковалев дернул головою, как конь, которому смотрят в зубы. Сделавши такую пробу, медик покачал головою и сказал:

— Нет, нельзя. Вы уж лучше так оставайтесь, потому что можно сделать еще хуже. Оно, конечно, приставить можно; я бы, пожалуй, вам сейчас приставил его; но я вас уверяю, что это для вас хуже.

— Вот хорошо! как же мне оставаться без носа? — сказал Ковалев. — Уж хуже не может быть, как теперь. Это просто черт знает что! Куда же я с этакою пасквильностию покажуся? Я имею хорошее знакомство; вот и сегодня мне нужно быть на вечере в двух домах. Я со многими знаком: статская советница Чехтарева, Подточина — штаб-офицерша… хоть после теперешнего поступка ее я не имею с ней другого дела, как только чрез полицию. Сделайте милость, — произнес Ковалев умоляющим голосом, — нет ли средства? как-нибудь приставьте; хоть не хорошо, лишь бы только держался; я даже могу его слегка подпирать рукою в опасных случаях. Я же притом и не танцую, чтобы мог вредить каким-нибудь неосторожным движением. Все, что относится насчет благодарности за визиты, уж будьте уверены, сколько дозволят мои средства…

140 — Верите ли, — сказал доктор ни громким, ни тихим голосом, но чрезвычайно увётливым и магнетическим, — что я никогда из корысти не лечу. Это противно моим правилам и моему искусству. Правда, я беру за визиты, но единственно с тем только, чтобы не обидеть моим отказом. Конечно, я бы приставил ваш нос; но я вас уверяю честью, если уже вы не верите моему слову, что это будет гораздо хуже. Предоставьте лучше действию самой натуры. Мойте чаще холодною водою, и я вас уверяю, что вы, не имея носа, будете так же здоровы, как если бы имели его. А нос я вам советую положить в банку со спиртом или, еще лучше, влить туда две столовые ложки острой водки и подогретого уксуса, — и тогда вы можете взять за него порядочные деньги. Я даже сам возьму его, если вы только не подорожитесь.

141 — Нет, нет! ни за что не продам! — вскричал отчаянный майор Ковалев, — лучше пусть он пропадет!

142 — Извините! — сказал доктор, откланиваясь, — я хотел быть вам полезным... Что ж делать! По крайней мере, вы видели мое старание.

143 Сказавши это, доктор с благородною осанкою вышел из комнаты. Ковалев не заметил даже лица его и в глубокой бесчувственности видел только выглядывавшие из рукавов его черного фрака рукавчики белой и чистой, как снег, рубашки.

144 Он решился на другой же день, прежде представления жалобы, писать к штаб-офицерше, не согласится ли она без бою возвратить ему то, что следует. Письмо было такого содержания:

«*Милостивая государыня*

    Александра Григорьевна!

Не могу понять странного со стороны вашей действия. Будьте уверены, что, поступая таким образом, ничего вы не выиграете и ничуть не принудите меня жениться на вашей дочери. Поверьте, что история насчет моего носа мне совершенно известна, равно как то, что в этом вы есть главные участницы, а не кто другой. Внезапное его отделение с своего места, побег и маскирование, то под видом одного чиновника, то, наконец, в собственном виде, есть больше ничего, кроме следствие волхвований, произведенных вами или теми, которые упражняются в подобных вам благородных занятиях. Я с своей стороны почитаю долгом вас предуведомить: если упоминаемый мною нос не будет сегодня же на своем месте, то я принужден буду прибегнуть к защите и покровительству законов.

Впрочем, с совершенным почтением к вам имею честь быть.

    Ваш покорный слуга

    Платон Ковалев».

«*Милостивый государь*

    Платон Кузьмич!

Чрезвычайно удивило меня письмо ваше. Я, признаюсь вам по откровенности, никак не ожидала, а тем более относительно несправедливых укоризн со стороны вашей. Предуведомляю вас, что я чиновника, о котором упоминаете вы, никогда не принимала у себя в доме, ни замаскированного, ни в настоящем виде. Бывал у меня, правда, Филипп Иванович

Потачников. И хотя он, точно, искал руки моей дочери, будучи сам хорошего, трезвого поведения и великой учености, но я никогда не подавала ему никакой надежды. Вы упоминаете еще о носе. Если вы разумеете под сим, что будто бы я хотела оставить вас с носом, то есть дать вам формальный отказ, то меня удивляет, что вы сами об этом говорите, тогда как я, сколько вам известно, была совершенно противного мнения, и если вы теперь же посватаетесь на моей дочери законным образом, я готова сей же час удовлетворить вас, ибо это составляло всегда предмет моего живейшего желания, в надежде чего остаюсь всегда готовою к услугам вашим

154

Александра Подточина».

155 «Нет, — говорил Ковалев, прочитавший письмо. — Она точно не виновата. Не может быть! Письмо так написано, как не может написать человек, виноватый в преступлении. — Коллежский асессор был в этом сведущ потому, что был посылан несколько раз на следствие еще в Кавказской области. — Каким же образом, какими судьбами это приключилось? Только черт разберет это!» — сказал он наконец, опустив руки.

156 Между тем слухи об этом необыкновенном происшествии распространились по всей столице, и, как водится, не без особенных прибавлений. Тогда умы всех именно настроены были к чрезвычайному: недавно только что занимали публику опыты действия магнетизма. Притом история о танцующих стульях в Конюшенной улице была еще свежа, и потому нечего удивляться, что скоро начали говорить, будто

нос коллежского асессора Ковалева ровно в три часа прогуливается по Невскому проспекту. Любопытных стекалось каждый день множество. Сказал кто-то, что нос будто бы находился в магазине Юнкера — и возле Юнкера такая сделалась толпа и давка, что должна была даже полиция вступиться. Один спекулатор почтенной наружности, с бакенбардами, продававший при входе в театр разные сухие кондитерские пирожки, нарочно поделал прекрасные деревянные прочные скамьи, на которые приглашал любопытных становиться за восемьдесят копеек от каждого посетителя. Один заслуженный полковник нарочно для этого вышел раньше из дому и с большим трудом пробрался сквозь толпу; но, к большому негодованию своему, увидел в окне магазина вместо носа обыкновенную шерстяную фуфайку и литографированную картинку с изображением девушки, поправлявшей чулок, и глядевшего на нее из-за дерева франта с откидным жилетом и небольшою бородкою, — картинку, уже более десяти лет висящую все на одном месте. Отошед, он сказал с досадою: «Как можно этакими глупыми и неправдоподобными слухами смущать народ?»

Потом пронесся слух, что не на Невском проспекте, а в Таврическом саду прогуливается нос майора Ковалева, что будто бы он давно уже там; что когда еще проживал там Хозрев-Мирза, то очень удивлялся этой странной игре природы. Некоторые из студентов Хирургической академии отправились туда. Одна знатная, почтенная дама просила особенным письмом смотрителя за садом показать детям ее этот редкий феномен и, если можно, с объяснением наставительным и назидательным для юношей.

158   Всем этим происшествиям были чрезвычайно рады все светские, необходимые посетители раутов, любившие смешить дам, у которых запас в то время совершенно истощился. Небольшая часть почтенных и благонамеренных людей была чрезвычайно недовольна. Один господин говорил с негодованием, что он не понимает, как в нынешний просвещенный век могут распространяться нелепые выдумки, и что он удивляется, как не обратит на это внимание правительство. Господин этот, как видно, принадлежал к числу тех господ, которые желали бы впутать правительство во все, даже в свои ежедневные ссоры с женою. Вслед за этим... но здесь вновь все происшествие скрывается туманом, и что было потом, решительно неизвестно.

III

159   Чепуха совершенная делается на свете. Иногда вовсе нет никакого правдоподобия: вдруг тот самый нос, который разъезжал в чине статского советника и наделал столько шуму в городе, очутился как ни в чем не бывало вновь на своем месте, то есть именно между двух щек майора Ковалева. Это случилось уже апреля седьмого числа. Проснувшись и нечаянно взглянув в зеркало, видит он: нос! — хвать рукою — точно нос! «Эге!» — сказал Ковалев и в радости чуть не дернул по всей комнате босиком тропака, но вошедший Иван помешал. Он приказал тот же час дать себе умыться и, умываясь, взглянул еще раз в зеркало: нос! Вытираясь утиральником, он опять взглянул в зеркало: нос!

160	— А посмотри, Иван, кажется, у меня на носу как будто прыщик, — сказал он и между тем думал: «Вот беда, как Иван скажет: да нет, сударь, не только прыщика, и самого носа нет!»
161	Но Иван сказал:
162	— Ничего-с, никакого прыщика: нос чистый!
163	«Хорошо, черт побери! — сказал сам себе майор и щелкнул пальцами. В это время выглянул в дверь цирюльник Иван Яковлевич, но так боязливо, как кошка, которую только что высекли за кражу сала.
164	— Говори вперед: чисты руки? — кричал еще издали ему Ковалев.
165	— Чисты.
166	— Врешь!
167	— Ей-Богу-с, чисты, сударь.
168	— Ну, смотри же.
169	Ковалев сел. Иван Яковлевич закрыл его салфеткою и в одно мгновенье с помощью кисточки превратил всю бороду его и часть щеки в крем, какой подают на купеческих именинах.
170	«Вишь ты! — сказал сам себе Иван Яковлевич, взглянувши на нос, и потом перегнул голову на другую сторону и посмотрел на него сбоку. — Вона! эк его, право, как подумаешь», — продолжал он и долго смотрел на нос. Наконец легонько, с бережливостью, какую только можно себе вообразить, он приподнял два пальца, с тем чтобы поймать его за кончик. Такова уж была система Ивана Яковлевича.
171	— Ну, ну, ну, смотри! — закричал Ковалев.
172	Иван Яковлевич и руки опустил, оторопел и смутился, как никогда не смущался. Наконец осторожно

стал он щекотать бритвой у него под бородою; и хотя ему было совсем несподручно и трудно брить без придержки за нюхательную часть тела, однако же, кое-как упираясь своим шероховатым большим пальцем ему в щеку и в нижнюю десну, наконец одолел все препятствия и выбрил.

Когда все было готово, Ковалев поспешил тот же час одеться, взял извозчика и поехал прямо в кондитерскую. Входя, закричал он еще издали: «Мальчик, чашку шоколаду!» — а сам в ту же минуту к зеркалу: есть нос! Он весело оборотился назад и с сатирическим видом посмотрел, несколько прищуря глаз, на двух военных, у одного из которых был нос никак не больше жилетной пуговицы. После того отправился он в канцелярию того департамента, где хлопотал об вице-губернаторском месте, а в случае неудачи об экзекуторском. Проходя чрез приемную, он взглянул в зеркало: есть нос! Потом поехал он к другому коллежскому асессору, или майору, большому насмешнику, которому он часто говорил в ответ на разные занозистые заметки: «Ну, уж ты, я тебя знаю, ты шпилька!» Дорогою он подумал: «Если и майор не треснет со смеху, увидевши меня, тогда уж верный знак, что все, что ни есть, сидит на своем месте». Но коллежский асессор ничего. «Хорошо, хорошо, черт побери!» — подумал про себя Ковалев. На дороге встретил он штаб-офицершу Подточину вместе с дочерью, раскланялся с ними и был встречен с радостными восклицаньями: стало быть, ничего, в нем нет никакого ущерба. Он разговаривал с ними очень долго и, нарочно вынувши табакерку, набивал пред ними весьма долго свой нос с обоих подъездов, приговаривая про себя: «Вот, мол, вам, бабье, куриный народ! а на дочке все-таки не женюсь. Так просто, par amour, — изволь!» И майор Ковалев с тех пор прогуливался как ни в чем не бывало и на Невском проспекте, и в театрах, и везде. И нос тоже как ни в чем не бывало сидел на его лице, не показывая даже вида, чтобы отлучался по сторонам. И после того майора Ковалева видели вечно в хорошем юморе, улыбающегося, преследующего решительно всех хорошеньких дам и даже остановившегося один раз перед лавочкой в Гостином дворе и покупавшего какую-то орденскую ленточку, неизвестно для каких причин, потому что он сам не был кавалером никакого ордена.

Вот какая история случилась в северной столице нашего обширного государства! Теперь только, по соображении всего, видим, что в ней есть много неправдоподобного. Не говоря уже о том, что точно странно сверхъестественное отделение носа и появленье его в разных местах в виде статского советника, — как Ковалев не смекнул, что нельзя чрез газетную экспедицию объявлять о носе? Я здесь не в том смысле говорю, чтобы мне казалось дорого заплатить за объявление: это вздор, и я совсем не из числа корыстолюбивых людей. Но неприлично, неловко, нехорошо! И опять тоже — как нос очутился в печеном хлебе и как сам Иван Яковлевич?.. нет, этого я никак не понимаю, решительно не понимаю! Но что страннее, что непонятнее всего, — это то, как авторы могут брать подобные сюжеты. Признаюсь, это уж совсем непостижимо, это точно... нет, нет, совсем не понимаю. Во-первых, пользы отечеству решительно никакой; во-вторых... но и во-вторых тоже нет пользы. Просто я не знаю, что это...

175 А, однако же, при всем том, хотя, конечно, можно допустить и то, и другое, и третье, может даже... ну да и где ж не бывает несообразностей?.. А все, однако же, как поразмыслишь, во всем этом, право, есть что-то. Кто что ни говори, а подобные происшествия бывают на свете, — редко, но бывают.

Annotations
to the Russian Text

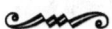

The Barber and His Wife

I

1.[1] *Марта 25 числа*. In the Russian tradition of citing dates, the day usually precedes the month. Here the inversion, as well as the use of the word *число* ("day"), are stylistic markers of nineteenth-century official announcements: newspaper articles and legal notifications. By using the official style in the first sentence of the story, the narrator assumes the role of a reporter and mimics journalese. The seriousness of the narrator's tone, the voice of a newspaper report in the first sentence contrasts with the subsequent events of the story.

    March 25 was an important religious holiday in Russia, the Feast of the Annunciation, commemorating the announcement of the Incarnation. (Unlike in the Catholic, Anglican, and Lutheran traditions, where the date of this feast can be moved, in the tradition of the Eastern Orthodox Church, it is a fixed holiday.) Thus, the first paragraph of the story juxtaposes two very different announcements made on March 25: the narrator's factual statement about an unusual occurrence in St. Petersburg (the appearance of the nose in the bread, as we learn a few lines down) and Archangel Gabriel announcing to Mary that she will conceive and bear a son. The narrator will maintain his slightly irreverent tone throughout the text. Since the story was first published in 1836, we may assume the action takes place in the early to mid-1830s.[2]

1. *Цирюльник Иван Яковлевич, живущий на Вознесенском проспекте*. The archaic word *цирюльник* (derived from Polish)

---

[1] The numbers at the beginning of each entry indicate the number of the paragraph in the Russian text of "The Nose."

[2] In the 1832 initial draft of the story, the action begins on "The 23 of 1832" with no indication of the month. In the 1833–1834 draft manuscript and the 1835 version, the nose disappears "This February 23." In the 1836 version published by *The Contemporary*, the date is "This April 25." In the version of "The Nose" published in 1942 in Gogol's *Works*, the date is "March 25."

and the more common *парикмахер* (from German), which was in use at the time, are synonyms, yet Gogol's choice of the former is of great importance. In Russia *цирюльники*, just as barbers in Europe, were engaged in not only haircutting, shaving, and hair styling, but also performing healers' duties, such as bloodletting, pulling teeth, and so on. Thus, the first lines of the story introduce the topics of illness and treatment, which run through the entire text. By the beginning of the twentieth century, the word *цирюльник* had disappeared from everyday usage.

The mention of a specific place of action—Voznesensky Prospect, located in the center of St. Petersburg, between the Fontanka River and the Moika River—creates a sense of reality and authenticity.

1. *...фамилия его утрачена, и даже на вывеске его — где изображен господин с намыленною щекою и надписью: «И кровь отворяют» — не выставлено ничего более.* In the first half of the nineteenth century, it was common for barbershops to hang signboards indicating the barber's name. The phrase *фамилия его утрачена* ("his surname is lost") sounds ambiguous: it can mean that the surname has faded or that it is missing. This detail introduces the motif of loss, further developed in the story of Major Kovalev, whose nose has disappeared.

    The expression *намыленная щека* ("a soapy cheek") resonates with the numerous mentions of facial features and body parts in the story. It brings to mind the expression *намылить шею* ("to soap up the neck"), which means "to punish," "to beat up," thus foreshadowing the theme of punishment running throughout the work.

    The words *И кровь отворяют* on the signboard suggest that the barber performs bloodletting. In nineteenth-century Russia, bloodletting was a popular method of treating high blood pressure as well as many other diseases. Although these signboards promised medical treatment, to Gogol's contemporaries they looked unwelcoming and even threatening, as blood was generally associated with violence.

Annotations to the Russian Text

The best hairdressing salons, which were run by French coiffeurs on Nevsky Prospect and other main streets of the city, looked very elegant. Conversely, the signboards of barbershops located in more remote areas seemed rather intimidating: they depicted jars with leeches. Popular in Gogol's time, these signs were still common in St. Petersburg in the early twentieth century. In his sketch "Signboards" (1925), Sergei Gornyi (pseudonym of prose and poetry writer Alexander Otsup) describes them in the following way: "The master standing behind the chair with unnaturally stiff hands, as if a sudden convulsion seized them, held the gentleman by his neck and head, and shaved him."[3] The work of hairdressers, as reflected in Russian literature, has often been compared to brutality. Roman Timenchik comments on the line *Власть отвратительна, как руки брадобрея* ("Power is disgusting, like the hands of a barber") from Osip Mandelshtam's poem "Ariost" (1933) by pointing out the affinity between shaving and death, hairdressers and executioners.[4] Nora Buks observes, "The tools—a razor and scissors, which easily become a weapon of murder—create a link between hairdressers and executioners."[5]

1. ...*услышал запах* (literally "heard the smell") is a colloquial expression common in the nineteenth century (the standard version is *почувствовал запах*, "sensed the smell"), analogous to the French verb *sentir*, which translates as "to smell" and "to feel." For the modern reader this expression may sound strange, since the verbs "to hear" and "to smell" refer to different

---

[3] Sergei Gornyi, *Sankt-Peterburg (Videniia)*, ed. A. M. Konechnyi (St. Petersburg: Giperion, 2000), 39.

[4] Roman Timenchik, "Ruki bradobreia," in *Chto vdrug, stat'i o russkoi literature proshlogo veka* (Moscow: Mosty kul'tury, 2017), 516–49.

[5] See her article on the hairdressing salon as a topic in Russian avant-garde art and Russian culture in general: Nora Buks, "Locus-poeticus: Salon de coiffure v russkoi kul'ture nachala XX veka," *Slavic Almanac* 10, no. 1 (2004): 2.

sensory organs, ears and nose. By using this expression in the story entitled "The Nose," Gogol draws his reader's attention to the oddness of this idiom.

4. *... для приличия надел сверх рубашки фрак.* The expression *для приличия* ("for propriety") suggests irony. At the beginning of the nineteenth century, the tailcoat was appropriate to wear for secular receptions and balls, as well as for horse riding. Men donned this garment in everyday life also, but not when having breakfast at home.

In general, in a literary work the purpose of describing clothes is to inform the reader of how the character looks or how other people perceive him or her. Consider an example from Leo Tolstoy's *War and Peace* (part 10, chapter 20). When Pierre Bezukhov travels to the headquarters of Field Marshal Kutuzov, officers there react to his green tailcoat and white hat with surprise. This eloquent detail demonstrates that to his comrades-in-arms Pierre seemed an outsider in the war. Gogol's descriptions, however, are very different from Tolstoy's realistic and psychological portrayals. The barber, like all Gogolian characters, is not a real person, but a caricature and a mask; his actions seem nonsensical.

5. *... Иван Яковлевич и руки опустил.* The expression *опустить руки* (literally "to lower one's hands," usually used in the passive voice: *руки опустились*), refers to a state of mind in which the ability or desire to do something is lost due to failure or a loss of hope. In other words, it means "to give up," usually because of some misfortune, and indicates that a person is desperate. Using the active voice instead of the passive, Gogol replaces the phrase's figurative meaning with the literal one. As a result, the idiom indicates a physical action—the lowering of hands. In fact, at that moment Ivan Yakovlevich raises his hands. This is clear from the next sentence, where he rubs his eyes. Yet, the figurative meaning of the idiom is still implicit—from the context, we know that the barber feels desperate when he finds the nose in the bread.

Annotations to the Russian Text

6. *Где это ты, зверь, отрезал нос? — закричала она с гневом. — Мошенник! пьяница! Я сама на тебя донесу полиции. Разбойник какой!* The reaction of the barber's wife to the sudden appearance of the nose and her words *зверь* ("beast"), *мошенник* ("swindler"), and *разбойник* ("bandit") bring us back to the inscription on the barber's signboard. The phrase *И кровь отворяют* now acquires strong criminal connotations. Gogol is toying with the idiomatic expression *оставить с носом* (literally "to leave someone with a nose" which means "to fool someone"). His protagonist, Major Kovalev, is left *without* a nose. The barber's wife's question "Where did you cut that nose off, you beast" implicitly suggests her suspicion that the barber has left someone without his nose. In the next chapter, this idiom appears in a more explicit form.

7. *Он узнал, что этот нос был не чей другой, как коллежского асессора Ковалева.* The phrase is odd because the verb *узнать* has different meanings depending on whether it is used with an animate or inanimate pronoun. *Узнать кого-то* means "to recognize somebody" and denotes a visual identification, whereas *узнать что-то* means "to find out something" and implies hearing new information. This sentence, comprising both meanings, sounds ambiguous and incomplete. Although Gogol writes that the barber "found out that this nose belonged to none other than the collegiate assessor Kovalev," the sentence also implies that the barber recognized the nose. Because of this ambiguity, the commentators of the original draft of the story explain in the footnotes that *узнал* means "saw" here.[6]

9. *Сухарь поджаристый! Знай умеет только бритвой возить по ремню, а долга своего скоро совсем не в состоянии будет исполнять, потаскушка, негодяй!* In this angry monologue,

---

[6] Nikolai Gogol, "Povesti," in his *Polnoe sobranie sochinenii v 14 tomakh*, vol. 3, ed. V. L. Komarovich (Moscow: AN SSSR, 1938), 381.

Part One. How "The Nose" Is Made

a resentful wife reproaches her husband. The colloquial word *сухарь* ("stale bread") usually refers to an insensitive person, and the adjective *поджаристый* ("crusty") intensifies the meaning of *callousness*. Praskovya Osipovna hints at the fact that the barber does not perform his conjugal duty. The jargon word *потаскушка* refers to a woman of easy virtue ("slut"). The use of the feminine-looking forms in reference to a man is not uncommon; some of these words, as, for example *сладкоежка* ("sweet tooth") sound neutral, whereas rude words of the feminine gender come across as particularly contemptuous and offensive when they are addressed to a man.

9. *... чтобы я духу его не слыхала!* This phrasing suggests that Praskovya Osipovna does not want the nose to be near her; in other words, this is her way of saying "Out!" Here Gogol distorts the set expression "Чтоб духу его тут не было" and is drawing the reader's attention to this awkward phrase, which literally means "I do not want to hear its smell."

10. *Иван Яковлевич стоял совершенно как убитый.* This phrase indicates that the barber is extremely upset when he finds a nose in his bread, because used in its figurative sense, the adjective *убитый* ("dead/killed") signifies "with a look of complete despair." However, the idiomatic expression *как убитый* ("as if dead/killed") that Gogol uses has a different meaning—it refers to a person in a state of immobility (thus, the expression *спит как убитый* designates a sound sleep). The merging of these two different idioms into one, *стоял как убитый* ("stood as if dead/killed"), creates a comic effect. Although devoid of logic, this expression was in use in Gogol's time. For example, it occurs in Alexander Bestuzhev-Marlinsky's story "Blood for Blood" (1825).

10. *Он думал, думал — и не знал, что подумать.* This phrase translates easily into English as "He thought and thought and didn't know what to think" and as such has humorous overtones. In Russian, the comic effect is somewhat stronger

Annotations to the Russian Text

because the verb *думать* is imperfective and thus stresses the process, which is further negated by the perfective verb *подумать*.

11. *Пьян ли я вчера возвратился или нет, уж наверное сказать не могу.* In the nineteenth century, the adverb *наверное* ("probably") held a meaning that was diametrically opposite to the modern one; it meant "definitely" (as the adverb *наверняка*, which has the same root). The statement is ironic: if the barber does not remember whether he returned drunk yesterday, then most likely he did.

12. *Наконец достал он свое исподнее платье и сапоги, натащил на себя всю эту дрянь и, сопровождаемый нелегкими увещаниями Прасковьи Осиповны, завернул нос в тряпку и вышел на улицу.* In the nineteenth century, *исподнее платье* referred to men's underwear. The phrase suggests that when the barber had breakfast at home, he was sitting at the table in his tailcoat, but was without underpants and trousers.

13. *Он хотел его куда-нибудь подсунуть: или в тумбу под воротами, или так как-нибудь нечаянно выронить.* The expression *подсунуть в тумбу под воротами* sounds absurd because the use of the preposition *в* implies that the object is hollow or has holes in it. *Тумба* (in nineteenth-century Petersburg) is a granite or cast-iron pillar with a diameter of 30–40 cm and a height of 140–150 cm or lower. Each stone house with a courtyard had four such curbstones—on the outer and inner sides of the arch. Some of them served as hitching posts, to which horses were tethered. *Нечаянно выронить* ("to drop accidentally") is a standard Russian expression despite the fact that it is slightly tautological—the verb *выронить* already implies an involuntary dropping. Gogol is playing with this expression by adding the verb *хотел* ("wanted"), thereby creating a conflict between intentionality and unintentionality in the expression *хотел нечаянно выронить*. The use of the adverb *как-нибудь* ("somehow") instead of *как будто* ("as if") intensifies this

conflict: the barber is not merely interested in making it look as if he drops the nose accidentally; he is actively looking for a way to do it.

The conjunction или/или ("either/or") suggests a choice between two actions, such as, for example, "slip it or drop it accidentally" or "slip it in one place or elsewhere." Gogol makes a logical shift when he writes, "Wanted to slip it somewhere: either [to put it] inside the pillar or to drop it accidentally." Despite the shift, this part of the sentence seems to mean that the barber wants to pretend that he dropped the nose accidentally.

13. ... *Иван Яковлевич должен был поднять нос*. This phrase hints at the idiom *ходить с поднятым носом* or *ходить задрав нос* ("to thumb one's nose"), which in Russian, just as in English, means "to openly show contempt or a lack of respect." It does not apply to the timid barber Ivan Yakovlevich, but foreshadows the personality of the story's main character, Major Kovalev, presented later in the text. In this story Gogol is toying with many Russian expressions containing the word "the nose."

14. *Он решился идти к Исакиевскому мосту: не удастся ли как-нибудь швырнуть его в Неву?* The barber's decision to get rid of the nose on St. Isaac's Bridge is odd and lacks logical motivation. In the 1830s, the now absent bridge, named after its neighbor St. Isaac's Cathedral, was a floating span crossing the Neva River. (The mention of a detachable bridge corresponds to Major Kovalev's "removable" nose.) The barber lives on Voznesensky Prospect, apparently close to Sadovaya Street, where, as we find out later, his client Major Kovalev resides. On his long walk to St. Isaac's Bridge, the barber first has to cross two bridges—one over the Catherine Canal (now called the Griboedov Canal) and the other over the Moika River. There are two other bridges in his neighborhood—one spanning the Fontanka and another the Obvodny Canal. It would have been much easier for the barber to discard the nose from one of the nearer bridges, rather than taking a long walk to the Neva.

Annotations to the Russian Text

One may assume that the barber decides on St. Isaac's Bridge because the Neva has a faster current and is deeper than the smaller rivers and canals in his neighborhood; however, the author does not say that. Ivan Yakovlevich's decision seems absurd for yet another reason: at St. Isaac's Bridge, he is more likely to be caught. An important thoroughfare that connected two central parts of the city—the Admiralty and the Vasilievsky Island—St. Isaac's Bridge was a crowded place: carriages raced across it and pedestrians crossed it day and night. Besides, in the 1830s and 1840s, the English embankment, connecting St. Isaac's Bridge and the Admiralty, served as a promenade where the nobility of St. Petersburg strolled in the spring.

15. ... *И хотя каждый день брил чужие подбородки, но его собственный был у него вечно небрит.* This sentence, which may be translated as "And although every day he shaved other people's chins, but his own was always unshaven," resonates with the Russian proverb *сапожник без сапог* ("shoemaker without shoes"; the English equivalent is "The cobbler always wears the worst shoes" or "The cobbler's children go barefoot"). The idea of the lack of something expected reverberates in the main event of the story—the disappearance of the nose from its owner's face.

15. *Фрак у Ивана Яковлевича (Иван Яковлевич никогда не ходил в сюртуке) был пегий; то есть он был черный, но весь в коричнево-желтых и серых яблоках; воротник лоснился, а вместо трех пуговиц висели одни только ниточки.* The collocation *в яблоках* (which means "dappled" and is usually used in reference to horses), suggests that the tailcoat is worn-out and extremely dirty.

The dress code in the Russian Empire was strict for all social strata, for courtiers as well as peasants. A brief glance at someone's tailcoat was sufficient to discern that person's status.

Tailcoats came into fashion after the 1812 return of the Russian Guards from Paris, and they were primarily worn by dandies. These coats had a front cutout, a rear flap, and a folding collar decorated with velvet. Buttons on both sides, made of silver, porcelain, or precious stones, narrow sleeves, and shoulders with wings gave the impression of sophistication and expense. When tailcoats became popular in the 1820s, people perceived them as extravagant. Compare Chatsky's ridicule of the Russian nobility's worship of foreign fashion near the end of Act 3 of Alexander Griboedov's comedy *Woe from Wit* (1825): "Хвост сзади, спереди какой-то чудный выем, / Рассудку вопреки, наперекор стихиям"[7] ("Tail in the back, in the front some outlandish cutout, / Contrary to common sense, braving the nature").

By the 1830s, tailcoats were gradually replaced by frock coats, which looked less extravagant and were more practical. Even in the best hairdressing salons on Nevsky Prospect and the city's main streets, coiffeurs worked in frock coats or vests.[8] The narrator's comment that the barber prefers tailcoats to frocks thus sounds ironic. Such dandyism makes the drunkard Ivan Yakovlevich look both ridiculous and pitiful: in his threadbare, greasy, and dirty coat with missing buttons, he looks utterly bizarre.

15. ... *понюхавши табаку, мылил ему за это и на щеке, и под носом, и за ухом, и под бородою.* The expression *понюхавши табаку* ("having sniffed") has an association with the colloquial expression *пропасть ни за понюх табаку* (literally "to perish for less than a snuff of tobacco"), which means "to perish purposelessly, for no [good] reason." This expression is echoed in the next chapter, when Major Kovalev complains about the disappearance of his nose: "но ведь пропал ни за что ни про что, пропал даром, ни за грош!" According to Vladimir

---

[7] A. S. Griboedov, *Gore ot uma, Komediia v chetyrekh deistviiakh v stikhakh* (Moscow: Detskaia literatura, 1967), 95.

[8] A. A. Konechnyi, et al., eds., *Byt pushkinskogo Peterburga: Opyt entsiklopedicheskogo slovaria*, 2 vols. (St. Petersburg: Izd. Ivana Limbakha, 2003), vol. 1, 165.

Dal's dictionary, in colloquial nineteenth-century Russian, the word *борода* ("beard") was also used in reference to *подбородок* ("chin"). In the narrative where a part of the face is one of the main characters, this inaccurate use of the word *beard* comes into focus.

16. *Он прежде всего осмотрелся; потом нагнулся на перила, будто бы посмотреть под мост: много ли рыбы бегает, и швырнул потихоньку тряпку с носом.* The phrase *много ли рыбы бегает* ("whether there were lots of fish running") is an example of a shift in idiomatic expressions containing verbs of motion. This lexical experiment has its "logic," however: if the nose can walk around the city, fish can run in the water.

16. *... отправился в заведение с надписью «Кушанье и чай» спросить стакан пуншу.* The remark contains an irony. *Пунш* was a common drink at young noblemen's friendly gatherings. See, for example, its mention in the introduction to Alexander Pushkin's *The Bronze Horseman*. In the eighteenth century the verb *пуншевать* ("to punch") was in use, and it meant "to drink punch in cheerful company." The recipe of this drink was rather complex: sugar had to be placed on a special grate, rum poured over the sugar, and the whole concoction then set on fire. The sugar melted and drained into the wine. This sophisticated drink was also served in expensive restaurants—for example, in the French restaurant Dumé, which Alexander Pushkin used to visit.[9] An eatery with the modest sign "Food and Tea" could hardly offer such a drink. It is more likely that Ivan Yakovlevich intends to have a simpler version of punch, the one that Dahl's dictionary defines as "boiling water with vodka or rum, sugar, sometimes also with lemon, etc."

---

[9] See Iuliia Demidenko, Restorany, traktiry, chainye: Iz istorii obschestvennogo pitaniia v Peterburge XVIII–nachala XX veka (Moscow: Tsentralpoligraf, 2011), 74–75.

Part One. How "The Nose" Is Made

16. ... *как вдруг заметил в конце моста квартального надзирателя благородной наружности, с широкими бакенбардами, в треугольной шляпе, со шпагою.* At St. Isaac's Bridge, the width of the Neva was about 500 meters, so for a person standing on one side of the bridge (or even in the middle of it) it was impossible to see the facial features of someone standing on the other side. As it is hard to discern a person's face even from a distance of 50–100 meters, this statement lacks logic.

16. ... *квартальный кивал ему пальцем.* The phrase contains a lexical shift. The verb *кивать* ("to nod") may be used only in reference to the noun "head." Apparently, the police officer is signaling the barber with his finger, asking him to come closer (there is a special verb for such a gesture in Russian: *поманить*). Just as the barber could not see the police officer standing at the other end of the bridge, the officer could not see the barber well either. This is especially so since in the next chapter the reader learns that by his own admission, the police officer was near-sighted and could not see anything without his glasses.

18. ... *зная форму, снял издали еще картуз.* The mention of *картуз* (a peaked cap) again suggests that Ivan Yakovlevich's outfit looked ridiculous. According to the dress code of the time, men wore tailcoats with tall hats and elegant shoes rather than peaked caps and boots. In chapter 10 of *The Gambler*, Dostoevsky describes ironically the outfit of a butler, who is wearing a tailcoat, a white tie, and a peaked cap. The same awkward outfit is found in Gogol's *Dead Souls*: when Chichikov's carriage drives up to the inn, a young man wearing a tailcoat and a peaked cap passes by with a backward glance.

The fact that the barber takes off his cap while still far away indicates that he is trying to please the police officer. Nevertheless, his greeting someone from afar is both ridiculous and awkward. Ivan Yakovlevich's gesture suggests a violation of etiquette. Compare, for example, an excerpt from Ivan

Turgenev's novel *On the Eve*: "'Good morning,' he said, approaching her and taking off his cap."[10]

19. **Желаю здравия вашему благородию!** The statutory formula for greeting a person of military rank is "Здравия желаю, ваше благородие" (which stands for "Hello, Your Honor," and literally means "I wish you good health, Your Honor"). Gogol turns this idiomatic expression into a literal one: instead of greeting the police officer, the barber wishes him good health. In Dostoyevsky's novel *The Double*, the scribe Ostafyev makes a similar "mistake" when he addresses Goliadkin.[11]

II

26. **... прыщик, который вчерашнего вечера вскочил у него на носу.** The verb of motion *вскочить* has two meanings, a literal one (to "jump up" or "jump out," used with animate nouns) and a figurative one ("to pop," said about a pimple). Gogol is playing with these two meanings when he writes that the pimple *вскочил* ("popped up") on Major Kovalev's nose, and a few lines down, he writes that Major Kovalev *вскочил* ("jumped out") of his bed. The parallel between these two actions suggests a logical connection with the story's plot: if the pimple can jump like a person, there is no reason the nose cannot walk like one. In the context of the 1830s, the mention of a pimple hints at the widespread disease syphilis.[12]

---

[10] I. S. Turgenev, *On the Eve*, trans. Gilbert Gardiner (London: Penguin Books, 1950), 96.

[11] Fedor Dostoevskii, "Dvoinik," in his *Polnoe sobranie sochinenii*, 30 vols. (Leningrad: Nauka, 1972), vol. 1, 189.

[12] See O. G. Dilaktorskaia, "Khudozhestvennyi mir peterburgskikh povestei," in N. V. Gogol', *Peterburgskie povesti*, ed. O. G. Dilaktorskaia, "Literaturnye pamiatniki" series (St. Petersburg: Nauka, 1995), 219.

The Barber on the Bridge

Annotations to the Russian Text

26. ... *и полетел прямо к обер-полицмейстеру*. The verb of motion *полететь* has two meanings, a literal one ("to start to fly," said about birds or airplanes) and a colloquial figurative one ("to start to run, walk, or ride very fast," said about a person). As can be seen from subsequent events, Kovalev did not run to the chief of police at that moment. Instead, first he went to the confectionary, then to Kazan Cathedral. *Обер-полицмейстер* is the head of the city police department, which dealt with petty criminal and civil cases.

27. *Коллежских асессоров, которые получают это звание с помощию ученых аттестатов, никак нельзя сравнивать с теми коллежскими асессорами, которые делались на Кавказе.* According to the Table of Ranks (*Табель о рангах*)—a list of positions and ranks in the government, military, and court of imperial Russia, introduced by Peter the Great in 1722—among the fourteen ranks, the highest was the first class. The rank of collegiate assessor belonged to the eighth class. The fact that Kovalev received that rank in the Caucasus suggests his lack of education. In the mid-1830s, it was much easier to reach the rank of collegiate assessor in the Caucasus and Siberia, where it could be obtained without taking exams and earning certificates. Here Gogol also derides Kovalev's desire for a quick and easy career.[13]

27. ... *а чтобы более придать себе благородства и веса, он никогда не называл себя коллежским асессором, но всегда майором.* According to the Table of Ranks, the civil rank of a collegiate assessor corresponded to the military rank of Major. Kovalev calls himself a Major because military ranks were more prestigious. He breaks the law, however; according to the decree of Catherine II of November 15, 1793, civilian officials

---

[13] See Irina Reyfman, *How Russia Learned to Write: Literature and the Imperial Table of Ranks* (Wisconsin: The University of Wisconsin Press, 2016), 108.

did not have the right to use military ranks. Gogol's comment suggests Kovalev's vanity and exaggerated preoccupation with rank.

27. «*Послушай, голубушка, — говорил он обыкновенно, встретивши на улице бабу, продававшую манишки, — ты приходи ко мне на дом; квартира моя в Садовой; спроси только: здесь ли живет майор Ковалев? — тебе всякий покажет»*. *Если же встречал какую-нибудь смазливенькую, то давал ей сверх того секретное приказание, прибавляя: «Ты спроси, душенька, квартиру майора Ковалева»*. Here Kovalev wants to show the women what an important personage he is. He is so noteworthy that everyone in St. Petersburg knows where he lives. The above statement contains several logical inconsistencies. His advice to the women to ask someone where his apartment is located is unreasonable, first, because Sadovaya Street was more than four kilometers long and, second, even though in the 1830s houses and apartments in St. Petersburg were numbered, they were still widely known by their owners' names. Kovalev suggests that his name is more famous than the name of the owner of the house in which he lives. In addition, the use of the conjunction *если* (if) accompanied by the emphatic particle *же* implies a contrast between the orders Kovalev gives to two different types of women: *бабы* (older peasant women) and *смазливенькие* (younger cuties). However, Kovalev gives them identical instructions. Although Gogol does not specify what *секретное приказание* (secret order) is, it is clear from the context that this also means Kovalev's invitation to the women to visit him. The word *смазливенькая* is generally translated as "cute," "pretty," or "nice," but it has a slightly derogative connotation and implies cheap prettiness.

28. *Воротничок его манишки был всегда чрезвычайно чист и накрахмален*. *Манишка* is a chemisette, a removable shirtfront. In the nineteenth century, those who could not afford to buy enough white shirts, which were worn under uniforms, resorted to removable shirtfronts, collars, and cuffs.

Annotations to the Russian Text

28. ... *эти бакенбарды идут по самой средине щеки и прямехонько доходят до носа.* Once again, Gogol draws the reader's attention to the peculiarities of the Russian verbs of motion: the verb *идти* ("to go / to walk") has two meanings: a concrete physical action and a figurative one. The narrator's statement that "the whiskers go in the middle of the cheek" anticipates the events Gogol introduces later: the nose's ability to walk. In the author's Petersburg tales, limbs and facial features often lead an independent existence. For example, in "The Portrait," the man in the painting seems so real that his eyes look as if they were cut out of a living person. At the beginning of "Nevsky Prospect," Gogol describes the mustaches, waists, noses, whiskers, and eyes of St. Petersburg's inhabitants walking independently of their owners.

29. ... *он должен был идти пешком, закутавшись в свой плащ и закрывши платком лицо, показывая вид, как будто у него шла кровь.* Major Kovalev pretends that his nose is bleeding; in other words, he acts as though he has a nose. This phrase hints at the idiomatic expression *кровь из носу*, which means "absolutely necessary / at any cost." Although this phrase does not come up in the story, it does fit the situation: Kovalev keeps saying that it is absolutely necessary for him to get his nose back.

29. ... *Хотя бы уже что-нибудь было вместо носа, а то ничего!* The absurdity of the sentence "There could be at least something instead of a nose, but there is nothing" is intensified through the use of the indefinite pronoun *что-нибудь* (with the particle *-нибудь*; "anything at all") rather than *что-то* (with the particle *-то*; "something specific").

30. *Он был в мундире, шитом золотом, с большим стоячим воротником; на нем были замшевые панталоны; при боку шпага. По шляпе с плюмажем можно было заключить, что он считался в ранге статского советника.* Only high-ranking members of the imperial court were allowed to don plumed hats, and solely on occasions when they wore court uniforms.

Part One. How "The Nose" Is Made

One can assume that the nose is not just a state councilor, but also an important person belonging to the highest echelons.[14]

32. ... *Ряд нищих старух с завязанными лицами и двумя отверстиями для глаз, над которыми он прежде так смеялся.* The old beggars covered their faces to hide traces of the "bad disease," indicative of their sinful past. One of the symptoms of syphilis is a collapse of the bridge of the nose. Women from the provinces and small villages who migrated to St. Petersburg to find work often became the prey of brothels or were forced to sell themselves on the streets.[15] This time Kovalev does not laugh at them, because he understands that they are his "sisters in misfortune."

37. ... *вы должны знать свое место.* This idiomatic expression has a direct analogue in English: "You have to know your place." As in many other instances, here the humorous effect derives from the interaction of the literal and the figurative meaning of the sentence. Kovalev suggests that his nose should be on his face. However, one may look at the situation from a different perspective. According to an imperial decree, on the Feast of the Annunciation officials had to attend church dressed in festive clothes.[16] The nose, who has the rank of a state councilor, is in its proper place: at the church.

40. ... *Какой-нибудь торговке, которая продает на Воскресенском мосту очищенные апельсины, можно сидеть без носа.* This sentence is another hint at the "bad disease." Kovalev is implying

---

[14] See Dilaktorskaia, "Khudozhestvennyi mir peterburgskikh povestei," 273; and also Reyfman, *How Russia Learned to Write*, 108.

[15] V. V. Iakovlev, ed., *Tri veka Sankt-Peterburga: Entsiklopediia*, 3 vols., vol. 2: *Deviatnadtsatyi vek*, book 5 (St. Petersburg: Fakul'tet filologii i iskusstv SPbGU, 2006), 707.

[16] O. G. Dilaktorskaia, "Fantasticheskoe v povesti N. V. Gogolia 'Nos,'" *Russkaia literatura* 1 (1984): 155.

that his status as collegiate assessor requires propriety in all matters, including his physical appearance and moral standing.

41. — *Ничего решительно не понимаю,* — *отвечал нос.* — *Изъяснитесь удовлетворительнее.* The style of the nose's response to Kovalev is markedly bureaucratic.

46. ... *открыл табакерку высокий гайдук с большими бакенбардами и целой дюжиной воротников.* This is a satirical depiction of the manners of St. Petersburg's inhabitants. People's conduct in the Orthodox Church was strictly regulated; they were expected to pray, light candles, bow before the icons, and kiss the icons. The footman's opening of the snuffbox in the church is clearly inappropriate. The comment about his clothes is also ironic. In Gogol's time, it was fashionable to wear several vests and several ties. By suggesting that the footman is wearing a dozen collars, Gogol takes the idea of excessiveness in clothes to an absurd level.

47. ... *Улыбка на лице Ковалева раздвинулась еще далее, когда он увидел из-под шляпки ее кругленький, яркой белизны подбородок и часть щеки, осененной цветом первой весенней розы. Но вдруг он отскочил, как будто бы обжегшись. Он вспомнил, что у него вместо носа совершенно нет ничего, и слезы выдавились из глаз его.* Kovalev's desire to flirt with a young lady in church indicates that his moral code is flawed. Oddly, he is preoccupied not with his missing nose but rather with the absence of anything on his face in place of the nose. He thinks that if there were something there, it would be appropriate for him to flirt.

48. *День был прекрасный и солнечный. На Невском народу была тьма.* In its figurative sense, the word *тьма* (lit. "darkness"), borrowed from the Turkic "tumen," means "multitude." By juxtaposing these two sentences, the first of which contains the word *солнечный* ("sunny"), Gogol creates a logical clash between the connotative and figurative meanings of the word *тьма*, thus creating a comical effect.

49. *А, черт возьми!* — *сказал Ковалев.* — *Эй, извозчик, вези прямо к обер-полицмейстеру!* Major Kovalev's visit to the chief of police's private residence during an important church holiday is highly unlikely. This ironic remark is meaningful: in this story, which is full of fantastic events, anything is possible.

50. «*Валяй во всю ивановскую!*» The expression *во всю ивановскую* (lit. "throughout the whole Ivan Square") is generally used when someone is shouting very loudly, at the top of the lungs (originally, the expression had to do with ringing Ivan the Great Bell Tower in the Kremlin). Gogol uses this idiom in reference to speed rather than to the intensity of sound. Kovalev gives the order to the coachman to go very fast because he is in a hurry, and also because he thinks of himself as an important person: "In St. Petersburg, unlike in Moscow, it was customary to travel very fast—this served as a sign of the high social status of the person sitting in the carriage."[17]

60. ... *Лошадь, на которой шерсть была длинная, как на болонке.* The statement is ironic, for unlike Bolognese dogs, horses (at least, in St. Petersburg) do not have long hair.

67. ... *В одной значилось, что отпускается в услужение кучер трезвого поведения.* Here the expression *отпустить в услужение* ("to let go into service) is a euphemism for "to sell" (a slave).

67. «*Кто здесь принимает объявления? — закричал Ковалев. — А, здравствуйте!*" The reality of Kovalev's visit to the newspaper office is questionable. Because of the ban on all types of work on the Feast of the Annunciation, all public offices were closed.

---

[17] Konechnyi A. A., et al., eds., *Byt pushkinskogo Petersburga: Opyt entsiklopedicheskogo slovaria*, 2 vols. (St. Petersburg: Izdatel'stvo Ivana Limbakha, 2005), vol. 2, 275.

67. ... *каждый день от восьми до трех часов утра*. The awkwardly phrased announcement "Every day from eight to three in the morning" reflects the absurdity of life in St. Petersburg. The advertisement would sound neutral if instead it stated, "Every day from eight o'clock in the morning to three o'clock in the afternoon," but it would not be a Gogolian phrase.

84. ... *все объявление состояло в том, что сбежал пудель черной шерсти. Кажется, что бы тут такое? А вышел пасквиль: пудель-то этот был казначей, не помню какого-то заведения.* "This poodle was a treasurer, I do not remember of which institution" is another instance of an awkwardly phrased statement. It would sound neutral if the narrator said, "It was not a poodle, but a treasurer, I do not remember of which institution." According to O. G. Dilaktorskaia, the mention of the "black poodle" (the devil) is a reference to Goethe's *Faust*, a book widely known to readers at the time.[18]

88. *Говорят, что есть такие люди, которые могут приставить какой угодно нос*. The idea of the artificial nose reflects the spirit of the time: in the 1830s, Petersburg hairdressers made wigs and overhead braids. In addition, the first dentures appeared. The expression *приставить нос* (another reference to syphilis) echoes the idiom *наставить/натянуть нос кому-нибудь* (colloq.), which means "to make a fool of someone" (lit. "to put a nose on someone").

90. ... *нюхая табак*. During the reign of Nicholas I, smoking in public places and on the streets was prohibited and was strictly enforced by the police. Because of the ban, many residents of the capital sniffed tobacco instead.[19]

---

[18] Dilaktorskaia, "Khudozhestvennyi mir peterburgskikh povestei," 274.

[19] S. F. Svetlov, *Peterburgskaia zhizn' v kontse XIX stoletiia*, "Zabytyi Peterburg" series, book 1 (St. Peterburg: Giperion, 1998), 74–75.

Part One. How "The Nose" Is Made

95. ... *описать это как редкое произведение натуры и напечатать эту статейку в «Северной пчеле».* The Northern Bee was a pro-governmental political and literary newspaper edited by Faddei Bulgarin, who had the reputation of being the most odious journalist in Russia. One of the newspaper's most popular sections, "Morals," informed readers about incidents that happened on St. Petersburg streets, paying particular attention to shady events. The clerk's suggestion is therefore ironic. The newspaper had a bad reputation because the information published in it was not reliable.[20]

95. ... *тут он утер нос.* The expression *утереть нос кому-то* (lit. "to wipe someone's nose") means "to outdo someone." Gogol is using this trope instead of the more general expression *вытереть нос*, which denotes merely the concrete meaning of a physical action. The expression refers not so much to the expedition clerk as to Major Kovalev, who is excessively proud of himself.

102. ... *отправился к частному приставу, чрезвычайному охотнику до сахару. На дому его вся передняя, она же и столовая, была установлена сахарными головами, которые нанесли к нему из дружбы купцы.* The comment about the police commissioner's love of sugar and the mention of the sugarloaves brought by merchants is a satirical remark about police officers, who enjoyed receiving bribes. A sugarloaf was the form in which refined sugar was produced until the late nineteenth century, when granulated sugar and sugar cubes were introduced. The expression *сахарная голова* (lit. "a sugar head") in the story about a runaway nose echoes the motif of the dismemberment of the human body. Gogol defamiliarizes this common metaphoric expression.

---

[20] Iakovlev, *Tri veka Sankt-Peterburga*, vol. 2, book 6 (St. Petersburg: Fakul'tet filologii i iskusstv SPbGU, 2008), 147.

Annotations to the Russian Text

104. ... *сама натура назначила, чтобы, наевшись, немного отдохнуть (из этого коллежский асессор мог видеть, что частному приставу были небезызвестны изречения древних мудрецов).* In the 1830s, afternoon rest was a common practice in everyday Russian life.[21] The phrase hints at verbal play, for it contains an allusion to the anonymous saying "После сытного обеда по закону Архимеда полагается поспать" ("After a hearty dinner, according to Archimedes's law, one is required to take a nap").

104. ... *много есть на свете всяких майоров, которые не имеют даже и исподнего в приличном состоянии и таскаются по всяким непристойным местам.* The statement "There are many Majors in the world that do not even have decent underwear but drag along to all kinds of lewd places" defies rationality. The police commissioner reproaches Kovalev for some kind of shady activity.

105. ... *не в бровь, а прямо в глаз.* This expression is generally used when something is said aptly. An English equivalent of this expression, "to hit the nail on the head," however, does not contain the words *бровь* ("brow") and *глаз* ("eye"), which are important in a story about a runaway nose. By using this expression in his response to the police commissioner's accusations, Kovalev admits his own wrongdoings.

105. *Признаюсь, после этаких обидных с вашей стороны замечаний я ничего не могу прибавить.* Kovalev's recognition would have sounded logical had he said that he had no objections to the officer's reproaches or that he had nothing to add to what he himself had already said. His admission that he has nothing to add to these reproaches suggests that he completely agrees with everything the officer said.

---

[21] Svetlov, *Peterburgskaia zhizn' v kontse XIX stoletiia*, 72.

106. *... лежа на спине, плевал в потолок и попадал довольно удачно в одно и то же место.* The expression *плевать в потолок* (colloq.; lit. "to spit at the ceiling") implies "spending time doing nothing," "sitting twiddling one's thumbs." By literalizing this idiomatic expression, Gogol increases the absurdity: it is impossible to spit at the ceiling; and it is even more impossible to hit the same spot twice.

109. *... без носа человек — черт знает что: птица не птица, гражданин не гражданин, — просто возьми да и вышвырни за окошко.* Kovalev is distressed that now he is a man without civil rights. According to the Russian code of laws at the time, people could not be hired as civil servants if they were terminally ill or had an "obvious lack of intelligence," or else were caught displaying inappropriate behavior.[22] The phraseology hints at the colloquial expression *важная птица* ("a big shot," lit. "an important bird"), which refers to a person occupying a high official or social position, possessing power and influence. Clearly, without his nose, Kovalev is no longer a *важная птица*.

109. *И пусть бы уже на войне отрубили или на дуэли.* This statement implies that Kovalev grieves not so much for the loss of his nose as for the fact that this loss has no meaningful explanation. His assumption that it would be better if the nose were cut off in war or in a duel sounds comical, as it profanes sentiments of military patriotism and of honor in duels.

109. *Иван, дурак, не принял, и я, верно, хватил ее.* Kovalev calls his servant, Ivan, "a fool" because the servant did not take the vodka remaining in the glass away after Kovalev had shaved (here vodka is an inexpensive alternative to the eau de cologne used by French coiffeurs). The epithet associates the servant with a popular character of Russian fairy tales, Ivan the Fool.

---

[22] Dilaktorskaia, "Khudozhestvennyi mir peterburgskikh povestei," 275.

In fact, if Kovalev drank this vodka, he himself would be the fool.

110. *Чтобы действительно увериться, что он не пьян, майор ущипнул себя так больно, что сам вскрикнул.* The phrase suggests that Major Kovalev did not believe that what was happening was real. However, it would make sense only if the Major pinched himself to make sure he was not dreaming rather than he was not drunk.

112. *… сказавши, что еще молод, что нужно ему прослужить лет пяток, чтобы уже ровно было сорок два года.* This phrase contains two absurdities. First, *лет пяток* ("approximately five years") conflicts with the phrase "exactly forty-two," which comes up later in the sentence. Second, the idea of marrying when one is exactly forty-two years old defies logic.

112. *И потому штаб-офицерша, верно из мщения, решилась его испортить и наняла для этого каких-нибудь колдовок-баб.* Kovalev assumes that the staff officer's wife, Podtochina, with whose daughter he had flirted, hired some sorceresses to ruin his health and reputation. The act of causing illness by casting a spell is traditionally called *наводить/навести порчу*. Gogol uses the verb *испортить*, which has the same root but has more literal meaning "to break," "to ruin," and thus creates the impression that Podtochina literally caused physical or moral damage to Kovalev. Dilaktorskaia observes that the motif of *порча* comes from folk medicine, popular in Russia at that time. Gogol was acquainted with all sorts of superstitions. By referring to *порча*, he ridicules folk medicine practices that border on witchcraft.[23]

116. *… полицейский чиновник… который в начале повести стоял в конце Исакиевского моста.* The juxtaposition of the "beginning of the story" and "the end of the St. Isaac's Bridge" creates an awkward stylistic construction: a comparison of unequal and

---

[23] Ibid., 218 and 271.

disparate items (somewhat similar to the English "apples and oranges").

117. ... *Вы изволили затерять нос свой?* The police officer's question "Did you deign to lose your nose" makes no sense, because the verb *изволить,* frequently used in the nineteenth century as formal marker of civil speech, literally means "to desire," "to wish," which is not compatible with the verb "to lose."

120. *Радость отняла у него язык.* This is a hint at the expression *язык отнялся от радости* ("Lost the ability to speak because of joy," lit. "Joy took away his tongue"), normally rendered in the passive voice. Here Gogol is using the active voice, thereby violating the idiom, as if suggesting that something or someone has taken away Kovalev's nose and his tongue.

121. ... *хотел уехать в Ригу.* The colloquial expression *поехать в Ригу* ("to go to Riga") is a euphemism for the verb *to vomit,* which derives from the assonance of *Riga* and the verb *рыгать* ("to belch" / "to burp").[24]

121. *Но, к счастию, были со мной очки, и я тот же час увидел, что это был нос. Ведь я близорук, и если вы станете передо мною, то я вижу только, что у вас лицо, но ни носа, ни бороды, ничего не замечу. Моя теща, то есть мать жены моей, тоже ничего не видит.* At the time, many Petersburgers had vision problems because they worked and read by candlelight during the dark autumn and winter evenings. It even became fashionable to be

---

[24] D. N. Ushakov, *Tolkovyi slovar' russkogo iazyka,* 4 vols. (Moscow: Gosudarstvennoe izdatel'stvo inostrannykh i natsional'nykh slovarei, 1939), vol. 3, 1358. Although it is hard to say when exactly this colloquial euphemism was first coined, it was in use in the nineteenth century. See Vladimir Korolenko's letter to D. Ia. Aizman from March 15, 1901, in Vladimir Korolenko, *Sobranie sochinenii,* 10 vols. (Moscow: Gosudarstvennoe izdatel'stvo khudozhestvennoi literatury, 1956), vol. 10, 141.

near-sighted.²⁵ Dilaktorskaia points out, however, that Russian officers and civil servants generally were not permitted to wear glasses. Permission to wear them was issued by special order as an exception to the rule. The police officer's remark about glasses indicates his possible disruption of the general bureaucratic order.²⁶

The police officer's comment about his mother-in-law and his explanation—"that is, the mother of my wife"—may sound comical, since the mother-in-law is not a blood relative, and so her nearsightedness is irrelevant to this. However, it is not as absurd as it may seem. Russian has an elaborate classification of words denoting relations by marriage: *теща, тесть* (parents of the wife); *свекровь, свекор* (parents of the husband), as well as many others, but these words are mostly used in provincial towns and villages. In large cities, except for *теща* ("mother-in-law"), the use of these words was confusing in Gogol's time as well as now. This confusion is clearly seen in the comic poem "Pop" ("Priest," 1844) by Ivan Turgenev, which contains the line *к попу приехала золовка* ("the priest's sister-in-law came to visit him"). The word *золовка* generally means "a sister of the husband."

122. *Ковалев был вне себя.* This phrase translates easily into English as *Kovalev was beside himself,* the idiom, which suggests that he was experiencing extreme joy. It also hints to the fact that Kovalev's nose was besides or out of his face.

124. *... еще третьего дня стащил он в одной лавочке бортище пуговиц.* The fact that the barber has stolen a dozen buttons does not seem surprising, as in the previous chapter we learned that his tailcoat was missing a few buttons. Further, the barber's inclination to steal will be mentioned again, but in an idiomatic form.

---

25 Konechnyi et al., *Byt Pushkinskogo Petersburga*, vol. 2, 53.

26 Dilaktorskaia, "Khudozhestvennyi mir peterburgskikh povestei," 276.

128. ... *увещевал по зубам одного глупого мужика, наехавшего с своею телегою как раз на бульвар.* The expression *увещевал по зубам* (lit. "exhorted on the teeth") is nonsensical; here it is a euphemism for "hitting on the teeth." The phrase implies that the police officer hit the peasant on the teeth. This euphemism constitutes a social commentary on Russian police officers' abusive practices.

137. ... *дал ему большим пальцем щелчка в то самое место, где прежде был нос.* Gogol satirizes the doctors of the time and their methods of treatment. Simultaneously, the doctor's action hints at the expression *щелкнуть по носу* ("to click on the nose"), which means "to put someone in one's place" or "to reprimand someone."

137. ... *как конь, которому смотрят в зубы.* This ironic phrase contains a hint at the proverb *Дареному коню в зубы не смотрят* ("Don't look a gift horse in the mouth," lit. "to a gift horse one does not look in the teeth"). The proverb refers to the practice of determining the age of a horse by examining its teeth. As noted by Dilaktorskaia, the phrase mocks fraudulent methods of medical treatment, popular in Russia at the time, in particular the method of "scaring the disease."[27]

138. *Оно, конечно, приставить можно; я бы, пожалуй, вам сейчас приставил его; но я вас уверяю, что это для вас хуже.* See the commentary on the expression *наставить нос* (paragraph 88), which means "to deceive someone." In a more general sense, the statement creates a sense of absurdity.

140. *А нос я вам советую положить в банку со спиртом или, еще лучше, влить туда две столовые ложки острой водки и подогретого уксуса.* This sentence contains a hint to one of the city's main sightseeing attractions, the Kunstkamera. Founded

---

[27] Ibid., 219.

by Peter the Great, this first Russian museum is known for its collection of anatomical rarities and anomalies, which includes parts of the human body preserved in alcohol.

153. *Если вы разумеете под сим, что будто бы я хотела оставить вас с носом, то есть дать вам формальный отказ.* Gogol draws the reader's attention to the expression *оставить с носом*, which means "to deceive," "to make a fool of."

154. *Александра Подточина.* The family name Подточина leads to an association with the expression *комар носа не подточит* (lit. "A mosquito will not sharpen its nose"), used in reference to something done so flawlessly that no defects can be found.[28] The verb *подточить* also means "to undermine." Specifically, the name hints at the fact that the sorcery, which caused the nose to disappear (Kovalev suspects that Podtochina is the culprit), was so ingeniously contrived and carefully executed that it could not be detected (that is, it was "a perfect crime"). Podtochina's first name is given as Palageya, but in her correspondence with Kovalev, her first name is Alexandra. There is no logical explanation for this inconsistency.

155. *Только черт разберет это!» — сказал он наконец, опустив руки.* The expression *опустив руки* ("having put his hands down") has a double meaning: a physical action and a moral state of perplexity. See the commentary to paragraph 5.

156. *... недавно только что занимали публику опыты действия магнетизма.* The German physician A. F. Mesmer (1734–1815) was well known in Russia. The followers of Mesmer's pseudoscientific theory believed in the existence of magnetism, that is, an energy transference between all animate and

---

[28] Sophia Lubensky, *Russian-English Dictionary of Idioms* (New York: Random House, 1995), 296.

Part One. How "The Nose" Is Made

inanimate objects. The so-called magnetizers claimed to have special healing powers.[29]

156. ... *о танцующих стульях в Конюшенной улице.* In December 1833 Pushkin wrote in his diary about a strange incident that occurred in St. Petersburg: in one of the buildings of the Imperial State Horse Breeding Office the furniture began to move and jump around. In January 1834, one of Pushkin's closest friends, Petr Vyazemsky, reported the same rumor in a letter to Alexander Turgenev.[30] In his Petersburg tales, Gogol describes the city as a place where rumors about fantastic events are part of everyday life.

156. ... *начали говорить, будто нос коллежского асессора Ковалева ровно в три часа прогуливается по Невскому проспекту.* At the beginning of the nineteenth century, strolls down the Nevsky Prospect were in fashion in St. Petersburg, especially the "sunny" side of Nevsky between Moika and Fontanka, from two to four o'clock in the afternoon. At the beginning of his short story "Nevsky Prospect," Gogol describes such walks in detail.

156. ... *Сказал кто-то, что нос будто бы находился в магазине Юнкера.* Магазин Юнкера was a fashionable hat store on Nevsky Prospect, 20.

156. ... *Один спекулатор почтенной наружности, с бакенбардами, продававший при входе в театр разные сухие кондитерские пирожки, нарочно поделал прекрасные деревянные прочные скамьи, на которые приглашал любопытных становиться за восемьдесят копеек от каждого посетителя.* Gogol is toying

---

[29] Konechnyi et al., *Byt Pushkinskogo Petersburga*, vol. 2, 46.

[30] S. Mashkinskii, ed., *Gogol' v vospominaniiakh sovremennikov*, "Seriia literaturnykh memuarov" (Moscow: Gosudarstvennoe izdatel'stvo khudozhestvnnoi literatury, 1952), 356.

with the obsolete word *спекулатор* and the more recent *спекулятор* (*спекулянт* in modern Russian), which have the same root. The former came from the Greek σπεκουλάτωρ (Latin *speculator*) through the Old Slavonic *спекоулаторъ*, and means "spy." The latter derived from the French *speculateur*, which, like the English *speculator*, has several meanings: "businessperson," "entrepreneur," "manipulator," "charlatan." The use of the word *theater* is ironic, as the spectacle is in fact secret and resembles peep shows.

156. ... *литографированную картинку с изображением девушки, поправлявшей чулок, и глядевшего на нее из-за дерева франта с откидным жилетом и небольшою бородкою.* Curious inhabitants of St. Petersburg are peering in the fashion shop window to see the nose; instead, what they see is a lithograph. The mention of this lithograph—a fashionable dandy watching the girl who shows her leg while fixing her stocking—continues the theme of forbidden peeking. In another Petersburg tale, "Nevsky Prospect," Gogol notes that in the windows of some shops on that avenue, one can see suspicious prints: "But as soon as dusk falls on the houses and streets, and the sentry, covering himself with a bast mat, climbs a ladder to light the lantern, and prints which do not dare show themselves in daytime peek out of the low shop windows, then Nevsky Prospect again comes to life and begins to stir."[31] In "The Overcoat," Bashmachkin grins passing a shop window with a similar picture in it.

157. ... *не на Невском проспекте, а в Таврическом саду прогуливается нос майора Ковалева, что будто бы он давно уже там; что когда еще проживал там Хозрев-Мирза.* Khozrev Mirza (1813–1875) was a Persian prince who headed the embassy after the murder of the Russian writer and diplomat A. S. Griboedov in Tehran. During his stay in St. Petersburg in 1829, Mirza lived in the

---

[31] Gogol, "Nevsky Prospect," 250.

Part One. How "The Nose" Is Made

Tauride Palace. There is no reasonable explanation as to why the nose is associated with his residence.

III

159. ... *Это случилось уже апреля седьмого числа*. In the nineteenth century, the Russians used the Julian calendar, which was twelve days behind the Western European (Gregorian) calendar. Hence the above phrase can be read in one of two ways: Kovalev finds his nose twelve days after he has lost it or he finds it on the next day, which suggests that he could have dreamed about the events. In an early draft of this story, Gogol planned the whole plot as Kovalev's dream.

159. ... *В радости чуть не дернул по всей комнате босиком тропака*. *Тропак* is a Russian and Ukrainian folk dance characterized by loud thumping sounds made with one's feet. That is why dancers traditionally perform it wearing boots. Cf. the description of this dance in Gogol's "Taras Bulba": "Near the young Zaporozhian four elderly Cossacks performed a dainty jig; suddenly they careened sideways with the force of a whirlwind, practically on to the heads of the musicians and then, just as abruptly, sank down and danced on their haunches, pounding the beaten earth with the silver heels of their boots. The answering rumble of the ground could be heard on all sides and the air carried into the distance echoes of the *hopaks* and *tropaks*, pounded out by the ringing heels of their boots."[32] The comment that Kovalev performs this dance barefoot is therefore deeply ironic.

163. ... *Как кошка, которую высекли за кражу сала*. A hint at two idiomatic expressions. The first one is *кошка съела* (lit. "The cat ate"), an ironic comment about an object that has disappeared (cf. "The dog ate it"). The second one is the expression *Знает*

---

[32] Nikolai Gogol, "Taras Bulba," in his *Village Evenings near Dikanka and Mirgorod*, trans. Christopher English (New York: Oxford University Press, 1994), 261–62.

кошка чье мясо съела (lit. "The cat knows whose meat he ate"), which refers to a person who realizes s/he is guilty ("A guilty conscience needs no accuser"). It is based on the idea that the behavior or appearance of the guilty person indicates that the person feels his/her guilt but, fearing punishment, does not admit it. The narrator implies that the barber is to blame for the loss of the nose.

164. *Говори вперед: чисты руки?* A reference to the first chapter, in which we learn that Kovalev told Ivan Yakovlevich that his hands always stank. Gogol is drawing the reader's attention to the figurative meaning of the expression *нечист на руку* (lit. "having impure hands"). It is said about someone who is suspected of petty theft. Indeed, earlier the police officer informed Kovalev that Ivan Yakovlevich had stolen a dozen buttons. The barber's inclination for theft suggests that he might have stolen the nose as well.

172. *Иван Яковлевич и руки опустил, оторопел и смутился.* As in the first chapter, here the expression *руки опустил* ("lowered his hands") has two different meanings. Hand lowering is a physical gesture. Besides, it is a hint at the barber's emotional state.

172. *... За нюхательную часть тела.* The fact that the nose is called *часть тела* ("part of the body") rather than an organ invites a psychoanalytical interpretation of the story.[33]

173. *Он весело оборотился назад и с сатирическим видом посмотрел, несколько прищуря глаз, на двух военных, у одного из которых был нос никак не больше жилетной пуговицы.* The small nose of a military man is compared to a button. The litotes contains a hint at the expression *с гулькин нос* (lit. "[as small] as a pigeon's nose").

---

[33] See chapter 5, "A Case of Castration Anxiety."

173. ... *набивал пред ними весьма долго свой нос с обоих подъездов.* Comparisons, metaphors, and exaggerations are Gogol's favorite stylistic devices. Here, the nose is compared with a house, and the nostrils with the house's main entrances.

173. ... *бабье, куриный народ*. *Бабье* is a derogatory collective noun derived from *бабы* ("women"). *Куриный народ* (lit. "chicken people") is a euphemism for "stupid people," by association with the idiom *куриные мозги* (lit. "chicken brain," in English "bird brain"). It has an association with the saying *Курица не птица, баба не человек* (lit. "A hen is not a bird; a woman is not a [real] person") and points to Kovalev's misogynistic views.

173. ... *остановившегося один раз перед лавочкой в Гостином дворе и покупавшего какую-то орденскую ленточку, неизвестно для каких причин, потому что он сам не был кавалером никакого ордена*. This sentence makes clear that Kovalev is preparing to rise in rank and to receive a decoration (which consists of a ribbon and medallion). A decoration was a mark of outstanding service or other achievements.

174. ... *пользы отечеству решительно никакой*. This phrase is deeply ironic. When Gogol reworked "The Nose," he added a polemic afterword to the story, which resembles a parody of the review published in *The Northern Bee*. Gogol parodies the reviewers' style and sneers at their potential reproaches. He is also mockingly controversial when he pretends to demand a moralizing attitude. The polemical ending is most likely Gogol's response to the review of Pushkin's work in *The Northern Bee* № 192, August 27, 1834, which contained attacks on the "implausibility" of Pushkin's *Tales of Belkin*.[34]

---

[34] See N. L. Stepanov's commentary to "The Nose" in Gogol', *Polnoe sobranie sochinenii*, vol. 3, 655.

Language Game as the Engine of the Plot

The concept of language game was formed by linguistic philosopher Ludwig Wittgenstein and became a central organizing principle in his *Philosophical Investigations* (published posthumously in 1953). In his book Wittgenstein points to the limitations of the Augustinian view of language as based on the idea that "the words in language name objects." He challenges the notion that "sentences are combinations of such names" and claims that a word or a sentence has meaning only as a byproduct of the "rules of the game" being played.[1] Given his tendency for obscurity, especially in his later work, Wittgenstein does not provide a strict definition of the expression "language game," but he notes that "language games" include various activities: describing an object, reporting an event, speculating about an event, making up a story and reading one, acting in a play, solving riddles, telling a joke, translating from one language to another, requesting, thanking, cursing, greeting, and praying.[2] We find many of these activities in the narrative canvas of "The Nose."

More specifically, the term "language game," the way it is used in the title of this section, corresponds to the following definition of this expression in *Stylistic Encyclopedic Dictionary of the Russian Language*:

> The "language game" is a certain type of speech behavior of speakers, based on a deliberate (conscious, thoughtful) violation of the systemic relationships of the language, i.e., on the destruction of the speech norm, in order to create non-canonical language forms and structures, which, as a result of this destruction, acquire expressive meaning and the ability to produce an aesthetic and, by and large, a *stylistic effect* on the listener/reader. Most often, "language game" is associated

---

[1] Ludwig Wittgenstein, *Philosophical Investigations*, trans. G. E. M. Anscombe, P. M. S. Hacker, and Joachim Schulte, revised 4th ed. by P. M. S. Hacker and Joachim Schulte (Hoboken, NJ: Wiley-Blackwell, 2009), sect. 1, 5e.

[2] Ibid., sec. 23, 15e.

with the expression of comic meanings in speech or with the desire to create a "fresh, new image." "Language game" is characteristic mainly of conversational, publicist, and artistic styles.[3]

In this section, I argue that in his language game with the reader, Gogol's narrator consistently *breaks the rules* with which the use of idiomatic expressions must comply, thus producing a special type of *skaz* in "The Nose."

According to linguistic conventions, idioms (also called idiomatic phrases, set phrases, or phrasemes) differ from "free phrases" in that their meaning bears little or no relation to the meaning of their parts. Thus, for example, the phrase "it's a piece of cake," which means "it's easy," should not be taken in its literal sense, namely as the sum of the words contained therein. Within a sentence idiomatic expressions function differently from the way "free expressions" do. Specifically, their compatibility with other elements of the text is limited (that is, none of the words should be replaced with another word, not even a synonym). In addition, idiomatic expressions have a fixed syntax. Even the smallest change in syntax usually produces a comic effect. A truncation of phraseological expressions (for example, the use of only some of their components) is also conventionally considered anomalous.[4] As examples given in the annotations to the Russian text of "The Nose" indicate, Gogol's narrator breaks these rules and conventions by twisting idioms, often "literalizing" them.[5]

Let us now examine a classification of the phraseological expressions Gogol uses or hints at in "The Nose," either breaking

---

[3] M. N. Kozhina, ed., *Stilisticheskii entsiklopedicheskii slovar' russkogo iazyka* (Moscow: Nauka, 2003), 547.

[4] V. Z. Sannikov, *Russkii iazyk v zerkale iazykovoi igry* (Moscow: Iazyki russkoi kul'tury, 1999), 298–99.

[5] Sannikov calls this device a "reanimation" of the original meaning of the words constituting an idiomatic expression, a practice that creates a comic effect. Ibid., 297.

Language Game as the Engine of the Plot

them or using them in their literal sense. These expressions fall into five major groups.[6]

Group 1—Expressions containing the word "nose" and words relating to smell

—*Чтобы духу (чьего) не было* (lit. "So I won't hear its smell")—highly coll. Used as an independent sentence. It is an order for someone to not appear someplace or quickly leave someplace and not reappear ever again. Eng.: "Get out of here!" [213].

—*Поднимать/поднять нос* (lit. "To raise one's nose")—highly coll. To behave arrogantly [414].

—*Хоть кровь из носу* <*из носа*> (lit. "Even if it makes my nose bleed")—highly coll. In reference to a demand or urgent need to do something. Eng. "No matter what," "Even if it kills me" [317].

—*Наставить нос кому* (lit. "To attach a nose to someone")—highly coll. 1. To deceive, to dupe. 2. To disgrace [414].

—*Утереть нос кому* (lit. "To wipe someone's nose")—highly coll. To prove one's superiority in something [414].

—*Щелкнуть по носу кого* (lit. "To snap someone's nose")—coll. To reprimand someone [417].

—*Комар носа не подточит* (lit. "A mosquito will not sharpen his nose")—coll. Used as an independent sentence or subordinate clause. Something is done so flawlessly that no defects can be found. Eng. "It is a very neat job" [296].

—*Ни за понюх табаку пропасть, погибнуть* (lit. "To perish / To destroy someone for less than a pinch of tobacco")—highly coll. To die, to have one's career destroyed needlessly, for no (good) reason [487].

As mentioned in the Introduction, the idiom that has a primary significance in the story is the expression *остаться с носом*, which means "to be fooled" (lit. "to be left with a nose"). The plot of "The

---

[6] In each group the expressions are accompanied by brief commentaries from Lubensky, *Russian-English Dictionary of Idioms*, with page numbers indicated in square brackets. The expressions are listed in the order in which they appear in the story.

Nose" evolves as a literalization of this expression. Gogol reverses the idiom and uses it in its literal sense: Major Kovalev learns that he is left *without* his nose. While trying to find it, the Major attempts to figure out who might have fooled him ("left him without a nose") — the barber Ivan Yakovlevich, the staff officer's wife Podtochina, or the devil.

As is often the case with idioms, because of their archaic nature, the genesis of the expression "to be left with a nose" is vague and unclear. According to the phraseological dictionary, this expression has nothing to do with the nose. Rather it is a homonym of the noun нос, which comes from the verb носить (to carry). In olden times, the word meant "an offering / a ransom" — something that is brought or delivered. The dictionary clarifies, "According to an ancient custom, the groom brought нос to his bride's parents, i.e., a gift, a ransom. If the bridegroom's marriage offer was refused, the gift was rejected and the bridegroom would remain 'with his ransom' ('with a нос')."[7]

Gogol seems to have been familiar with the origin of this idiomatic expression. The story contains the theme of a marriage proposal and a (non-)refusal of the hand of a daughter. Significantly, it is the staff officer's wife, Podtochina, who uses this idiom in a letter to Kovalev: "You also mention a nose. If by that you mean that I supposedly led you by the nose and intended to refuse you formally (*будто бы я хотела оставить вас с носом, то есть дать вам формальный отказ*), I am surprised that you speak of it, since I, as you know, was of the completely opposite opinion, and if you were to propose to my daughter in a lawful fashion right now, I would be ready to satisfy you at once, for this has always constituted the object of my liveliest desire, in hopes of which I remain, always ready to be at your service."[8]

---

[7] A. K. Birikh, V. M. Mokienko, and L. I. Stepanova, eds., *Slovar' russkoi frazeologii: Istoriko-etimologicheskii spravochnik* (Saint Petersburg: FolioPress, 1998), 409.

[8] Nikolai Gogol, "The Nose," in *The Collected Tales of Nikolai Gogol*, 321.

There is also a slightly different explanation of this idiom: in times past, the word нос signified "offering/bribe," and thus the expression meant "to be left with an unaccepted offering/bribe, i.e., without making a deal."[9] Since bribery is one of the main themes in the story, Gogol was familiar with this meaning as well. Thus, the central idiom of the story, "to be left with a nose," creates a triple focus: on Kovalev's loss of his nose, on his inability (or unwillingness) to marry Podtochina's daughter, and on the problem of bribery common among government officials of the time. All these meanings remain obscure not only for those who read the story in translation but also for many modern readers with a native knowledge of Russian.

Group 2—Words denoting various parts of the body and parts of the face other than the nose

—Намылить шею (lit. "Lather the neck")—substand. To beat someone severely [812].

—Опускать / опустить руки (lit. "To lower hands")—coll. To become disheartened and lose the desire or ability to act. Eng. "X gave up" (in despair) [568].

—Не в бровь, а прямо в глаз (lit. "Not in the brow but straight in the eye")—coll. To say something apt, exactly right. Eng. "Hit the nail on the head" [33].

—Язык отнялся (lit. "The tongue fell away")—coll. Someone suddenly lost the ability to speak. Eng. "X lost his tongue" [830].

—Дареному коню в зубы не смотрят (lit. "One should not look a gift horse in the mouth")—saying. One should not complain about or look for faults in something that is freely offered. Eng. "Don't look a gift horse in the mouth" [302].

—Нечистый на руку / нечист на руку (lit. "With impure hands")—coll. One who is inclined to steal or swindle. Eng. "X is sticky-fingered" [574].

---

[9] Birikh, Mokienko, and Stepanova, *Slovar' russkoi frazeologii*, 409.

Gogol's manipulation of these expressions creates a favorable background for the central literalized idiom *остаться с носом* (lit. "to be left with a nose"), which becomes the basis for the development of the plot.

Group 3—Idioms and other fixed expressions relating to emotional states, personal characteristics, and human behavior

—*Как убитый* (lit. "As if killed")—coll. About someone sleeping very soundly, someone falling into a deep sleep; Eng. "Dead to the world" [721].

—*Сапожник <всегда ходит> без сапог* (lit. "A bootmaker never has boots")—highly coll. To do something very poorly or clumsily [584].

—*Знать свое место* (lit. "To know one's place")—occas. derog. To act or behave in keeping with one's position. Eng. "To know one's place" [363].

—*Во всю ивановскую* (lit. "So that the whole Ivanovskaya hears it")—highly coll. Someone who does something at a very high level of intensity [263]. Usually used with sound verbs: to shout, to snore.

—*Плевать в потолок* (lit. "To spit at the ceiling")—coll. To idle, do absolutely nothing [499].

—*Поехал в Ригу* (lit. "Went to Riga")—old-fash., euph., past tense, highly coll. To vomit, usually as a result of excessive intoxication [545].

—*Знает кошка, чье мясо съела* (lit. "The cat knows whose meat it ate")—saying. The person knows that he is guilty (said of a person whose behavior suggests that he is aware of his wrongdoing). Eng. "That's your <his> guilty conscience speaking" [309].

Most of the expressions in these three groups have no direct equivalents in English, which makes translation difficult. Only a few of them can be rendered in English without any loss in meaning, such as, for example, the expression "to know one's place." The narrator uses it in the episode in Kazan Cathedral when Kovalev addresses his nose to tell him/it that the nose "must know his/its place." The phrase figuratively implies that the nose must behave in keeping with his position, whereas literally it means that it must return to Kovalev's face. The humor of this remark can be easily preserved in translation.

Another example of a linguistic equivalence is the episode when Kovalev, examined by the doctor, pulls his head "like a horse who is looked in its teeth." The phrase brings a strong association with the English proverb "Don't look a gift horse in the mouth," which means "Don't be ungrateful." In Russian, this ancient proverb is phrased as *дареному коню в зубы не смотрят* (lit. "one should not look a gift horse in the teeth"). The hint at this proverb creates a double entendre: the doctor examines Kovalev as if he is not a human being but an animal, thus behaving very unprofessionally.

In most cases, however, the narrator's language game becomes lost in translation, as, for example, the most brilliant instance of a literalization—the episode in which the narrator reports that Kovalev's servant, Ivan, *лежа на спине, плевал в потолок* (lit. "lying on his back, spat at the ceiling"). In Russian, the idiomatic expression *плевать в потолок* (to spit at the ceiling) signifies "to do nothing" (the English equivalent is "to sit twiddling one's thumbs"). Gogol gives a literal meaning to this expression, thus creating a comic effect and a sense of absurdity. The subsequent remark that the servant *попадал довольно удачно в одно и то же место* (lit. "successfully hit the same place") makes the joke hilariously funny in Russian and introduces an even greater degree of absurdity.

There are various strategies to translate idiomatic expressions, such as paraphrasing (translation by description), idiom-to-idiom translation, word-for-word (literal, calque) translation, or omission.[10] In English translations of "The Nose," this passage is usually rendered word for word. Here are some examples:

---

[10] See Margarita Strakšiene, "Analysis of Idiom Translation Strategies from English into Lithuanian," *Studies about Languages* 14 (2009): 18; and eadem, "Analysis of Idiom Translation Strategies from English into Russian," *Studies about Languages* 17 (2010): 31.

—"Going into the front room, he saw his lackey Ivan on his back on the soiled leather sofa, spitting at the ceiling and hitting the same spot quite successfully";[11]

—"When he entered the hall he saw his footman Ivan lying on the grubby leather couch, aiming gobs of spit at a point on the ceiling, a target which he hit with some measure of success";[12]

—"Walking up to the front room, he saw his footman, Ivan, lying on his back across the dirty leather couch, spitting repeatedly at the same spot on the ceiling and hitting it each time."[13]

In all three translations the phrase about Ivan spitting at the ceiling seems meaningless and is attributed to the general absurdist mode of the story, but in a wrong way. In the Russian original, in this case the sense of absurdity is created not by the lack of logic but by the language game.

Group 4—Idioms consisting of interjections containing the word "devil" (*черт*)

Kovalev uses such expressions eleven times: *Черт его знает, как это сделалось* ("Devil knows how it happened");[14] *Черт знает что, какая дрянь* ("Devil knows, what rubbish!");[15] *Черт его знает, как это сделать!* ("Devil knows how to go about it!");[16] *Черт возьми!* ("Ah, devil take it!");[17] *Черт хотел подшутить надо мною!* ("The

---

[11] Nikolai Gogol, *The Collected Tales of Nikolai Gogol*, trans. Richard Pevear and Larissa Volokhonsky (New York: Pantheon Books, 1998), 315.

[12] Nikolai Vasilyevich Gogol, *Petersburg Tales, Marriage, The Government Inspector*, trans. Christopher English (Oxford: Oxford University Press, 1995), 51.

[13] Nikolai Gogol, *The Nose*, trans. Ian Dreiblatt (London: Melville House, 2014), 29.

[14] Gogol, "The Nose," 302 (Pevear and Volokhonsky's translation).

[15] Ibid., 306.

[16] Ibid., 307.

[17] Ibid., 309.

devil's decided to make fun of me!");[18] *Чтоб черт побрал ваш табак!* ("Devil take your snuff!");[19] *Но без носа человек — черт знает что!* ("But lacking a nose, a man is devil knows what");[20] *Это просто черт знает что* ("This is simply devil knows what");[21] *Только черт разберет это!* ("The devil alone can sort it all out!");[22] *Хорошо, черт побери* ("Good, devil take it!");[23] *Хорошо, хорошо, черт побери!* ("Good, good, devil take it").[24] All of these expressions are easily translated.

Curiously, in the 1830–1840s, because of the popularity of Gogol's stories, these interjections came into fashion among the youth of St. Petersburg. In an essay published in the historical journal *Russian Antiquity* (*Russkaia starina*), the Russian critic V. V. Stasov wrote:

> Since Gogol's time, a completely new language was established in Russia; we liked it endlessly for its simplicity, strength, accuracy, amazing glibness and closeness to nature. All Gogol's constructions and expressions quickly entered common use. Even Gogol's favorite exclamations—"the devil take it," "to the devil," "the devil knows you," as well as many others—suddenly became popular as never before. All young people began to speak Gogol's language. Later we began to recognize Gogol's deep poetry and were filled with the same admiration for it as for his humor.[25]

---

[18] Ibid., 312.

[19] Ibid., 314.

[20] Ibid., 315.

[21] Ibid., 320.

[22] Ibid., 322.

[23] Ibid., 323.

[24] Ibid., 325.

[25] V. V. Stasov, "Gogol' v vospriiatii russkoi molodezhi 30-40-kh gg.," in *N. V. Gogol' v vospominaniiakh sovremennikov*, ed. S. I. Mashinskii (Moscow: Gosudarstvennoe izdatel'stvo khudozhestvennoi literatury, 1952), 396.

Gogol was not the first Russian writer to use these interjections in a literary work. One such expression is contained in the first stanza of the first chapter of Pushkin's *Eugene Onegin*. Pushkin uses the same device of literalization in the lines *Вздыхать и думать про себя, / Когда же черт возьмет тебя* ("While thinking under every sigh: / The devil take you, Uncle. Die!").[26]

Years before Gogol wrote his story, in 1822 or early 1823 young Pushkin used the expression "to be left with a nose" in its literal sense. In a humorous letter to his close friend the poet Petr Vyazemsky, Pushkin included an epigram on a taboo topic—syphilis, which was widespread at the time and one of whose symptoms was the collapse of the bridge of the nose:

> *Лечись — иль быть тебе Панглоссом,*
> *Ты жертва вредной красоты, —*
> *И то-то, братец, будешь с носом,*
> *Когда без носа будешь ты.*[27]
>
> Go take a medication—otherwise you will become a Pangloss,
> You are a victim of harmful beauty,—
> And so, brother, you will be left with a nose,
> When you will be left without a nose.[28]

It is not out of the question that Gogol was familiar with Pushkin's epigram.

---

[26] Alexander Pushkin, *Eugene Onegin*, trans. James E. Falen (Oxford: Oxford University Press, 2009), 15.

[27] A. S. Pushkin, *Polnoe sobranie sochinenii v 16 tomakh* (Moscow: Izdatel'stvo AN SSSR, 1937–1959), vol. 2, book 1: *Stikhotvoreniia, 1817–1825. Litseiskie stikhotvoreniia v pozdneishikh redaktsiiakh*, ed. M. A. Tsiavlovskii et al. (1947), 206.

[28] The reference to Voltaire's character Pangloss—who explained that the syphilis he had acquired from a prostitute was necessary and designed for the greater good—is Pushkin's mockery of the philosophy of ungrounded optimism.

Group 5—Literalized collocations

Gogol uses expressions containing verbs of motion in a figurative sense, such as *прыщик вскочил* ("a pimple popped up") and *бакенбарды идут* ("whiskers go"). In the story about the nose running away, these expressions stand out as personifications: the pimple jumps, whiskers walk, the nose rides in a carriage. By making the reader pause and think about these commonly used formulaic phrases, Gogol draws our attention to the fact that these expressions are in fact funny.

Occasionally Gogol breaks the rules—he makes alterations in the syntactic forms of these phraseological units. Thus, for example, he changes the fixed expression *поехал в Ригу* ("went to Riga") into a statement about the nose wanting to go to Riga (*хотел уехать в Ригу*). He transforms the expression *Комар носа не подточит* ("A mosquito will not sharpen its nose") into the last name Podtochina. He turns the fixed expression *нечист на руку* ("with impure hands") into a question, *Чисты руки?* ("Are your hands clean?"). He converts the fairy-tale cliché name *Иван-дурак* ("Ivan the Fool") into a statement about Ivan's (Kovalev's servant) foolishness. Instead of the expression *наводить порчу*, which figuratively means "to put a spell on someone," he uses the verb *испортить*, which has the same root but a literal meaning, "to break / to ruin," thus creating a sense that there is something mechanical rather than human in Kovalev's personality.

As mentioned above, tradition has it that idioms are not meant to be taken literally; their figurative meaning is not deducible from their individual words. To be sure, the writer was perfectly aware of this linguistic and stylistic requirement. Gogol studied the Russian language carefully. He enjoyed reading and compiling various dictionaries. His *Book of all Sorts of Things* (*Kniga vsiakoi vsiachiny*, 1826–1832) contains the "Dictionary of Ukrainian Lexicon." In the second half of the 1830s, he wrote notes on the grammar and vocabulary of the Russian language. After returning to Russia from Italy in 1848, he was engaged in the collection of *Materials for a Dictionary of the Russian Language*. While working on this project, he used the *Dictionary of the Academy of Russia* and Karl-Philippe

Reiff's *Russian-French Dictionary*, which included an etymological lexicon of Russian and provided literal and figurative meanings of Russian words. In the preface to *Materials*, Gogol wrote:

> Having studied the Russian language for many years, marveling more and more at the accuracy and intelligence of its words, I am growing more and more convinced of the essential need for such an explanatory dictionary. A dictionary that would show the true face of Russian words (*выставил лицом русское слово*), so to speak, in their direct meaning; that it would illuminate the word; would show more tangibly its dignity, which is so often unnoticed; and would discover partly its very origin.[29]

Occasionally Gogol's awkward phrasing has been interpreted as an inadequate mastery of Russian. From the late 1830s to the early 1840s, writers with purist views claimed that Gogol's language was irregular and ungrammatical. Nikolai Polevoi found "gross linguistic irregularities (*большие неправильности в языке*)" in the second book of Gogol's *Evenings on a Farm near Dikanka*. Osip Senkovsky sensed that Gogol's style was "accompanied by a sad disorder of the phrase and a lack of ability to speak the language" in *Arabesques*. Konstantin Masalsky found a number of "stylistic irregularities and negligence" in *Dead Souls*. Faddei Bulgarin spoke ironically about Gogol's language. Even Vissarion Belinsky, despite his admiration for Gogol's prose, noted that it had its shortcomings: "incorrectness in language (*неправильности в языке*)." Belinsky's verdict was apologetic: "Gogol has something that makes one not notice the negligence of his language—he has style."[30]

A century later Andrey Bely pointed out Gogol's "grammatical inaccuracy" and recorded the writer's incorrect use of cases. He noted that Gogol's "verbs do not fare particularly well," "the gerunds

---

[29] N. V. Gogol', "Materialy dlia slovaria russkogo iazyka," in *Polnoe sobranie sochinenii*, vol. 9, *Nabroski, Konspekty, Plany, Zapisnye knizhki*, ed. N. F. Bel'chikov (1952), 441.

[30] Quoted in Vinogradov, "Iazyk Gogolia i ego znachenie v istorii russkogo iazyka," 61.

Language Game as the Engine of the Plot

are terrible," "there is a confusion of verbal aspect and mood," "there is a great deal of abominable phrasing and grammatical nonagreement," Gogol's "prepositions stumble throughout," his "usage of adverbs is clumsy, and "it would take flypaper to catch all the Gallicisms, Polonisms, and Ukrainianisms."[31] Bely buttressed each of these statements with numerous examples from Gogol's works (though none of these examples is from "The Nose"). On the whole, his opinion resembles that of Belinsky. Bely admits Gogol's "grammatical inaccuracy" is a flaw but claims that this flaw does not undercut the beauty of Gogol's literary style.

Without doubt, Gogol was aware that fixed expressions cannot be broken into parts, that their components are not interchangeable and must stand in a certain order, that they have figurative rather than literal meaning. It is not Gogol who destroys the integrity of the idioms and changes their syntactic functions, but his narrator — the mask Gogol creates for the narrative of "The Nose." This constructed "speech mask" determines the author's special narrative position. The narrator makes comments with a serious tone, but behind his mask, one can sense Gogol's irony and rhetorical strategy.

The language game in "The Nose" suggests that here we are dealing with a special form of *skaz* — the introduction of living oral speech into literary texture, an orientation of the narrative towards a particular manner of speech. The author creates a narrator who is an utterer of oral speech with its characteristic spontaneity and conversational nature.

"The Nose" has been defined as *skaz* rarely and briefly.[32] The theoretical studies of *skaz* were undertaken by formalist scholars

---

[31] Bely, *Gogol's Artistry*, 351–53.

[32] Donald Fanger applies this term to "The Nose" in his *Creation of Nikolai Gogol* (Cambridge, MA: Harvard University Press, 1979), 119. Vladimir Markovich suggests that *skaz* is present in all of Gogol's Petersburg tales, though he does not discuss "The Nose" specifically; V. M. Markovich, *Peterburgskie povesti N. V. Gogolia* (Leningrad: Khudozhestvennaia literatura, 1989), 40. He also points

Boris Eikhenbaum and Yuri Tynianov, as well as by Victor Vinogradov, who associated with the formalists, and by Mikhail Bakhtin. Although these scholars wrote extensively on Gogol, none of them discussed the presence of *skaz* in "The Nose." Let us recall their main points.

In "The Illusion of *skaz*" (1918), Eikhenbaum viewed the major characteristic of *skaz* as the orientation of the narrative toward oral speech and articulatory expressiveness. By means of this narrative technique, the word is introduced into a literary work as "a lively, mobile activity formed by voice, articulation, intonation, which are also joined by gestures and facial expressions."[33] In his path-breaking essay "How Gogol's 'Overcoat' is Made" (1919), Eikhenbaum elaborated on the idea that in *skaz* the personal tone of the narrator plays a key role in the narrative: it organizes the composition of the work.[34] Differentiating between the "narrating" *skaz*, in which the characteristic manner of narration reflects the narrator's mental outlook and character, and the "reproducing" *skaz*, in which the narrator functions as an actor and a carrier of language masks, Eikhenbaum assigned Gogol's "The Overcoat" to the latter type. In "Literary Today" ("Literaturnoe segodnia," 1924), Yuri Tynianov supplemented Eikhenbaum's typology of *skaz*, distinguishing between the humorous *skaz* launched by Nikolai Leskov and the lyrical and poetic *skaz* that is found in Alexey Remizov.[35]

Objecting to Eikhenbaum's assumption of an exhaustive criterion, Victor Vinogradov argued that the orientation toward

---

out that in the Petersburg tales we hear two contrasted voices, one belonging to the narrator and the other to the author: "The simple-minded narrator and the inspired and insightful (or ironic) author successively alternate with each other in each of Petersburg tales. Everywhere Gogol's narrative fluctuates between bookish and spoken languages" (49).

[33] B. M. Eikhenbaum, "Illiuziia skaza," in his *Skvoz' literaturu: Sbornik statei* (Leningrad: Academia, 1924), 152.

[34] B. M. Eikhenbaum, "Kak sdelana 'Shinel'" Gogolia," in *Skvoz' literaturu*, 172.

[35] Iu. N. Tynianov, "Literaturnoe segodnia," in his *Poetika; Istoriia literatury; Kino* (Moscow: Nauka, 1977), 160.

oral speech is typical not just of *skaz*, but of many genres, such as literary notes, memoirs, and diaries.[36] In "The Problem of *Skaz* in Stylistics" (1926), Vinogradov offered a different criterion for *skaz*—artistic recreation of "the oral monologue of the narrative type" set against a literary language background.

Mikhail Bakhtin's objections to the formalists' approach to *skaz* as an orientation toward oral speech was somewhat similar to Vinogradov's. In his *Problems of Dostoevsky's Poetics* (1929, 1963), Bakhtin made a distinction between the author's speech and someone else's speech (whether a storyteller's or a character's). He detected the idiosyncrasy of *skaz* in the merging of two voices, in the verbal interaction of two different types of speech and two different types of consciousness—one belonging to the author and the other to "someone else" (the narrator or a character).

According to Bakhtin, the purpose of *skaz* is to introduce a different socially colored voice. He observed:

> It seems to us that in most cases *skaz* is introduced precisely for the sake of someone else's voice, a voice socially distinct, carrying with it precisely those points of view and evaluations necessary to the author. What is introduced here, in fact, is a storyteller, and a storyteller, after all, is not a literary person; he belongs in most cases to the lower social strata, to the common people (precisely this is important to the author)—and he brings with him oral speech.[37]

Despite the fact that none of these scholars suggested the presence of *skaz* in "The Nose," the story holds most of its basic characteristics. While in the "The Overcoat," as Eikhenbaum suggested, the organizing compositional principle lies in the narrator's intonation, in "The Nose" the evolution of the plot is determined by the narrator's toying with idiomatic expressions.

---

[36] V. V. Vinogradov, "Problema skaza v stilistike," in his *O iazyke khudozhestvennoi prozy* (Moscow: Nauka, 1980), 44.

[37] Mikhail Bakhtin, *Problems of Dostoevsky's Poetics*, ed. and trans. Caryl Emerson (Minneapolis: University of Minnesota Press, 1984), 192.

Part One. How "The Nose" Is Made

In tune with Tynyanov's classification, "The Nose" contains a comic type of *skaz*—there are no lyrical or poetic digressions in the story.

"The Nose" also illustrates Vinogradov's idea about the interaction between spoken and literary language in *skaz*, because here the elements of oral speech contrast and blend with the background literary language in which the story is written.[38] Overall descriptions are rendered in a literary style, such as, for example, the passage in which Kovalev is introduced to the reader:

> But meanwhile it is necessary to say something about Kovalev, so that the reader may see what sort of collegiate assessor he was. Collegiate assessors who obtain that title by means of learned diplomas cannot in any way be compared with collegiate assessors who are made in the Caucasus. They are two entirely different sorts. Learned collegiate assessors . . . But Russia is such a wondrous land that, if you say something about one collegiate assessor, all collegiate assessors, from Riga to Kamchatka, will unfailingly take it to their own account. . . . Major Kovalev had come to Petersburg on business—namely, to seek a post suited to his rank: as vice-governor if he was lucky, or else as an executive in some prominent department. Major Kovalev would not have minded getting married, but only on the chance that the bride happened to come with two hundred thousand in capital. And therefore the reader may now judge for himself what the state of this Major was when he saw, instead of

---

[38] In his "Studies on Gogol's Style" ("Этюды о стиле Гоголя," 1926), which provide a deep and detailed analysis of the oral techniques in Gogol's *skaz*, Vinogradov comments on "The Nose" very briefly: "It is well known that the whole story of 'The Nose' is built on the play with a string of metaphorical and metonymic displacements of the symbol of 'the nose,' and above all, on the replacement of the hero with his nose." V. V. Vinogradov, "Etudy o stile Gogolia," in *Poetika russkoi literatury*, 287. Vinogradov's other essay—"The Language of Gogol" ("Iazyk Gogolia," 1936)—is devoted not so much to the evolution of Gogol's artistic language as a whole, but to the last stage of the writer's creative career. V. V. Vinogradov, "Iazyk Gogolia," in *Iazyk i stil' russkikh pisatelei: Ot Karamzina do Gogolia*, ed. D. S. Likhachev and A. P. Chudakov (Moscow: Nauka, 1990), 271–330.

a quite acceptable and moderate nose, a most stupid, flat, and smooth place.[39]

This passage contains elements of both literary and oral narrative. Its style is neutral, devoid of the lyricism or excessive rhetoric characteristic of other works by Gogol, but it is a literary style. The word "reader," used twice, also suggests this is a literary narrative. On the other hand, the mention of the act of speaking ("if you say something") introduces the motif of rumors and gossip, which will further evolve in the episode of the newspaper expedition, and then again at the end of the story:

> Meanwhile, rumors of this remarkable incident spread all over the capital, and, as usually happens, not without special additions. Just then everyone's mind was precisely attuned to the extraordinary: only recently the public had been taken up with experiments on the effects of magnetism. What's more, the story about the dancing chairs on Konyushennaya Street was still fresh, and thus it was no wonder people soon began saying that the nose of the collegiate assessor Kovalev went strolling on Nevsky Prospect at exactly three o'clock.[40]

This passage clearly illustrates how citywide rumors spread by the inhabitants of Petersburg became incorporated into the literary narrative addressed to readers. The act of storytelling thus acquires a certain weight. Vladimir Markovich keenly observes, "In essence, each of Gogol's stories is a symbiosis of the two most popular forms of urban folklore—an anecdote and a legend. From an anecdote in St. Petersburg tales there are plot situations which appear to be extraordinary but real incidents, as if snatched from the stream of everyday life."[41] Markovich writes that in Petersburg stories we hear two contrasting voices, one belonging to the narrator and the other

---

[39] Gogol, "The Nose," 305.

[40] Ibid., 322.

[41] Markovich, *Peterburgskie povesti N. V. Gogolia*, 40.

to the author: "The simple-minded narrator and the inspired and insightful (or ironic) author successively alternate with each other in each of the Petersburg stories. Everywhere Gogol's narrative fluctuates between bookish and spoken language."[42]

Occasionally, literary and colloquial styles begin to merge in "The Nose," thus illustrating the theory of *skaz* that Mikhail Bakhtin offered. This double-voicedness manifests itself in the merging of the author's voice with that of the narrator. Long sentences and bookish constructions blend with oral speech, saturated with idioms and colloquial expressions. What makes *skaz* special in "The Nose" is that here "someone else's" speech does not belong to a single individual, whose voice is socially defined and expressively colored. Here the nonauthorial speech is the language of folk wisdom manifesting itself in idioms. The double-voicedness is maintained by two different tones: the serious one belonging to the narrator and the ironic one belonging to the author.

The narrator's voice emerges in the first-person pronoun "I" at the beginning of the story: "He decided to go to St. Isaac's Bridge: might he not somehow manage to throw it into the Neva? . . . But *I* am slightly remiss for having said nothing yet about Ivan Yakovlevich, a worthy man in many respects."[43] It comes up again numerous times at the end:

> *I* am speaking here not in the sense that *I* think it costly to pay for an announcement: that is nonsense, and *I* am not to be numbered among the mercenary. . . . *I* just do not understand, *I* decidedly do not understand! But what is strangest, what is most incomprehensible of all is how authors can choose such subjects. . . . *I* confess, that is utterly inconceivable, it is simply . . . no, no *I* utterly fail to understand.[44]

---

[42] Ibid., 49.

[43] Gogol, "The Nose," 303. My italics.

[44] Ibid., 325. My italics.

Language Game as the Engine of the Plot

At the beginning of the story the narrator sounds perfectly serious, whereas at the end, merging with the author's voice, his voice becomes filled with irony.

By hinting at commonly used idioms, collocations, and sayings, Gogol draws the reader's attention to the fact that these expressions have lost their original meaning, that they have become verbal clichés and petrified expressions, worn out and stilted by their automatic use. This resonates with what Walter Redfern, the author of *Clichés and Coinages,* writes on the use of idioms: "Nobody, for instance, can literally run with the hare and hunt with the hounds. We can only lay a false trail or whoop in joint pursuit. It could be that some people use idioms because they do not understand their meaning, but wish to borrow glamour or authority from their support."[45] Gogol, it seems, would have agreed with this assertion.

By using these expressions in their literal rather than figurative sense, Gogol creates an effect of "defamiliarization" (*остранение*), a phenomenon described by Viktor Shklovsky in his essay "Art as Device" (1917). The technique, according to Shklovsky, puts into focus what has become taken for granted, and thus is automatically perceived, in order to make it look and sound strange. By making the familiar idioms seem strange, Gogol does more than create a comic effect. He refreshes our perception of the language by defamiliarizing the idiomatic expressions.

As a result, Gogol's "The Nose" emerges as a story not so much about Major Kovalev as about the Russian language. The idea of dismembering the human body goes hand in hand with "dismembering" idiomatic expressions. The absurdities in the style correspond to the absurdities in content. At the very end of the story, language completely falls apart when the narrator mumbles: "And yet, for all that, though it is certainly possible to allow for one thing, and another, and a third, perhaps even.... And then, too, are there not incongruities everywhere?... And yet, once you reflect on it, there really is something to all this."[46]

---

[45] Walter Redfern, *Clichés and Coinages* (Oxford: Basil Blackwell, 1989), 125.

[46] Gogol, "The Nose," 326.

Part One. How "The Nose" Is Made

A characteristic feature of idioms is their special role in organizing storytelling. Idioms often function as evaluative devices, as authorial comments.[47] In oral narratives, the typical model of "observation plus comment" has a communicative function and thus is used often in everyday stories and anecdotes. The linguist Michael McCarthy specifies:

> Evaluative clauses in narratives forestall the embarrassing question *So What? (Why should I want to listen to this story? What's exciting/special/funny about it?)*. Equally, listeners add their evaluation of events, commenting on the story's general worth, its effects on them, and so on. Evaluation is not an optional extra in storytelling; without it there is no story, only a bland report.[48]

Besides creating the effect of defamiliarization in "The Nose," the narrator's use of idioms performs both nominative and communicative functions, indicating the relation between the speaker and the described person or event.

The evaluating function of idiomatic expressions allows the narrator of "The Nose" to make additional comments on the characters, their actions, and events. For example, the expression *поднять нос* ("to raise one's nose") is a hint at Kovalev's arrogance; the phrase *нечист на руку* ("with impure hands") stresses that the barber has an inclination to steal and therefore might have stolen the Major's nose.[49] The expression *хотел уехать в Ригу* suggests that the nose's attempt to go to Riga is due to his (or his owner's) excessive intoxication and so on.

Finally, the language game in "The Nose" makes idiomatic expressions stand out as what the formalists call "the motivations"

---

[47] See R. Moon, "Textual Aspects of Fixed Expressions in Learners' Dictionaries," in *Vocabulary and Applied Linguistics*, ed. P. J. Armaud and H. Béjoint (Basingstoke, UK: Macmillan, 1992), 13–27.

[48] Michael McCarthy, *Spoken Language and Applied Linguistics* (Cambridge: Cambridge University Press, 1998), 134.

[49] Gogol, "The Nose," 318.

Language Game as the Engine of the Plot

of the major event of the plot. They introduce at least six possible causes for the disappearance of the nose.

1. The blame for the disappearance of the nose lies with Ivan Yakovlevich. Asking the barber whether his hands are clean, Kovalev implies that he is capable of stealing. The assumption of his guilt is intensified by the narrator's use of the saying *знает кошка, чье мясо съела* (lit. "the cat knows whose meat it ate"), said of a person whose behavior suggests that he or she is aware of his or her wrongdoing.

2. The blame for the disappearance of Kovalev's nose lies with the staff officer's wife, Podtochina. Although in her letter to Kovalev she denies that she decided to "leave him with a nose" (*оставить его с носом*), Kovalev is convinced that she has hired witches to cause him harm. The very name Podtochina echoes the saying *Комар носа не подточит* ("A mosquito will not sharpen its nose") and suggests that the misdeed was committed without the slightest slip.

3. Kovalev himself is to blame for the loss of his nose because absorbed by his thoughts of his social status he regards other people with contempt. The person's arrogance is expressed figuratively by the idiom *ходить задрав нос* ("to walk sticking one's nose up in the air / "turning up one's nose"), which means "to regard / to treat other people with disdain or scorn." This idiom is hinted at in the story. Speaking metaphorically, the nose runs away because Kovalev sticks up his nose in the air.

4. Kovalev's servant, Ivan, is to blame for the disappearance of the nose. Kovalev ponders, "Maybe, by mistake somehow, instead of water I drank the vodka I use to pat my chin after shaving. That fool Ivan (*Иван дурак*) didn't take it away, and I must have downed it."[50] In this phrase the fairy-tale cliché "Ivan the Fool" is rendered literally. Being a fool, the servant neglected his duties.

---

[50] Ibid., 316.

Part One. How "The Nose" Is Made

5. The devil is the cause of the nose's disappearance. Eleven expressions containing the word *черт*, which the Major Kovalev swears with, can be reduced to two major ones:

a) Черт возьми ("The devil take it!") and

b) Черт знает что ("The devil knows what").

Gogol endows these expressions with their literal meaning. As if following Kovalev's swearing *черт возьми*, the devil takes his nose away. The Major's curse, *черт знает*, implies that only the evil spirit knows the true state of affairs.

6. Finally, blame for these events lies in the Petersburg fog, which is mentioned twice in the story. At the end of the first and second chapters, Gogol writes: *"но здесь вновь все происшествие скрывается туманом, и что было потом, решительно неизвестно"* (lit. "But here the incident becomes covered by the fog, and of what happened further decidedly nothing is known"). The fog obstructs the visibility of the events both literally and figuratively. The expression *Напускать/напустить туману, наводить/навести туману* ("Let out the fog") means to present an issue in an unclear, muddled fashion (usu. to hide the true state of affairs).[51] Fog prevents one from seeing clearly; it blinds one's eyes in both a figurative and a literal sense. When at the end of the first and second chapters Gogol writes that "Here the whole incident is covered by the fog," he gives the word "fog" its literal and figurative meanings. The very city of Petersburg, with its watery element—canals, rivers, and frequent precipitations—*напускает туман* ("lets out the fog"), that is, blinds and misleads its inhabitants, as wel as the story's readers. Such is the image of this city in the so-called Petersburg text of Russian Literature—the term launched by V. N. Toporov and later elaborated by Yuri Lotman, both of whom examined the Petersburg theme in Russian literary works by Pushkin, Gogol, Dostoevsky,

---

[51] Lubensky, *Russian-English Dictionary of Idioms*, 716. In its figurative sense, the expression is used in reference to Khlestakov in Gogol's *The Inspector General*, and in reference to the ladies of the town in his *Dead Souls*.

Blok, Andrei Bely, and others, based on the myth of the semi-sacred, semi-profane city.[52]

However different these motivations are, there is a common denominator to them: the idiomatic Russian language that Gogol is challenging in "The Nose."

Gogol was against restricting the narrative to the narrow framework of the standard literary style. In his essay "The Language of Gogol and Its Importance in the History of the Russian Language" (1953), Victor Vinogradov observes that "Gogol viewed his main task as bringing the language of fiction closer to the living and precise colloquial language of the common folk."[53] Just like his literary idol Pushkin, Gogol did not mind using colloquial speech and the ungrammaticality of the vernacular. He believed that in artistic prose one can and should use constructions and forms characteristic of oral speech more freely. Elsewhere, analyzing the plot and composition of "The Nose," Vinogradov observes that "Gogol built the world of 'fantastic nonsense' by means of the artistic development of the 'new logic of things,' which he extracted from forms of colloquial, often 'nonliterary' language."[54]

---

[52] If one considers that "The Nose" belongs to the cycle of Gogol's Petersburg tales (though Gogol did not conceive it as such and never labeled a cycle of stories as "Petersburg tales"—this happened after his death), one might say that the reason the nose disappeared has to do with the place of action, namely Petersburg. According to its literary myth, anything can happen in this most fantastic and abstract city, as Dostoevsky once defined it. Yet, despite the fact that the events in "The Nose" take place in Petersburg, this story has not received much attention in "Petersburg Text of Russian Literature." See V. N. Toporov, *Peterburgskii tekst russkoi literatury, Izbrannye trudy* (Saint Petersburg: Iskusstvo-SPb, 2003), and Yuri M. Lotman, "The Symbolism of St. Petersburg," in his *Universe of the Mind: A Semiotic Theory of Culture*, trans. Ann Schukman, introd. Umberto Eco (Bloomington: Indiana University Press, 1990), 191–202.

[53] Vinogradov, "Iazyk Gogolia i ego znachenie v istorii russkogo iazyka," 56.

[54] V. V. Vinogradov, "Naturalisticheskii grotesk: Siuzhet i kompozitsiia povesti Gogolia 'Nos,'" in *Poetika russkoi litetaruty*, 44.

Part One. How "The Nose" Is Made

Gogol's mastery of artistic language was praised by many critics and scholars as a considerably more significant and important aspect of his literary legacy than its content. At the conclusion of his book on Gogol, Vladimir Nabokov wrote, "His work, as all great literary achievements, is a phenomenon of language and not one of ideas."[55] The philosopher Vasily Rozanov called Gogol a "genius of form." In the eponymous essay, he wrote about Gogol's art: "After all, there is nothing here! No plot! No content! - Content? . . . Indeed, no! But the form, the way it is narrated, is amazing."[56] Elsewhere, Rozanov expressed his opinion in more radical terms: "And all Gogol, all—except for "Taras <Bulba>" and Ukrainian pieces in general—is vulgarity in terms of conception, in terms of content. And—a genius in form, in 'how' it is said and narrated."[57]

The symbolist poet and writer Andrey Bely examined a variety of literary devices in Gogol's prose, such as "alliterations," "refined arrangements of words," "complex epithets," "impressionistic use of verbs," abundance of "intentionally banal rhetoric," comparisons, parallelisms, and semi parallels. He illustrated these devices in Gogol's stories "Viy," "A Terrible Vengeance," "Ivan Fyodorovich Shponka and His Aunt," and the novel *Dead Souls*. At the conclusion, Bely wrote: "I cannot list here even one-hundredth of all those conscious tricks to which Gogol's style resorts. I know only one thing: this stylistics reflects the most sophisticated soul of the nineteenth century. Gogol's superhuman torments were reflected in superhuman images; and in Gogol's oeuvre these images gave rise to a superhuman work on the form."[58] Gogol's manipulation of the idioms in the story "The Nose" is one example of the writer's

---

[55] Vladimir Nabokov, *Nikolai Gogol* (New York: New Directions Publishing, 1961), 150.

[56] V. V. Rozanov, "Genii formy," in *Gogol' v russkoi kritike: Antologiia*, ed. S. G. Bocharov (Moscow: Fortuna, 2008), 234.

[57] V. V. Rozanov, "Iz 'Uedinennogo' i 'Opavshikh list'ev,'" in Bocharov, *Gogol' v russkoi kritike*, 305.

[58] Belyi, "Gogol'," 277.

many "conscious tricks" that he uses to achieve his mastery of form.

The single device that has been discussed in this chapter relates not only to the story's plot but also to its epilogue written in 1842, in which the narrator asks numerous rhetorical questions about the events he has described. What seems most amazing to him "is how authors can choose such subjects" (как авторы могут брать подобные сюжеты). To be sure, the statement is ironic. The noted scholar Donald Fanger does not find it strange, but reads Gogol's "The Nose" as a manifesto,

> because the story as a whole mocks a serious attitude toward plot (the accepted notion of significant form), mocks ordinary assumptions about intentionality (the very notion of language as the carrier of messages), insists openly on this mockery, and at the end encourages the beleaguered reader's assumption that "all the same, when you think it over, there really is something in all this."[59]

The question of "how can authors chose such subjects" is illumined by Thomas Seifrid's argument that "The Nose" records Gogol's search for a form of discourse, a form of literary narrative, and "presents itself as Gogol's meditation on the possibilities for narrative in Russia."[60] Seifrid views "The Nose" as an embodiment of Gogol's concerns about creating an autonomous Russian discourse and regards the story as Gogol's commentary on a post-Petrine crisis of national identity.

For Gogol, the problem of "how the authors can choose such subjects" was more acute than it was for any other Russian writer. He admitted that he did not know how to invent stories. As legend has it, and as Gogol himself claimed, the plots of *The Inspector General* and *Dead Souls* were suggested to him by Pushkin. It seems that the plot of "The Nose" was prompted by language itself.

---

[59] Donald Fanger, *The Creation of Nikolai Gogol* (Cambridge, MA: Harvard University Press, 1979), 121–22.

[60] Thomas Seifrid, "Suspicion toward Narrative: The Nose and the Problem of Autonomy in Gogol's 'Nos,'" *The Russian Review* 52, no. 3 (July 1993): 389.

Part One. How "The Nose" Is Made

What Joseph Brodsky said in his Nobel lecture about a poet also applies to Nikolai Gogol: "But regardless of the reasons for which he takes up the pen, and regardless of the effect produced by what emerges from beneath that pen on his audience—however great or small it may be—the immediate consequence of this enterprise is the sensation of coming into direct contact with language or, more precisely, the sensation of immediately falling into dependence on it, on everything that has already been uttered, written, and accomplished in it."[61]

That said, being an engine of the plot, language sets into motion other forms of energy in the story. As Robert A. Maguire comments in his book *Exploring Gogol*, "Gogol himself would have been appalled, at any stage of his career, by the notion that language can be divorced from 'thought' or 'knowledge.' Readers who see 'The Nose' as merely a joke miss the sad, even tragic spectacle of a compulsion-driven hero who ultimately learns nothing from his experiences."[62] To avoid the mistake Robert Maguire warns about, other forms of energy will be considered in the following chapters.

---

[61] Joseph Brodsky, "Nobel Lecture," in *From Nobel Lectures: Literature, 1981–1990*, trans. Barry Rubin, editor-in-charge Tore Frängsmyr, ed. Store Allén (Singapore: World Scientific Publishing, 1993), 114.

[62] Robert A. Maguire, *Exploring Gogol* (Stanford: Stanford University Press, 1994), 339.

Part Two

Interpretations

1
Joke, Farce, Anecdote

When in 1836 the literary magazine *The Contemporary* published Nikolai Gogol's story "The Nose," the journal's editor, Alexander Pushkin, prefaced it with a lively note: "For a long time N. V. Gogol would not agree to publish this farce (*шутка*). But we have found in it so much unexpected, fantastic, funny and original, that we have persuaded him to allow us to share with the public the pleasure which his manuscript has afforded us."[1]

In the above quotation of Pushkin's laconic preface in Herbert E. Bowman's translation, *шутка* is rendered as "farce," and there are reasons for this. The word is an appropriate definition of the story's literary genre, as "The Nose" contains exaggerated and improbable situations and an element of absurdity. Pushkin could have used the word *фарс* (farce) or *фарса* (the Russified feminine version that was in use in Pushkin's time). However, he used *шутка*, which primarily translates as "joke" and thus may simply refer to the humorous nature of the story.

Pushkin admired the comic aspect of Gogol's works and laughed heartily when he listened to Gogol reading them, though occasionally it was a laughter through tears. Gogol recalls, "When I began to read the first chapters of *Dead Souls* to Pushkin, in the form in which they formerly were, Pushkin, who always laughed at my readings (he loved laughter), slowly became gloomier and gloomier, and finally he was completely somber. When the reading was finished, he uttered in an anguished voice: 'God, how sad is our Russia!'"[2]

---

[1] Quoted in Herbert E. Bowman, "The Nose," *The Slavonic and East European Review* 31, no. 76 (December 1952): 204.

[2] Nikolai Gogol, *Selected Passages from Correspondence with Friends*, trans. Jesse Zeldin (Nashville: Vanderbilt University Press, 1969), 105.

1. Joke, Farce, Anecdote

What could Pushkin have meant when he called "The Nose" *шутка*? In the nineteenth century, as in modern Russian, this word meant "an entertaining anecdote," "a story with a funny punchline," "a prank"—something people say or do for fun to evoke laughter. Vladimir Dahl's dictionary defines the verb *шутить* as "to say, to do what is only for fun, entertainment, laughter, amusement; to joke, to play the buffoon; to act naughty, to be mischievous, to amuse yourself and other people with idle and funny make-believe."[3]

The word *шутка* appears in Pushkin's story "The Queen of Spades" (1833). The old countess utters it right before she dies when she tells Hermann that the anecdote about three winning cards was nothing but *шутка*, that is, just a joke. Her explanation of the anecdote contrasts with two other interpretations provided at the beginning of "The Queen of Spades": *случай* ("chance") presenting the winning as accidental and *сказка* ("fairy tale") giving the anecdote a supernatural aura, whereas the countess's utterance of *шутка* ("joke") hints that it was just a funny story, that Hermann should not have taken it too seriously.

Pushkin's remark about Gogol "not agreeing to publish 'The Nose' for a long time" was also a joke. Originally, Gogol hoped to publish the story in the literary magazine *The Moscow Observer*, edited by S. P. Shevyrev and M. P. Pogodin. Anticipating that censors would find the episode of the nose praying in an Orthodox church irreverent and disrespectful, in his letter to Pogodin dated March 18, 1835, Gogol wrote, "I am sending you the nose. . . . In case your stupid censors insist that the nose should not be in Kazan Church, then perhaps he can be moved to a Catholic one. However, I don't think that they would be out of their minds to such a degree."[4] Not having heard from the editors for a month, on April 17, 1835, Gogol wrote to Pogodin again: "Perhaps just the devil knows what

---

[3] Vladimir Dahl, *Tolkovyi slovar' zhivago velikoruskago iazyka*, 4 vols., repr. 1863–1866, 2nd ed. (Moscow: Izdanie knigoprodavtsa-tipografa M. O. Vol'fa, 1880), vol. 4, 649–50.

[4] N. V. Gogol', "Pis'ma, 1820–1835," in his *Polnoe sobranie sochinenii*, vol. 10, ed. N. L. Meshcheriakov, commentaries N. L. Stepanov (1940), 355.

is going on with the nose! I sent it properly, wraped in oilcloth, with an address to Moscow University. I can't even think that it could have disappeared somehow.... Please, pester the local postmaster. To make sure it didn't hide somewhere between the fat parcels because of its miniature size."[5]

The editors of *The Moscow Observer* were on friendly terms with Gogol and had invited him to contribute to the journal; nonetheless, they did not seem to appreciate his sense of humor in "The Nose" and rejected the manuscript. As the literary critic Vissarion Belinsky elucidated several years later, Pogodin and Shevyrev refused to publish it on the grounds that it was "dirty," "vulgar," and "trivial."[6] Other conservative critics of the 1830s and 1840s shared this view. Thus, in 1843, in his review of Gogol's *Works* for *Biblioteka dlia chteniia*, O. I. Senkovsky (whose pen name was Baron Brambeus) wrote about the author of "The Nose," "With one hand he grabbed a butting satire by the horns, and with the other, as usual, a vulgar and completely non-literary anecdote ... proclaimed himself a comical-satirical-philosophical-poet and attacked, without style, without imagination, without evidence of his subtle taste and sense of decency, the whole world, all its oddities, vices and shortcomings."[7]

Pushkin was of a different opinion about "The Nose" and gladly agreed to publish the story in *The Contemporary*. Before sending it to Pushkin for publication, Gogol slightly revised the text, and radically changed the ending. In the new version he decided not to resolve the disappearance of the nose as just Kovalev's dream and wrote a new conclusion.

In May 1836, a few months before the publication of "The Nose," Gogol reflected upon the nature of laughter. Wounded by the lack of hearty laughter in the audience at the end of the

---

[5] Ibid., 363–64.

[6] V. G. Belinskii, "Stat'i i retsenzii, 1842–1843," in his *Polnoe sobranie sochinenii*, 13 vols. (Moscow: Izdatel'stvo AN SSSR, 1955), vol. 6, ed. N. F. Bel'chikov, 504.

[7] Quoted in V. V. Vinogradov, "Shkola sentimental'nogo naturalizma," in *Poetika russkoi literatury*, 151.

1. Joke, Farce, Anecdote

premiere of his comedy *The Inspector General*, he wrote a short play, *Leaving the Theater after the Presentation of a New Comedy*. In it, Gogol distinguished between two types of laughter—a light laugh that serves as idle amusement and a "more important and profound" laugh that holds the highest status and has a special purport:

> No, laughter is more important and profound than they think. Not that laughter that is born of a momentary exasperation, a sick and bilious disposition; nor that easy laughter that caters to people's shallow enjoyment and pleasure—but that laughter which surges out of man's sunny nature, which surges out because a spring hidden inside it bubbles eternally at its base, and it so enlarges its object that what would otherwise have slipped past is thrown into sharp relief; without its penetrating power, life's triviality and emptiness would not strike such terror into men. The degrading and the mediocre, examples of which he walks past with unruffled composure every day would not swell up before him into such a terrible, almost grotesque force that he cries out with a shudder: "Are there really such people?" even as his own experience tells him that there are even worse people. No, those who claim that laughter is disturbing are unjust. It only disturbs what is murky, but laughter is luminous ... cheerful laughter is something only a deeply virtuous person is capable of.[8]

Scholars generally agree that the first type of laughter characterizes Gogol's early stories belonging to the cycle *Evenings on a Farm near Dikanka* (1829–1832), whereas the second type is characteristic of his later works—*The Inspector General* (1836) and *Dead Souls* (1842). In "An Author's Confession" (1847), Gogol schematically divided his life into two halves, corresponding to these two types of laughter. As he explained, he wrote his early works "to entertain [himself]; [he] invented everything ridiculous that I could invent." During the second period of laughter, Gogol

---

[8] Nikolai Gogol, *Leaving the Theater after the Presentation of a New Comedy*, trans. Isabel Heaman, in N. Gogol, *Hanz Kuechelgarten, Leaving the Theater, and Other Works*, ed. Ronald Meyer (Ann Arbor, MI: Ardis, 1990), 89–90.

Part Two. Interpretations

claimed "Pushkin made [him] take the matter seriously."[9] "The Nose," written between the "two periods of laughter," does not fully belong to either period; rather it serves as a transition from the first phase of laughter to the second one, containing features of both periods: the story amuses as well as instructs. It was written when Gogol was already socializing with Pushkin (they first met in 1831).

When the story first came out, Pushkin was alone in his opinion that in "The Nose" there was "so much unexpected, fantastic, funny and original." Critics, however, barely noted the publication of the story. According to N. L. Stepanov's commentary in the fourteen-volume edition of Gogol's collected works, the publication of the story was overshadowed by the appearance of Gogol's other works. In 1836 critics were busy reviewing Gogol's *Mirgorod* and *Arabesques* and discussing the premiere of *The Inspector General*. When the story was published again in 1842, they were occupied with the recent appearance of *Dead Souls*.[10] Stepanov writes, "Most often, 'The Nose' was put on a list of Gogol's 'farces' and 'anecdotes' by his contemporary critics, being considered only with the totality of his other works. Shevyrev, in his article on *Dead Souls*, even speaks of 'The Nose' as Gogol's failure."[11] During the next two decades the story was perceived in a similar vein. In 1856, in his essay "Sketches of the Gogolian Period," Nikolai Chernyshevsky wrote that "The Nose" was merely a "retelling of a well-known anecdote."[12] At the time, the word "anecdote" (*анекдот*) designated a short story; not necessarily funny, just a curious one.

At the turn of the twentieth century, when poets, writers, and scholars began to write abundantly on Gogol and his style, "The

---

[9] N. V. Gogol', "Avtorskaia ispoved'," in *Polnoe sobranie sochinenii*, vol. 8, *Stat'i*, ed. N. F. Bel'chikov (1952), 439.

[10] N. L. Stepanov, commentaries to Gogol', *Polnoe sobranie sochinenii*, vol. 3 (1938), 659.

[11] Ibid.

[12] N. G. Chernyshevskii, "Ocherki gogolevskogo perioda russkoi literatury," in his *Polnoe sobranie sochinenii*, ed. V. Ia. Kirpotin, 15 vols. (Moscow: OGIZ GIKHL, 1947), vol. 3, 15.

1. Joke, Farce, Anecdote

Nose" was no longer read as a mere anecdote. In 1890 the symbolist poet and critic Innokenty Annensky argued that Gogol's artistic goal in the story was something more profound, that its purpose was to "make people feel the vulgarity (*пошлость*) surrounding them."[13] A few decades later, the idea of Gogol's treatment of *пошлость* as part of the writer's aesthetics was further elaborated by Vladimir Nabokov and Vasily Zenkovsky.

In his essay "The Problem of Gogol's Humor" (1906), Annensky approached humor in Gogol from a different perspective. Annensky drew a parallel between "The Nose" and "The Portrait" suggesting that both contained what he called the "humor of creation":

> Gogol wrote two stories: he devoted one to the *nose*, and the other one to the *eyes*. . . . If we put these two emblems—of *physicality* and *spirituality*—next to one another and imagine the figure of Major Kovalev, who is buying, for some unknown reason, an order ribbon, and the shadow of Chartkov dying in a crazy delirium, then at least for a moment we will feel all the impossibility, all the absurdity of a creature that combines the nose and the eyes, the body and the soul. . . . But it may also be that a higher manifestation, not accessible to us, of the *humor of creation* appeared here and that the human mystery, painful for us, is most easily solved in the sphere of higher categories of being.[14]

Annensky's poetic observation on Gogol's humor allows one to view "The Nose" as belonging to the writer's "second period of laughter," when he "took the laughter seriously."

The first scholarly classification of Gogol's comical devices was offered by I. E. Mandel'shtam in his book *On the Character of Gogol's Style* (1902).[15] Mandel'shtam dedicated a whole chapter to Gogol's humor, in which he provided a summary of the evolution

---

[13] Innokentii Annenskii, "O formakh fantasticheskogo u Gogolia," in his *Kniga otrazhenii*, "Literaturnye pamiatniki" series (Moscow: Nauka, 1979), 211.

[14] Innokentii Annenskii, "Problema Gogolevskogo iumora," in *Kniga otrazhenii*, 19–20.

[15] Mandel'shtam, *O kharaktere gogolevskogo stilia*.

of comical devices in Gogol, as well as a classification of different types of humor: "of vulgar expressions," "of proper names," "of judgments that have no logic," as well as many other types of humor. Mandel'shtam described two periods in the history of laughter in Gogol's work and provided numerous examples from Gogol's works but not from "The Nose."

In his path breaking essay "Naturalistic Grotesque: Plot and Composition in Gogol's tale 'The Nose,'" written in 1920, Victor Vinogradov returned to the "anecdotal" nature of the story. The innovative spirit of his essay emerged from his discovery that "nosological" anecdotes and puns were widespread in the 1820s and 1830s. He observed that in Gogol's time, Russian journals published "panegyrics" to the nose, expressing its tremendous significance for people and the nose's connection with honor and the intellectual process.[16] Anecdotes about the nose's misadventures circulating in the form of rumors were often published in these periodicals. One of them, entitled "French Joke," was a semicomical, semisad confession of a man who turned into a nose. His appearance aroused so much disgust that everyone ridiculed him mercilessly. Gogol was familiar with this story, published in the literary supplement to the *Russian Invalid* on September 9, 1831—he mentions it in a letter to Pushkin. Gogol also was familiar with another anecdote, published in *Molva* in 1831—a translation from German of a humorous panegyric to the nose—about the enormous significance of noses for people of different ages and social strata.

Numerous satirical anecdotes and puns (каламбуры) containing the word "nose" were collected in the encyclopedic almanac *Pictures of the World*, published by Alexander Vel'tman in 1836. This almanac came out before "The Nose," which might have given Gogol the impetus to write his story. These anecdotes narrated stories about severed, vanished, and transplanted noses. Among these stories there were poetic experiments and many puns from Russian

---

[16] Vinogradov, "Naturalisticheskii grotesk," 8. Vinogradov assigns the word *anekdot* (anecdote) its old meaning of a short, an amusing, but not necessarily a funny story. By "nosological puns" he means brief stories that embrace expressions containing the word "nose."

1. Joke, Farce, Anecdote

phraseology. Stories about noses' misadventures circulating in the form of rumors, and often published in periodicals, were satirical; they were rather innocent and not caustic satires on Russian society.

Vinogradov argued that Russian intermediary publications and genres served as a link between Gogol's "The Nose" and Laurence Sterne's novel *The Life and Opinions of Tristram Shandy* (1759).[17] Although Sterne's novel was translated into Russian in 1804–7, Gogol was familiar with it through the works of authors who imitated Sterne's imagery and style. Among them was the Russian writer of French origin Yakov de Sanglen (Jacques de Saint-Glin), author of the novel *The Life and Opinions of the New Tristram* (1825).

The popularity of nosological anecdotes, Vinogradov maintains, also owed to the emergence of rhinoplasty (plastic surgery to reconstruct the nose) in 1817. The new medical trend soon came to the attention of the public after a translation into Russian of *Rhinoplasty*, authored by the German surgeon Karl Ferdinand von Gräfe. Newspapers and magazines published excerpts from this book, often with humorous details and nosological puns.

Because of the general popularity of the nosological theme in the 1830s, noses appear in many of Gogol's works, Vinogradov observed. In "The Tale of How Ivan Ivanovich Quarreled with Ivan Nikiforovich," the narrator ponders, "I confess I don't understand why it's so arranged that women grab us by the nose as deftly as if it were a teapot handle."[18] Nosology defines Ivan Nikiforovich and Agafya Fedoseevna's relationship. As the narrator comments, "And despite the fact that Ivan Nikiforovich's nose somewhat resembled a plum, she still grabbed him by that nose and led him around

---

[17] More recently, the Israeli literary scholar Efraim Sicher took Vinogradov's "conclusions further to consider Gogol's story as a form of metafiction . . . that parodies the conventions of plot construction." Sicher traces the parodic strategies of "The Nose" in Sterne's *Tristram Shandy*. See Efraim Sicher, "Dialogization and Laughter in the Dark, or How Gogol's Nose was Made: Parody and Literary Evolution in Bachtin's Theory of the Novel," *Russian Literature* 28 (1990): 213.

[18] Nikolai Gogol, "The Tale of How Ivan Ivanovich Quarreled with Ivan Nikiforovich," in *The Collected Tales of Nikolai Gogol*, 210.

with her like a little dog."[19] The motif of a severed nose figures in "Nevsky Prospect," in the episode of the drunkard Schiller. An echo of nosology is heard in "The Diary of a Madman," where the theme of the nose's independent existence is adumbrated: "And that's why the moon itself is such a delicate sphere that people can't live on it and now only noses live there. And for the same reason, we can't see our own noses, for they're all in the moon. And when I pictured how the earth is a heavy substance and in sitting down may grind our noses into flour, I was overcome with such anxiety that, putting on my stockings and shoes, I hurried to the state council chamber to order the police not to allow the earth to sit on the moon."[20] In Vinogradov's view, the centrality of this theme in "The Nose" suggests the anecdotal nature of the plot.

In the 1920s several Russian literary scholars belonging to the formalist circle, with whom Vinogradov was affiliated, wrote extensively on Gogol. The formalists and their associates—Boris Eikhenbaum, Yuri Tynianov, Alexander Slonimsky, and Vladimir Propp—were interested in various aspects of the comic in Gogol, but surprisingly almost none of their works was about "The Nose."[21]

---

[19] Ibid.

[20] Nikolai Gogol, "The Diary of a Madman," in *The Collected Tales of Nikolai Gogol*, 298.

[21] Thus, Boris Eikhenbaum proposed the idea of a "purely comic *skaz*" in Gogol's "Overcoat," without any mention of "The Nose." See Boris Eikhenbaum, "How 'The Overcoat' is Made," in *Gogol from the Twentieth Century: Eleven Essays*, ed. Robert A. Maguire (Princeton: Princeton University Press, 1974). Yuri Tynianov traced numerous comic devices in Gogol's work, such as the use of hyperboles, parallelisms, inversions, combinations of the high and the low, tragedy and comedy, abundant sound repetitions, and the use of masks (verbal as well as physical), but without any reference to "The Nose." See Yuri Tynianov, *Dostoevskii i Gogol' (k teorii parodii)* (St. Petersburg: Opoiaz, 1921). In "The Technique of the Comic in Gogol" (1923) Alexander Slonimsky looked more closely at Gogol's humor. See Alexander Slonimsky, "The Technique of the Comic in Gogol," in *Gogol from the Twentieth Century*, 323. The general principles of Slonimsky's study were similar to those of the Russian formalists, but they were complemented by psychological aesthetics. In the prefatory note the author specifies his methodology: "My method is not formalistic, as it might appear at first glance, but rather 'esthetic.' I examine

1. Joke, Farce, Anecdote

In 1918–1919, a collective work was undertaken at the Moscow Linguistic Circle to analyze "The Nose." Presentations were made by Petr Bogatyrev, Osip Brik, Roman Jakobson, and Aleksey Buslaev, in which each scholar offered his own version of the formal analysis of the story. A special study dedicated to "The Nose" was prepared by Yuri Tynianov. Their presentations have not been published.[22]

Mikhail Bakhtin, in the final pages of his dissertation on Rabelais (written in the 1930s and first published as an essay in 1973 under the title "Rabelais and Gogol"), focused on the grotesque aspect of laughter in Gogol.[23] He claimed that Gogol's *Mirgorod* and *Taras Bulba* were saturated with a carnivalesque spirit, just as

'technique' only insofar as it has teleological value and serves certain esthetic ends" (324). Slonimsky argued that the nature of Gogol's humor manifests itself in the fusion of the comic and the serious, and that in Gogol "the rise of humor is intimately associated with romanticism" (325). Slonimsky's essay provides many examples of Gogol's technique of the comic in *The Inspector General*, "How the Two Ivans Quarreled," and "The Overcoat," but not in "The Nose." In his *On the Comic and Laughter* (1928), the folklorist and literary scholar Vladimir Propp delved into the sphere of Gogol's humor from a more theoretical perspective. See Vladimir Propp, *On the Comic and Laughter*, ed. and trans. Jean-Patrick Debbèche and Paul Perron (Toronto: University of Toronto Press, 2009). The diversity of Propp's chapters, titled "The Comic of Similarity," "The Comic of Difference," "Humans as Things," "Ridiculing the Professions," "Parody," "Comic Exaggeration," "Duping," and "Incongruity," points to a very broad arsenal of comic devices. Each of these rubrics contains numerous examples from the works of many European and Russian writers. Among these, Gogol earned the highest number of references, being quoted six dozen times. However, "The Nose" is mentioned there only once and then very briefly. A few decades later, in 1962, Propp gave a lecture titled "On the Nature of the Comic in Gogol" at Leningrad University's Philological Department, in which he elaborated on Henri Bergson's concept of the comic and its application to Gogol. See V. Ia. Propp, "Priroda komicheskogo u Gogolia," ed. V. I. Eremina, *Russkaia literatura* 1 (1988): 27–43. Propp's comments on "The Nose" are extremely sparse, however.

[22] In the list of Tynyanov's unpublished works of the early 1920s there is an article entitled "On literary history of Gogol's story 'The Nose.'" For more details see Vinogradov, *Poetika russkoi literatury*, 483.

[23] The introduction and an addition were written in 1970. In 1975 the essay was published in the magazine *Voprosy literatury i estetiki* under a slightly different title. See I. L. Popova, "'Rable i Gogol' kak nauchnyi siuzhet M. M. Bakhtina," *Izvestiia RAN, seriia literatury i iazyka* 68, no. 6 (2009): 12–18.

his Petersburg tales were: "In the Petersburg tales, and in all of Gogol's subsequent work, we find other elements of the culture of folk humor (народно-смеховая культура), and first of all, *in their very style*. There is no doubt about the direct influence of the forms of the booth folk (балаганная народная) comedy."[24] Bakhtin did not write much about "The Nose." He just stated that "the images and the style of 'The Nose' are, of course, related to Sterne and Sternian literature: these images were common in those years. But at the same time, there was a nose, most grotesque and striving for an independent life, as well; Gogol found these themes in the puppet shed of Petrushka, our Russian Pulcinella."[25]

In art and literature, the grotesque usually implies a combination of the comic and elements of the mysterious, fantastic, terrible, ugly, and irrational. Therefore, the carnivalesque laughter Bakhtin proffered was very different from Gogol's definition of laughter—both the "easy laughter that caters to people's shallow enjoyment and pleasure" of the first period of his creative career and the "luminous laughter" of the second one. Launching the concept of the grotesque body, with its emphasis on the mouth and the lower stratum, Bakhtin advanced the principle of grotesque realism, which implied the lowering of the spiritual and the ideal to the material and physical level.

According to R. M. Mirkina's notes of Bakhtin's lectures made in late 1922–early 1923, Bakhtin viewed Gogol's laughter as complex and multifaceted, related neither to realism nor to romanticism. Gogol did not reflect reality; instead he performed brilliant experiments on reality by immersing an event in the "void of life." Gogol

> would take an event, immerse it in a certain environment and show how it would develop there. This environment is the void of life. Gogol collected the emptiness spread everywhere,

---

[24] M. M. Bakhtin, "Rable i Gogol'" (Iskusstvo slova i narodnaia smekhovaia kul'tura), in his *Sobranie sochinenii*, vol. 4, book 2, ed. I. L. Popova (Moscow: Iazyki slavianskikh kul'tur, 2010), 514.

[25] Ibid.

1. Joke, Farce, Anecdote

thickened it, plunged the event into it and watched how it would occur in a condensed atmosphere of idleness and emptiness. Gogol touches this topic so deeply that it reveals the eternal nature of idleness in the world, which has always existed and will always exist.[26]

Bakhtin's application of the concept of Western carnivalesque culture and the Rabelaisian "grotesque body" to Gogol was not welcomed among several Russian scholars, such as Yuri Mann, Yuri Lotman, and Boris Uspensky.[27] Caryl Emerson explains, "As a rule, Gogol specialists are not enthusiastic about Bakhtin's 'carnivalization' of their writer's weird, demon-ridden landscapes. They consider Bakhtin too quick to lighten the situation up, to romanticize the effects of Gogol's grotesque, to see humor and spiritual receptivity where in fact there is nothing but blank, voided space."[28]

Innokentii Annensky, Boris Eikhenbaum, Yuri Tynianov, Alexander Slonimsky, Vladimir Propp, and Mikhail Bakhtin all wrote about the comic in Gogol but did not illustrate their ideas and insights with samples from "The Nose." This omission may not be accidental. It indicates that humor and laughter in this story are deeply idiosyncratic. The humor in "The Nose" does not have much in common with the comic element in Gogol's other works. It is not related to proper names. It is not built on hyperboles and litotes. As I have demonstrated in section "How 'The Nose' is Made," in many instances in "The Nose" the comic effect is created by the narrator's language game and wordplay. Besides, humor in "The Nose" borders on satire and the absurd—topics considered in the

---

[26] M. M. Bakhtin, "Dopolneniia," in *Sobranie sochinenii*, vol. 2, 422.

[27] See, for example, Yuri Lotman, "Gogol' i sootnesenie smekhovoi kul'tury s komicheskim i ser'eznym v russkoi natsional'noi traditsii," *Materialy Pervogo vsesoiuznogo simpoziuma po vtorichnym modeliruiushchim sistemam* 5 (1974): 131–33.

[28] Caryl Emerson, "Coming to Terms with Bakhtin's Carnival: Ancient, Modern, sub Specie Aeternitatis," in *Bakhtin and the Classics*, ed. R. Bracht Branham (Evanston, IL: Northwestern University Press, 2002), 17.

next chapters. It enters into "serious" contexts of sexual symbolism and into the sphere of the religious and sacrilegious; thus it is multidimensional and complex.

This must be why the translation of the word *шутка*, which Pushkin applied to Gogol's "The Nose," is so complex; it includes the whole spectrum of meanings, including those noted by Pushkin himself, who found in it "so much unexpected, fantastic, funny and original."

2
Social Satire

Among various definitions of what distinguishes satire from humor, one concerns the author's intention when creating a literary work. Humor serves to amuse the audience, whereas satire ridicules existing vices and gives a moral lesson. A product of the author's dissatisfaction, discontent, or pain regarding reality, satire is based on conflicts and contradictions, usually of a moral or social nature. In Matthew John Caldwell Hodgart's definition, satire implies the author's engagement with and disengagement from the world: "True satire demands a high degree both of commitment to and involvement with the painful problems of the world, and simultaneously a high degree of abstraction from the world."[29]

Selected Passages from Correspondence with Friends demonstrates that Gogol was deeply and painfully concerned with the problems of Russian society. His fictional works—the comedy *The Inspector General* and the novel *Dead Souls*—denounce various kinds of vice and folly: corruption, greed, and vanity. "The Nose," a transitional work between the early stage of Gogol's literary career and the late one, has been interpreted as a satirical indictment of life in Russia in the 1830s.

In 1835, before "The Nose" was published, Vissarion Belinsky wrote the following about Gogol's early works: "The humor of Mr. Gogol is calm, calm in its very indignation, good-natured in its very deceit. But in [his] work there is another humor, menacing and open; it bites until one bleeds, digs into the body to the bones, pulls no punches, slashes right and left with its scourge of twisted hissing snakes, bilious humor, poisonous, merciless."[30] What this critic describes indicates satire more than humor. A year later

---

[29] Matthew Hodgart, *Satire: Origins and Principles,* with a new introduction by Brian A. Connery (New Brunswick, NJ: Transaction Publishers, 2010), 11.

[30] V. G. Belinskii, "O russkoi povesti i povestiakh g. Gogolia," in *Gogol' v russkoi kritike, antologiia* (Moscow: Fortuna EL, 2008), 28.

Part Two. Interpretations

Belinsky was the only critic who responded to the publication of "The Nose." In his review of Gogol's Works, published in 1842, he emphasized the satirical orientation of the story and the typicality of Major Kovalev. He praised Gogol for his portrayal of Russian "types":

> Do you know Major Kovalev? Why did you become so interested in him? Why does he amuse you with the incredible adventure of his unfortunate nose? "Because he is not Major Kovalev, but the Majors Kovalevs, so after you have met him, even if you have met a whole hundred Kovalevs at once, you will immediately recognize them, distinguish them among thousands." Typicality is one of the basic laws of creativity; without it there is no creativity.[31]

In Belinsky's view, it was not only the protagonist who had typical features, but other characters also, as, for example, the footman in the newspaper office telling a story about the countess's missing dog. Referring to the footman's story, Belinsky writes:

> These few words characterize the whole social stratum, all servile people (*лакейский люд*), with their way of thinking and their way of expressing themselves; and, besides this, in these few words one can find a person who looks like many other people in this category, and who, at the same time, looks like only himself, and no one else. We could cite a lot here as an example of such typical features and outlines, but it would take us too far and would distance us from the subject.[32]

In his review Belinsky also noted the improvement in the revised version of "The Nose": "This arabesque, carelessly sketched by a pencil of the great master, has been changed in its denouement significantly and for the better."[33] His comment referred to Gogol's removal of the explanation that the "incredible incident" happened

---

[31] V. G. Belinskii, "Stat'i i retsenzii 1839 i 1840," in *Polnoe sobranie sochinenii*, vol. 3, ed. B. I. Bursov, 52–53.

[32] Ibid., 54.

[33] V. G. Belinskii, "Retsenzii i zametki, ianvar' 1843," in *Polnoe sobranie sochinenii*, vol. 3, 661.

2. Social Satire

in a dream and the addition of an ironic afterword, a parody of the reviews published in the conservative literary and political newspaper *The Northern Bee*.

Belinsky's reading of "The Nose" was challenged in the late-nineteenth and early-twentieth centuries but it established a critical approach that remained mainstream in Soviet Russia in the 1930s-50s. The most radical interpretation of Gogol's satire was purely utilitarian and functional. Vladimir Ermilov, a Marxist critic advocating the party line in literature, observed that "The Nose" contained "anti-serfdom explosive material (*антикрепостнический взрывчатый материал*). In a pompous and bombastic style, he wrote about political awareness in "The Nose":

> Shame on the social system where one person rises above another not because of his moral, mental, and spiritual qualities, but on external grounds that have nothing to do with *human worth*! Shame on a society where a person is equated with a thing, with an animal, where all human relationships are distorted, like in a nightmare! Shame on a society where nullities in hats with plumes boss around, where Misters Kovalevs cover the deadly decay of their class with an external noble appearance! These are the conclusions from Gogol's images—even though he himself did not draw them thoroughly.[34]

Many critics of a different ideological orientation also viewed "The Nose" as a biting and cutting attack on Russian society in Gogol's time, as a satire on the mores and vices of the social milieu of the 1830s, in which the fantastic element was simply a means of exposing social evils. This perspective was shared by literary scholars of different persuasions and scholarly interests.

Even Vasily Gippius, who did not profess the established Soviet position about Gogol's protest against social evil, considered "The Nose" a satire, in line with *The Inspector General*. According to Gippius, the target of satire in "The Nose" is the official bureaucracy

---

[34] V. Ermilov, *N. V. Gogol'* (Moscow: Sovetskii pisatel', 1952), 165.

in Petersburg. In the figures of the Major and his nose, Gippius discerned features of a satirical grotesque:

> Gogol derived a satirical effect from such a grotesque motif as the nose's turning into an official. A high and important official, who is "reputed to be very learned," pious, and arrogant, upon closer inspection turns out to be a fraudster and an impostor, moreover, not at all a man, but only the nose of Major Kovalev, who escaped from his "place." Motifs, which are later developed in *The Inspector General* and *Dead Souls,* are outlined here by means of a light sketch and in terms of deliberate grotesque.[35]

Commentators on Gogol's *Complete Works*, published in 1937–1952, note that due to its satirical orientation, "The Nose" suffered from censorship interference more than the rest of the writer's works. This is why Gogol had to exclude the scenes of Major Kovalev's meeting with the nose in Kazan Cathedral, as well as the mention of a bribe Kovalev offers to the policeman.[36]

The renowned Soviet literary scholar Grigory Gukovsky, who in his youth associated with the circle of Russian formalists, claimed that the plot of "The Nose" was based on the satirical metonymy inherent in Gogol's general artistic method. Gogol's metonymy suggests that in the "abnormal" (*противоестественный*) world of Saint Petersburg of the 1830s, a nose can occupy a responsible position. This phenomenon was widespread, as too many venerable people who played an important role in society and government in reality were nothing but soulless parts of the body. Thus Gogol is trying to tell his readers that society was organized in an abnormal way. An angry satirist, Gogol sees society as an unnatural phenomenon, more unnatural than the disappearance of the nose.[37] Gukovsky writes:

---

[35] V. V. Gippius, "Tvorcheskii put' Gogolia," 84.

[36] N. V. Gogol', "Povesti," in his *Polnoe soranie sochinenii*, ed. V. L. Komarovich, 14 vols. (Moscow: AN SSSR, 1937–52), vol. 3, 653–54.

[37] G. A. Gukovskii, *Realizm Gogolia* (Moscow: Gosudarstvennoe izdatel'stvo khudozhestvennoi literatury, 1959), 290–91.

2. Social Satire

The author, as it were, tells the reader: Do you find the adventures of Major Kovalev's nose unnatural and bizarre? Of course they are wild. But you shouldn't be wondering at them. They are not at all wilder than the great number of life phenomena that surround you daily, to which you are accustomed and which seem normal and natural to you. The major ones have already been discussed: rank, position, falsehood of the title absorbed human being and became more important. This is what is fantastic, not the fact that the nose can walk along Nevsky.[38]

Georgy Makogonenko maintained that in Soviet literary criticism, scholars were primarily attracted to the satirical, "accusatory" nature of the story, imbued with sparkling humor. With the exception of Yuri Mann's books *On the Grotesque in Literature* (*O groteske v literature*, 1966) and *Poetics of Gogol* (*Poetika Gogolia*, 1978), they did not pay attention to the story's grotesque and fantastic elements.[39]

For an overview of the spectrum of vices exposed in this satirical tale, we start with the main character's professional dishonesty. Major Kovalev has reached the rank of collegiate assessor in a dubious way, and not by passing an exam and earning a certificate. He is one of those collegiate assessors who were "made in the Caucasus." As mentioned in the annotations, the phrase refers to the common practice at the time of obtaining rank in a remote area of Russia for a quick and easy career. Besides, Kovalev acts fraudulently in other areas of his career also. To look and feel more noble, reputable, and authoritative, he unlawfully claims that he is a Major, a military rank more prestigious than a civil one.

Thus, "The Nose" satirizes the veneration of rank and position. In the first half of the nineteenth century, a Russian nobleman's life was determined by his rank, and a uniform was more prestigious than a frock coat. High position and rank were valued more than personality or cultural attainment. Flattery of high-

---

[38] Ibid., 286–87.

[39] G. P. Makogonenko, *Pushkin i Gogol'* (Leningrad: Sovetskii pisatel', 1985), 187.

ranking officials—Kovalev's wicked characteristic—was common in this milieu. Strolling along Nevsky Prospect and meeting his acquaintances, Kovalev tries to please his superiors by addressing them with higher honorifics than the ones they actually have earned. When he meets a court councillor, he calls him colonel, especially when other people are around.

Having discovered in Kazan Cathedral that his nose has a higher status than he himself does, Kovalev feels shy and speechless. He hesitates to start a conversation with a person of higher rank, mumbling, "How shall I approach him? By all tokens, by his uniform, by his hat, one can see he's a state councillor. Devil knows how to go about it!"[40] In his mind, rank is sacred; it cannot be joked about, mentioned in vain, or criticized in theatrical plays.

Another target of Gogol's satire is Kovalev's cynical attitude toward women. When he meets female merchants selling shirtfronts on the street or comely young girls strolling down the streets, Kovalev invites them to his apartment. The only marriage he can think of is a marriage of convenience: he would wed only if the bride had two hundred thousand rubles in capital. In church, instead of praying, he casts his eyes on young girls. "A rounded chin of a bright whiteness and part of a cheek glowing with the color of the first spring rose" make him smile broadly until he suddenly realizes that any approach is unlikely to succeed because his nose is missing and therefore he has an inappropriate look.[41]

Kovalev courts the daughter of the staff officer's wife, but although Podtochina is happy to hand over her daughter to him, he "kept avoiding a final settlement."[42] Kovalev's immoral and wicked behavior toward women distinguishes him from Gogol's other characters. Unlike Poprishchin (in "The Diary of a Madman") dreaming about his boss's daughter or the artist Piskarev (in "The

---

[40] Gogol, "The Nose," 307.

[41] Ibid., 308.

[42] Ibid., 316.

2. Social Satire

Nevsky Prospect") imagining a feminine ideal and sublime beauty, Kovalev is very pragmatic. According to Vasily Gippius, Major Kovalev has much in common with the mediocre officer Pirogov, who also behaves inappropriately with women,[43] though Kovalev is even more cynical than Pirogov. At the end of the story, thinking of Podtochina, he murmurs to himself, "There, that's for you, females, hen folk! And even so I won't marry the daughter. Just like that—par amour, if you please!"[44]

Another important target of satire in the story is bribery. The police officer takes bribes; several barbers shave him for free, and Kovalev offers him a large sum of money—a red banknote worth ten rubles, which was a significant amount at the time (enough to buy five pounds of tobacco). The police commissioner is presented as a "great lover of sugar."[45] His entire dining room is laden with sugar loaves, which merchants bring to him as bribes. The police commissioner does not reject objets d'art, though he prefers money over everything else.

Gogol also ridicules doctors and the way they treat their patients. The doctor in the story pretends that he treats them because he is honorable and not because he seeks to make a profit, and he says he takes their money "solely so as not to give offense by refusing."[46] The doctor's so-called honor manifests itself exclusively in his posture and in his thorough tooth brushing. He is a person without a face, without eyes, and without hands: "Kovalev did not even notice his face but, plunged into profound insensibility, saw only the cuffs of his shirt, clean and white as snow, peeking out from the sleeves of his black tailcoat."[47]

Satire transpires when almost none of the characters in "The Nose" behaves in accordance with his or her position. The barber,

---

[43] V. V. Gippius, "Tvorcheskii put' Gogolia," 84.

[44] Gogol, "The Nose," 325.

[45] Ibid., 314.

[46] Ibid., 320.

[47] Ibid., 320.

whose profession involves giving a hygienic shave and a medicinal bloodletting, turns out to be dirty, a drunkard, and a thief. The doctor is unable to cure his patient. The nose turns out to be a state councillor. In Petersburg, "everything is not what it seems to be," as Gogol writes at the end of the story "Nevsky Prospect."

The advertisements brought to the newspaper office demonstrate the depersonalization and dehumanization of Saint Petersburg society as a whole. Here, people and objects are sold together: a coachman, a carriage, a peasant girl, another carriage, a horse, turnip seeds, a cottage, horse stalls, a garden, and old soles. Residents of Petersburg do not live by the news; they live on rumors about fantastic events: the effects of magnetism, chairs dancing on Konyushennaya Street, the nose walking along Nevsky Prospect and in Tauride Garden.

Gogol criticizes immorality, wickedness, villainy, impurity, and corruption, but the story does not convey a corrective or didactic message. Major Kovalev does not draw a moral lesson from his misfortune. At the beginning of the story, we learn that he came to Saint Petersburg "on business—namely, to seek a post suited to his rank: as vice governor if he was lucky, or else as an executive in some prominent department."[48] At the end of the story, nothing has changed as he goes "to the office of the department where he had solicited a post as vice governor or, failing that, as an executive."[49]

Although Belinsky's interpretation of "The Nose" as social satire predominated in Soviet Russia in the 1930s–1950s and was still salient during the next two decades, "The Nose" continued to have an independent life, and its bizarre imagery required delving into other spheres. By the 1980s, the social satire approach to "The Nose" was no longer mainstream, giving way to new interpretations.

---

[48] Ibid., 306.

[49] Ibid., 324.

3
Mockery of the Demonic and of the Sacred

Some interpreters of Gogol's art have argued that the "luminous" and "cheerful" laughter "surging out of man's sunny nature," which Gogol wrote about in his short play *Leaving the Theater after the Presentation of a New Comedy*, had a ghastly side. Approaching Gogol from religious and philosophical perspectives, they claimed that this dark humor was a natural consequence of Gogol's spiritual strivings.

The Russian religious thinker and literary critic Dmitry Merezhkovsky opens his 1906 essay "Gogol and the Devil" with the following passage:

> "How to present the Devil as a fool"—this, by his own acknowledgement, was the central idea of all of Gogol's life and thought. "My sole concern has long been that after my work people should have a good hearty laugh at the Devil."
>
> In Gogol's religious outlook, the Devil is a mystical essence and a real being, in which eternal evil, a denial of God, has been concentrated. Gogol the artist investigates the nature of the mystical essence in the light of laughter; Gogol the man contends with this real being using laughter as a weapon: Gogol's laughter is man's struggle with the Devil.[50]

Merezhkovsky focuses on the late stage of Gogol's creative career, which was troublesome: Gogol had visions and was tormented by insomnia. At that time, he was under the influence of Father Matvei Konstantinovsky, a religious fanatic who condemned all of Gogol's literary works.

According to Merezhkovsky, the writer exposed the devil, tore off his mask, and demonstrated that the devil's face is terrible not because it is extraordinary, but because it is perfectly ordinary. The devil Gogol mocks is an embodiment of banality, rather than

---

[50] Dmitry Merezhkovsky, "Gogol and the Devil," in *Gogol from the Twentieth Century: Eleven Essays*, 57.

originality. Merezhkovsky does not discuss "The Nose," yet the major thrust of his essay applies to the story: by mocking Major Kovalev's arrogance, pomposity, and strivings for high status and rank, Gogol is making a fool of the devil—an embodiment of vanity and conceit.

In Soviet times the religious aspect of Gogol's work was not explored. The most authoritative Gogol scholar, Yuri Mann, notes, "Gogol's description of the devilry is based on an explicit or semi-explicit analogy between the demonic and the human."[51] However, several Russian émigré spiritual thinkers and scholars—Nikolai Berdyaev, Nikolai Ulyanov, Vasily Zenkovsky, Paul Evdokimov, and Alexander Obolensky—approached Gogol's treatment of evil from a religious perspective. They drew attention to the grim side of Gogol's laughter.

The Russian religious philosopher Nikolai Berdyaev labeled Gogol as "infernal artist" and described the images in his works as "shreds of people, nonhumans, people's grimaces."[52] In his *Spirits of the Russian Revolution* (*Dukhi russkoi revoliutsii*, 1918), Berdyaev observed that Gogol had depicted monstrous images that would later evolve during the Russian Revolution. Speaking about these evil images, Berdyaev used the word "uncanny": "Gogol hid himself and carried away some unsolved mystery to the grave. Truly there is something uncanny (жуткое) in him. Gogol is the only Russian writer in whom there was a sense of Magism—he artistically conveys the action of the dark, evil, magical forces."[53]

In 1959 *Novyi zhurnal*—a literary journal of the Russian diaspora published in New York—featured an essay on Gogol by the Russian émigré and historian Nikolai Ulyanov, who between 1956 and 1973 taught Russian history and literature at Yale University. In this essay Ulyanov called "The Nose" a picturesque representation of the triumph of evil spirits, similar to the images that appear in the

---

[51] Iurii Mann, *Poetika Gogolia: Variatsii k teme* (Moscow: Coda, 1996), 23.

[52] Nikolai Berdiaev, *Dukhi russkoi revoliutsii* (Moscow: T8 RUGRAM, 2018), 15.

[53] Ibid., 11.

3. Mockery of the Demonic and of the Sacred

paintings of Hieronymous Bosch (ca. 1450–1516) and Pieter Bruegel the Elder (ca. 1525–1569):

> Considering all the parallels between Gogol and Bosch, it is impossible not to mention that besides Bosch and Bruegel, it is hard to find a painter who created ugly creatures by representing them as separate parts of the body that have turned into independent beings. On their paintings one can see live heads on tiny legs, giant bellies, ears, and in the middle of Bosch's famous *The Haywain Triptych*, there is a figure that one can take for a nose. The appearance of the Nose is the pinnacle of the darkening of minds, and the most vivid expression of the world's ghostly character.[54]

Ulyanov maintained that just as with Bosch's and Bruegel's paintings, Gogol's story encompassed nightmarish visions that combined the comical and the diabolical, that is, grotesque features: "However, with Bosch, almost all of his evil spirits are comical, each incarnation of Satan is executed in a grotesque manner. And we know where this tradition comes from—it is of medieval origin. In miracles played out on public square stages, the devil was supposed to provoke laughter; he was comic."[55]

Ulyanov's juxtaposition of Gogol's prose and Hieronymus Bosch's paintings is somewhat reminiscent of Mikhail Bakhtin's association of Gogol with François Rabelais, especially because Bosch and Rabelais were virtually contemporaries. The chapter titled "The Grotesque Image of the Body and Its Sources" in Bakhtin's book on Rabelais, focusing on bodily excesses and delight in the obscene,

---

[54] N. Ul'ianov, "Arabesk ili apokalipsis?," *Novyi zhurnal* 57 (1959): 127. Wolfgang Kayser also drew a parallel between Gogol's "The Nose" and Bosch's paintings in *The Grotesque in Art and Literature*, trans. Ulrich Weisstein (1957; repr., New York: McGraw Hill, 1963), 125. The parallel between Gogol and Bosch also dovetails with my juxtaposition of Gogol and Salvador Dalí in chapter 9, which is not surprising because surrealists considered Bosch their forerunner. Dalí contemplated the work of Bosch in Madrid and of Magritte in the museums in the Netherlands. In 1936 Bosch's canvases appeared at a surrealist exhibition at the Museum of Modern Art in New York.

[55] Ibid., 128.

has visual analogues in Bosch's licentious and eerie imagery. Even though Ulyanov does not use the word "carnivalesque," in essence he writes about the same phenomenon. Like Bakhtin, he associates Gogol's laughter with European late-medieval theater performances staged in open public spaces—various mystery plays based on biblical narratives, which often contained lore about devils; comical plays; as well as other festivities. These parallels must be purely coincidental, for Ulyanov, whose essay was published in 1959, could hardly have been familiar with Bakhtin's essay on Gogol and Rabelais, written in the 1930s but first published as an essay in the Soviet Union in 1973.

According to Ulyanov's reading of "The Nose," Gogol's spiritual task was to expose and mock a godless reality: "The world that has forgotten God is losing the image of its Creator. An invisible intangible change occurs: something flies away, some eclipse sets in. People continue to count money, take bribes, serve in the chancery, marry, court, but all this, as in an ant heap—blindly following their noses, from subject to subject, looking down at the ground, not raising their eyes to the sky."[56] Ulyanov defines "The Nose" as an apocalyptic vision: "The world—God's creation—becomes an illusion and is replaced by the creation of the devil."[57] He maintains that just as with Bosch's and Bruegel's paintings, Gogol's story is full of grotesque imagery, among which is a crowd of old women at Kazan Cathedral with bandaged faces and two slits for eyes, a horse covered with long hair like a lapdog, and a black poodle who "turned out to be a treasurer," to name just a few. On March 25, Annunciation Day, when the coming of the Savior is announced, the presence of the nose (a monster in the spirit of Bosch-Bruegel-Goya) in the temple acquires symbolic and apocalyptic significance.[58]

---

[56] Ul'ianov, "Arabesk ili apokalipsis?," 122.

[57] Ibid., 125.

[58] Ibid., 128.

3. Mockery of the Demonic and of the Sacred

Ulyanov's essay evoked a wide range of responses among his compatriots. In Vasily Zenkovsky's book on Gogol that came out two years later, the Russian religious philosopher, an émigré living in Paris, refers to Ulyanov's essay as follows: "Not so long ago it was said about Gogol's 'The Nose' that this 'joke,' as Pushkin put it, is actually connected with devilry ('stupidity and vulgarity are the conditions for the advent of dark forces in the world,'—this is how Ulyanov sums up his provocative interpretation of 'The Nose')."[59] Zenkovsky argues that the diabolical theme in Gogol has two primary sources: Russian folklore with its demonology and German romanticism. He stresses that the imagery of these artistic sources reflects the religious world of Gogol, who doubted neither the existence of God nor the reality of evil forces. In his early career, Gogol drew attention to all kinds of moral deformities and depicted their manifestations. Over time, he began to think about the causes of the existence of evil in the world. Zenkovsky writes:

> An aesthetic attitude to all kinds of vulgarity (пошлость), which determined Gogol's early artistic conceptions, also meant a moral repulsion from everything that was low, unworthy, and evil. Gogol vigilantly noticed all those deformities that were generated by the action of evil movements in the soul—and hence his pathos of exposure: this was Gogol's artistic path. But why are all these deformities possible, where is the root of all abominations, untruths, and vulgarity? At first, Gogol simply portrayed all the manifestations of ugliness in life, but then his thought began to concentrate on the question of the causes of evil in the world.[60]

Zenkovsky stresses that Gogol's belief in the reality of evil did not mean that he was possessed by evil spirits. During the second half of his life, the writer thought that evil could be conquered and eliminated. That is why he believed that Christianization and transfiguration of life were of paramount importance. In *Gogol's*

---

[59] V. N. Zen'kovskii, *N. V. Gogol'* (Paris: YMCA-Press, 1961), 195.

[60] Ibid., 196.

Spiritual Journey (1934), the Russian literary scholar and Christian thinker Konstantin Mochulsky, who also lived in Paris, made a similar observation on Gogol's stories of the years 1834–1835, stating that Gogol "sees the world in the power of dark forces and with a merciless eye follows the struggle between man and the devil."[61]

Alexander Obolensky, an American scholar of Russian descent, later approached the problem of Gogol's artistic representation of evil.[62] Like Ulyanov, Obolensky observed that Hieronymus Bosch had anticipated Gogol's imagery: "This anxious atmosphere which the painter and the writer conjure up, delight in and convey in their works testifies to the fact that both visions, the written and the drawn, may be superimposed one upon the other in complete unison. The two artists portray anomalous beings who belong to both realms and can mediate across the boundaries of the real and the transcendental."[63] Juxtaposing some of Gogol's texts and Bosch's paintings, Obolensky draws vivid parallels between these artists' frightful and fantastic landscapes born from their inner vision, as well as between their common themes of death, hell, and the Last Judgment.

"The Nose" does not figure in Obolensky's essay, but it does in Paul Evdokimov's work on Gogol and Dostoevsky that came out in 1961 in French. An Orthodox Christian theologian, professor at Saint Sergius Orthodox Theological Institute, Evdokimov argued that in "The Nose" Gogol treated the essence of evil as an absence rather than a presence, a mix of being and nonbeing. His arguments go as follows: The devil (διάβολος) is a parasite, impostor, and imitator, whose goal is to make the world a parody of the Kingdom

---

[61] Konstantin Mochul'skii, *Dukhovnyi put' Gogolia* (Paris: YMCA-Press, 1976), 27.

[62] A. Obolensky, "Gogol and Hieronymous Bosch: A Comparative Essay," in *Transactions of the Association of the Russian-American Scholars in the USA* (New York: Association of Russian-American Scholars in the USA, 1984), 115–32.

[63] Obolensky, "Gogol and Hieronymous Bosch," 120.

3. Mockery of the Demonic and of the Sacred

of Heaven.[64] In "The Nose," instead of the divine world, we see an imitation and a parody of it. Referring to Ulyanov's essay, Evdokimov stresses the importance of the date of action: the Feast of the Annunciation is the day when people go to local churches to attend service. On that joyful day, the nose walks triumphantly into Kazan Cathedral as someone who has power over the world, a gruesome parody of the Master of the Temple.

After a long period of silence, in the post-Soviet era, discussion of the religious perspective reenters Gogol studies in Russia. The prominent literary scholar Sergei Bocharov applies Pavel Florensky's triad лик-лицо-личина (roughly translated as "spiritual face-physical face-mask") to Gogol's idiosyncratic way of portraying the human face. Faces in Gogol's works are never neutral, he claims—they are always shifted and deformed: "The deformation of the face appears as an unmotivated, fundamental attribute of the Gogolian world which arises both from the objective state of that world and the Gogolian person and from the author's subjective view of them."[65]

The motif of the "humiliation" of the human face, which comes up so often in Gogol, Bocharov argues, goes back to Christ's being slapped on the cheek. Bocharov maintains that Florensky's analysis of a face (лицо) that has lost contact with the person's soul helps us to read the portrayals of Gogol's characters. As Florensky formulates it, "The phenomenon of personality breaks away from its essential nucleus, exfoliates, and becomes a shell."[66] Bocharov concludes that the existential problem that lies at the core of "The Nose" is the problem of selfhood.

Starting in the 1990s, a number of scholars took the opposite approach. Israeli scholar Mikhail Vaiskopf, translator of and

---

[64] Paul Evdokimov, *Gogol et Dostoïevski ou la Descente aux enfers* (Paris: Desclée de Brouwer, 1961), 78.

[65] Sergei Bocharov, "Around 'The Nose,'" in *Essays on Gogol: Logos and the Russian Word*, ed. Susanne Fusso and Priscilla Meyer (Evanston, IL.: Northwestern University Press, 1992), 25.

[66] Ibid., 29.

commentator on biblical texts, makes the most radical suggestion by stating that in "The Nose" Gogol mocks liturgical practice.[67] Vaiskopf begins by posing two questions—why does the nose appear in the loaf of bread, and what does the nose's later personification mean? Vaiskopf finds answers to both questions in the plot's parallels with biblical and liturgical events. At the beginning of the story we see a repulsive couple—the barber and his grumpy wife living in defiance of God's words "Be fruitful and multiply" and ignoring the counsel "to become one single flesh." Thus, from the very start corporeality is interpreted both literally and symbolically. The flight of the nose thus relates to the collapse of a single flesh.[68]

Time and place also bear religious symbolism, Vaiskopf maintains. The barber lives on Voznesensky Prospect (the Russian word *вознесение* means "ascension"), and "peddler women sell peeled oranges on Voskresensky Bridge" (the word *воскресение* means "resurrection"). The action of the plot is confined to March–April, which signifies that Gogol associated the time with the most important Christian holiday—Christ's Resurrection. On the other hand, the Feast of the Annunciation falls on a Friday in the story, and thus the nose's supernatural separation resonates with Jesus's crucifixion. This resonance is emphasized in Major Kovalev's exclamation "My God, my God! Why is this misfortune?'" which is similar to Christ's exclamation on the cross. Another biblical parallel is the childless couple—the barber and his wife—a hidden caricature of Joseph the Betrothed and the Virgin.[69]

Vaiskopf observes that as the author of *Meditations on the Divine Liturgy*, Gogol knew perfectly well the Orthodox Christian

---

[67] Mikhail Vaiskopf, "Nos v Kazanskom sobore: O genezise religioznoi temy u Gogolia," in his *Ptitsa troika i kolesnitsa dushi. Raboty 1978–2003* (Moscow: Novoe literaturnoe obozrenie, 2003), 164–85. Earlier, this interpretation of "The Nose" appeared in M. Vaiskopf, *Siuzhet Gogolia. Morfologiia; Ideologiia; Kontekst* (Moscow: Radiks, 1993), reprinted in 2002.

[68] Ibid., 167.

[69] Ibid., 170.

3. Mockery of the Demonic and of the Sacred

tradition of preparing the holy bread, as well as the procedure an Orthodox priest must follow before he conducts the *Proskomedia* (a service of offering gifts to God in preparation for the Sacrament of the Holy Eucharist in the Divine Liturgy). During the Offertory Service the priest takes the bread in his left hand and the lance in his right, and touching the lance to the seal of the *prosphoron* (a small loaf of leavened bread), he elevates both hands to the level of his head and says a prayer. Tracing the parallels between the beginning of Gogol's story and the beginning of the Orthodox liturgy, Vaiskopf reaches the conclusion that the barber's splitting of the bread into two halves and the appearance of the nose comically symbolize the events described in the Gospel—the appearance of the risen Christ before the Ascension.[70] He writes, "In the subsequent scene of the Nose's triumphal visit to the Cathedral, it is not difficult to identify the shocking parody of Christ's union with the Church."[71] The scene demonstrates that the church in "The Nose" is a graceless and dead corporeal entity, a kingdom of "empty forms."

Vaiskopf argues that the mockery of the liturgy in "The Nose" testifies to the writer's secret hostility to ecclesiastical, ritualized, and materialized Christianity, which replaced the spirit with flesh. His hypothesis is the following: Gogol was influenced by the antichurch movement of the Doukhobors, whose views harkened back to the Gnostic denial of the "carnal" as a "dungeon" and the kingdom of evil. Thus Gogol's spirituality was anticonfessional. He believed that ritual differences only obscured the common Christian truth, and that ecclesiasticism was detrimental for all Christian denominations. This is why Gogol did not mind moving Kovalev's encounter with his nose from the Orthodox cathedral to the Catholic one in case there was a problem with censorship. Gogol's close study of Eastern patristics, his reading of *The Philokalia*—a collection of texts written between the fourth and fifteenth centuries by spiritual masters of the Eastern Orthodox Church's mystical hesychast tradition—gave rise to his mysticism. Gogol's true innovation was

---

[70] Ibid., 171.

[71] Ibid.

Part Two. Interpretations

his stunningly courageous projection of medieval archaism onto the modern literary process, Vaiskopf concludes.[72]

Other scholars elaborated on the topics launched by Vaiskopf. Thus, S. A. Goncharov considered the concept of "smell" as "spirit" (дух) as a broad topic in mystical literature. He also reads the story symbolically: "The triumph of 'flesh' in the context of Petersburg tales becomes the embodiment of a metaphysical Void, asserting its limitless power in sacred time (Annunciation) and sacred space (the noseless Kovalev and the 'devout' nose in Kazan Cathedral)."[73]

In the twenty-first century, philosophical and religious studies of "The Nose" continue to develop at full pace. The Italian Slavist Franca Beltrame reminds us that Gogol's Christian faith and his spiritual quest often acquire paradoxical forms, in the same way that Gospel parables express truth in paradoxes. "The Nose," revealing problems of faithlessness and spiritual emptiness, is no exception to this quest.[74] More globally, Beltrame writes, the story addresses the spiritual crisis in the Russian society of the early

---

[72] Vaiskopf elaborates on Dmitry Chizhevsky's hypothesis that Gogol was influenced by the eighteenth-century Ukrainian philosopher and mystic Grigory Skovoroda. Chizhevsky briefly mentions this hypothesis in his essay on Gogol's "The Overcoat." Vaiskopf notes that in his fundamental work on Skovoroda, written decades later, Chizhevsky abandoned this idea, because he had came to the conclusion that Gogol and Skovoroda were influenced by the same sources—the spiritual teachings of Church Fathers as well as Ukrainian theological writers of the seventeenth and eighteenth centuries. Vaiskopf, "Nos v Kazanskom sobore," 146-47. On Gogol and Skovoroda, see Dmitry Chizhevsky, "About Gogol's 'Overcoat,'" in *Gogol from the Twentieth Century: Eleven Essays*, ed. Robert A. Maguire, 315. Svetlana Evdokimova also sees the Gospel as a "thematic key to the story." However, she disagrees with Vaiskopf that Gogol mocks the liturgy in "The Nose": "Gogol mocks not the churchliness but the lack of it." Svetlana Evdokimova, "Gorod zemnoi i grad nebesnyi: Peterburg v povesti Gogolia 'Nos,' in *Peterburgskaia tema i "Peterburgskii tekst" v russkoi literature XVIII-XX vekov*, ed. V. M. Markovich (St. Petersburg: Izdatel'stvo S.-Peterburgskogo universiteta, 2002), 48.

[73] S. A. Goncharov, *Tvorchestvo Gogolia v religiozno-misticheskom kontekste* (Saint Petersburg: Izd-vo RGPU im. A. I. Gertsena, 1997), 155.

[74] Franka Bel'trame, "K voprosu o paradoksal'nosti bogoiskaniia v povesti Gogolia 'Nos,'" in *Gogol' kak iavleniie mirovoi literatury*, ed. Iu. V. Mann (Moscow: IMLI RAN, 2003), 168–77.

3. Mockery of the Demonic and of the Sacred

1830s. Thus, on the Feast of Annunciation, Nevsky Prospect is flooded with people, whereas Kazan Cathedral is almost empty. Beltrame maintains that the nose's praying piously in the church is noticeably hypocritical. The episode serves as a reference to the biblical parable of the Pharisee and the Publican (Luke 18:9–14). A typical Pharisee, the nose is contrasted with women with covered faces sitting outside the church. Unlike the arrogant Kovalev, these women are humble sinners in the spirit of the Publican. Overall, marking Gogol's transition to religious prose, "The Nose" reveals a messianic tendency, Beltrame concludes.

History of science scholar John F. Cornell also examines theological allusions in "The Nose." According to his reading, the story is inspired by a biblical narrative, specifically by the Sermon on the Mount. The tale reflects Gogol's artistic interpretation of Christ's declaration that it is better to remove an offending eye or limb than to risk hell (Matthew 5:29–30 and 18:8–9). Cornell makes the point that the story "takes off from the Gospel's image of the body gone out of control and presents us with a comical case study of a fractured identity that is a fruit of scandal."[75] The word "scandal" as used here is a literal rendering of the Greek noun σκάνδαλον, which means something that gives offense: the nose literally scandalizes Kovalev.

In part, in his essay Cornell provides a reading of Gogol's "The Nose"; in part he interprets the Gospel scene. This double task makes his essay intriguing. He writes, "Admittedly, my commentary is speculative—indeed it hangs on a chain of highly unorthodox conjectures. But theology and biblical scholarship should not be permitted to hijack the art of reading." Among other biblical allusions Cornell, similarly to Vaiskopf, points to the reference to the Gethsemane scene: "Near the culmination, the Noseless One's afflictions have a familiar ring. 'My God, my God!' he exclaims like

---

[75] John F. Cornell, "Anatomy of a Scandal: Self-Dismemberment in the Gospel of Matthew and in Gogol's 'The Nose,'" *Literature and Theology: An International Journal of Religion, Theory, and Culture* 16, no. 3 (September 2002): 275.

Christ on the cross, 'Why is this misfortune?'"[76] This, and other details, all contribute to what Cornell calls "the evangelical satire," without specifying what might have inspired Gogol to explore this genre.

The Russian scholar L. P. Rassovskaya, who specializes in Pushkin, Gogol, mythology, and folk literature, elaborates on the motifs of the Annunciation, Incarnation, and Resurrection in "The Nose," as pointed out by Vaiskopf. She claims that in "The Nose" Gogol creates a religious parody, just as Alexander Pushkin does in his early humorous poem *The Gabrieliad* (1822).[77] These motifs acquire blasphemous connotations in the story. The incarnation of the nose on the day of God's miraculous Immaculate Conception is blasphemous; so is the fact that the nose does not sink in water, does not burn in the furnace, and thus bears a resemblance to imperishable holy relics. In these motifs of death and resurrection, Rassovskaya sees the symbolism of an ancient rite of passage. The nose leaves Kovalev's face, passes the ritual of initiation, and thus acquires a new life. Now he belongs to the Petersburg bureaucratic community.

The transformation remains incomplete, however, since the nose, not being human, cannot fully become an official. The initiation turns out to be imaginary. Being a mirage and a phantom, the new state councillor disappears, but the parody remains. His "body" remains imperishable, so that on April 7 he reunites with his "father," Major Kovalev. According to Rassovskaya, this happens on Easter Sunday because in 1835, when Gogol first tried to publish his story, Orthodox Easter fell on April 7. Had Gogol used April 7 in his 1835 version, his censors would have interpreted it as obvious blasphemy, but in the 1842 version the paschal connotations of the date were no longer evident.

Comparing the blasphemous works of two Russian authors—Pushkin's *The Gabrieliad* and Gogol's "The Nose"—Rassovskaya

---

[76] Ibid., 279.

[77] L. P. Rassovskaia, "Koshchunstvennye proizvedeniia Pushkina i Gogolia ('Gavriiliada' i 'Nos')," *Vestnik SamGU*, special issue (2003): 32–44.

3. Mockery of the Demonic and of the Sacred

concludes that despite all the differences in these authors' views on art and religion, in their two works their positions coincide, perhaps for the first time in their artistic practice. This intersection implicitly suggests the influence of the Pushkin spirit on Gogol's "The Nose."

In her more recent book on Gogol, the American scholar Kathleen Scollins, explores the motif of Annunciation in "The Nose" in more detail, suggesting that the travestied Gospel scene "inverts the classical biblical hierarchy of the senses to climax, not in sexless incarnation but in carnal separation."[78]

Scollins reads "The Nose" as a story about triple separation. The first one takes place on the level of the plot: the nose disappears from a fragmented face. The second separation occurs in space: in Saint Petersburg, the dis-integrated city concealed in fog. Kovalev lives on Sadovaya Street (representing values deemed negative in the city: lowborn, peasant, and religious) but prefers to walk along Nevsky Prospect (associated with values considered positive in the city—status, position, and wealth). The fragmentation of the city owes to its early uneven development, enforced by Peter the Great. Petersburg, a city of parts, lacks harmony, just as a noseless face does.

The third separation is a disintegration of self, society, and speech, argues Scollins. The plot unfolds on Annunciation Day, the feast commemorating the Logos-centric initiation of the Incarnation, but the Major "loses the ability to perceive the 'living word' of God," and the following happenings invert and parody the events in the New Testament."[79] Scollins concludes that Gogol portrays Petersburg as a city devoid of the divine Logos, and its citizens as devoid of spirit: "Over the course of the tale, Kovalev's face, the city of Petersburg, and the narrative form itself are all revealed to

---

[78] Kathleen Scollins, *Acts of Logos in Pushkin and Gogol: Petersburg Texts and Subtexts* (Boston: Academic Studies Press, 2017), 134.

[79] Ibid., 171.

Part Two. Interpretations

be resolutely fragmentary, the constituent parts of all three liable to break away and escape at any moment."[80]

The variety of religious approaches to "The Nose" makes it clear that the story exceeds the parameters of a joke, anecdote, or social satire. Rather, it has the depth and breadth of a spiritual inquiry, but the content and the purpose of this inquiry are ambiguous. The claim of Gogol's mockery of the demonic is consonant with Konstantin Mochulsky's observation that Gogol's Christianity was based on pagan beliefs and fears.[81] Ridicule of the devil is common in Slavic folklore, where the devil (черт) is put to shame. Gogol's mockery of the sacred in "The Nose" is debatable, however, for it challenges a more traditional view of Gogol as a Christian Orthodox artist and thinker despite his sympathy for Catholicism and mystical teachings.

A compact and convincing formulation of Gogol's spirituality was provided by Michael Holquist, who observed that "the animating principle in Gogol's life as in his work was a compulsion to overcome the yawning gap he perceived between the banalities and beastliness of the profane, and the heights of the totally other realm of the sacred."[82] Holquist's observation applies to "The Nose": the gap between the heights of the sacred and the banality of the profane reaches its peak in the scene, in which on the Feast of Annunciation the nose is praying in Kazan Cathedral.

In the philosopher Paul Evdokimov's words, this apocalyptic scene, in which the nose (an imposter), as well as other people with no faces, take possession of the Temple of God, was distressing for Gogol.[83] Evdokimov views this scene as a parody of the Feast of Annunciation not because in it he sees Gogol's mockery of the

---

[80] Ibid., 172.

[81] Mochul'skii, *Dukhovnyi put' Gogolia*, 10.

[82] Michael Holquist, "The Tyranny of Difference: Gogol and the Sacred," in *Cold Fusions: Aspects of the German Cultural Presence in Russia*, ed. Gennady Barabtarlo (New York: Berghahn Books, 2000), 78.

[83] Evdokimov, *Gogol et Dostoïevski*, 78.

3. Mockery of the Demonic and of the Sacred

sacred, but because in it "fear penetrates the heart of Gogol, and from now on, he will feel more and more this metaphysical cold which will chase him with its icy breath until his death."[84]

The religious readings of "The Nose," complementing the "secular" ones, provide additional possibilities and choices. To interpret the timing of the events (the Feast of the Annunciation) as an omen of Gogol's blasphemy or as his harmless joke; to see Voznesensky Prospect as a travestied sacred space (given that *вознесение* means "ascension") or as part of a public place in central Petersburg, where Gogol himself lived;[85] to consider the cutting of the bread in the opening of the story as a mockery of the Orthodox liturgy or as an everyday triviality that contrasts with the most fantastic and bizarre events that follow.

---

[84] Ibid., 85. My translation.

[85] All four apartments where Gogol lived—on Gorokhovaya Street 46, Kazanskaya Street 39, Ekaterininsky Canal Embankment 68, and Malaia Morskaia 17—were in close proximity to Voznesensky Prospect. On Gogol's mystification about one of these buildings, in which his character Poprishchin lives in "The Diary of a Madman" and where Gogol himself lived, see Ksana Blank, "Po zakoldovannym mestam Gogolia," *Novoe literaturnoe obozrenie* 11 (1995): 177–80.

Annunciation Day

4
Chronicle of Folk Superstitions

Some scholars claim that "The Nose" is riddled with allusions to the superstitions of nineteenth-century "lower" urban culture. The Russian semiotician and historian of culture Boris Uspensky suggests that besides religious connotations associated with the Feast of the Annunciation, the dates in "The Nose" reflect folk beliefs linked with calendar holidays.[86] In his essay dedicated to the problem of time in "The Nose," Uspensky points out that Slavic folk traditions crop up not only in Gogol's Ukrainian cycle but also in his Petersburg tales. Uspensky's ethnographic insights suggest that time in the story propels the events in the plot.

As mentioned in the annotations, the nose disappears on March 25 and reappears on Kovalev's face on April 7, which hints at the possibility that everything happened in Kovalev's dream; the twelve days between the two dates represent the time difference in the nineteenth century between the Julian calendar (followed at the time in Russia) and the Gregorian one (followed in the West). Many scholars stress that these dates might suggest that Kovalev finds his nose on the next day rather than twelve days after he has lost it, and therefore have dreamed about the events. Uspensky uses a different approach to the time difference than most scholars do. Drawing attention to popular beliefs, he notes that in areas where Orthodox Christians used the Julian calendar and Catholics used the Gregorian calendar, the interval between the Orthodox and Catholic religious holidays of the same name could have been considered "unclean," "nonexistent," and dangerous, like Kasyan's Day (February 29, the extra day in leap year). It was perceived not as real time, but as virtual time.

---

[86] B. A. Uspenskii, "Vremia v gogolevskom 'Nose' ('Nos' glazami etnografa)," in his *Istoriko-filologicheskie ocherki* (Moscow: Iazyki slavianskoi kul'tury, 2004), 49–68.

Uspensky maintains that Gogol, who was interested in folk customs and collected ethnographic data, may have been familiar with various kinds of beliefs associated with those days. He notes that the dates March 25 and April 7 do not appear in the text of the story until its final version, published in 1842, and that during his prolonged stay abroad Gogol witnessed the Feast of the Annunciation in Rome in 1837, 1838, 1839, and 1841. In one of those years, Gogol inserted the dates March 25 and April 7 into his story, thus giving the plot a new twist. Uspensky argues that this most likely happened in 1837, the year Gogol was in Rome when the Catholic capital celebrated Annunciation according to the new style, on March 25, and a few days later Gogol must have celebrated the Russian Annunciation in one of Rome's Orthodox churches, in keeping with the old style.

By comparing several editions of the story, Uspensky concludes that in the process of working on the text, its plot and composition acquired shape by 1832. All subsequent work on the text came down to the search for the motivation of the plot, which would clarify the author's attitude to the events.[87] Eventually, the motivation was associated chiefly with the time at which the events occur, that is, March 25–April 7.

Uspensky's insights demonstrate that the time of action in "The Nose," just like its place of action, is concrete and specific but at the same time mythical and symbolic. Both time and place serve as motivations of the events. Petersburg, as presented in the Petersburg text of Russian literature, is a mythical space where mysterious events often take place. Similarly, the span of March 25–April 7 is an unreal time when strange occurrences happen, and then for no apparent reason reverse themselves, and everything goes back to normal.

---

[87] Gogol wrote its initial draft in 1832. The first draft edition was finished in 1833–1834. The edited manuscript that Gogol sent to *The Moscow Observer* is dated 1835. It was first published in 1836 in *The Contemporary*, a Russian literary, social, and political journal edited by Alexander Pushkin. The final version of the story appeared in the third volume of Gogol's *Works* in 1842.

4. Chronicle of Folk Superstitions

In her essay accompanying Gogol's Petersburg tales in the Literaturnye pamiatniki series, O. G. Dilaktorskaia also examines the influence of popular culture on "The Nose."[88] She finds it significant that the nose is missing on Friday morning and that Gogol's original plan was to motivate it by the dream because of a common Russian folk belief that Thursday dreams are prophetic. Although Gogol withdrew this motivation in the later versions, the dream/sleep motif remained in the story—all three chapters begin with the characters' awakening. Besides, Kovalev occasionally thinks that what happened to him happened in a dream. Like other motifs in this story, dreams were subject to popular superstitions of the time and the practice of consulting books interpreting dreams was widespread in nineteenth-century Russia.[89] Among other information, these books explained what it meant to have a dream about doctors and barbers and about the loss of a body part. Thus, for example, "The dream about losing a nose was considered a sign of harm and loss."[90]

In Russian folk culture Friday was traditionally seen as an unlucky day associated with evil spirits, which may have been influenced by the Christian understanding that Jesus Christ was crucified on a Friday. The fact that the story's action begins on a Friday is notable for yet another reason—according to popular belief, Friday's patroness in Russian culture is Paraskeva Friday (*Параскева Пятница*), an image that carries features of the Christian saint Paraskeva and of Mokosh—the main female deities of the East Slavic pantheon. The image of Paraskeva Friday is associated with

---

[88] Dilaktorskaia, "Khudozhestvennyi mir peterburgskikh povestei," 207–57.

[89] In the twentieth century, these books circulated in *samizdat*.

[90] Among such books was a famous fortune-telling volume by the Moscow merchant S. I. Komissarov, entitled *An Ancient and New Everlasting Fortune-Telling Oracle, Found after the Death of One-Hundred-Year-Old Elder Martin Zadek*, published in 1821 under the pseudonym Martyn Zadek in Moscow (third edition), in which one section was dedicated to the interpretation of dreams. An earlier fortune-telling book, by Lev Prokhorov, entitled *A Magic Mirror Revealing the Secrets of the Great Albert, and Other Famous Egyptian Sages and Astronomers*, was released in Moscow in 1814 (fourth edition).

marriage and childbearing. In folk consciousness, her image merges with the image of the Mother of God. By virtue of this, it is logical that Major Kovalev, who is cynical about marriage, is avenged on Friday, March 25, concludes Dilaktorskaia.

Besides its significance as one of the major feasts, traditionally Annunciation Day was associated with signs, omens, and the practice of fortune-telling.[91] For Gogol's contemporaries, the meaning and symbolism of the day and date were obvious. Dilaktorskaia concludes, "It is likely that the specific dates and days of the story, indicated by Gogol, are meant for the common perception of his contemporaries, for whom the mention of spells (*порча*) and marriage would be sufficient so that the story's real and artistic details become illuminated with additional meanings."[92]

Tracing Gogol's references to folk culture, social mores, prejudices, and superstitions of the time, Dilaktorskaia demonstrates that in "The Nose" the fantastic is born from the intersection of two kinds of quotidian culture: social and folk. For today's reader, she argues, most of the allusions remain concealed, but for Gogol's contemporaries, these references were obvious and funny. A whole spectrum of social and mythological allusions in the text serve as catalysts for incidents, phenomena, images, and details.

Just like Gogol and his first readers, the protagonist of the story, Major Kovalev, perceives everything in the spirit of his time, for his consciousness is influenced by the everyday culture of the 1830s. For example, Kovalev assumes that his nose's disappearance is due to witchcraft instigated by the staff officer's wife, who "probably in revenge, decided to put a spell on him, and to that end hired some sorceresses, because it was by no means possible to suppose that the nose had been cut off."[93] This remark reveals Kovalev's fear of spells. Kovalev believes that the staff officer's wife, Podtochina,

---

[91] Thus, the folk custom of freeing birds from the cages became part of the annual celebration of the Orthodox Feast of the Annunciation.

[92] Dilaktorskaia, "Fantasticheskoe v povesti N. V. Gogolia 'Nos,'" 159.

[93] Gogol, "The Nose," 316.

4. Chronicle of Folk Superstitions

hired sorceresses because she was displeased that the Major did not want to marry her daughter.

The idea of spoiling by magic was rooted in the archaic concept that hatred or anger toward someone could send an ailment to that person. Spoiling could be done by request and sometimes for money. Kovalev's exclamation "the devil wanted to play a trick on me!" reflects the same type of folk belief, since the idea of spoiling is attributed to evil spirits. His assumption that the nose has disappeared because after he shaved he accidentally drank some vodka that remained in the glass instead of drinking water also belongs to the realm of superstitions. In particular, it was believed that destructive power could be transferred to another by putting a curse on that person's food or drink.[94]

The spells motif in "The Nose" is tied with the motif of a disease that was common in those days—the incurable syphilis, unofficially called the "French disease" or "bad disease," Dilaktorskaia writes. Kovalev's preoccupation with a pimple on his nose hints at his fear that this might be an early symptom of syphilis. The advanced stage of the disease—the collapse of the bridge of the nose—thus serves as a hidden mover of the plot. This explains Kovalev's argument with his nose in Kazan Cathedral: "For me to go around without a nose is improper (*неприлично*, literally "indecent"), you must agree. Some peddler woman selling oranges on Voskresensky Bridge can sit without a nose, but having prospects in view . . . being acquainted, moreover, with ladies in many houses."[95]

In Gogol's time, folk medicine, based on oral tradition rather than on scientific evidence, was practiced far and wide. The drawing of blood, mentioned in the first lines of "The Nose," was used for all kinds of diseases, including those caused by spells. Vladimir Nabokov begins his book on Gogol by writing about Gogol's final illness and the doctors' unprofessional assistance, which led to the writer's premature death. Nabokov bitterly writes that the

---

[94] Linda Ivanits, *Russian Folk Belief*, with a foreword by Felix J. Oinas (Armonk, NY: M. E. Sharpe, 1989), 107.

[95] Gogol, "The Nose," 307.

bloodletting administered to Gogol—"the hideous black clusters of chaetopod worms sucking at his nostrils"—was as useless as it was humiliating.[96]

Gogol had been interested in folk ethnography since he was young. While working on his Ukrainian stories, in his letters to his mother he asked her to provide him with information on various folk beliefs and superstitions. In the 1840s he collected various ethnographic materials and wrote them down. These included detailed descriptions of various medicinal herbs, folk customs and beliefs associated with plants, as well as materials on agricultural holidays.[97] In his reminiscences about Gogol, the literary critic P. V. Annenkov wrote, "We can say that he showed the nature of the southern man even with his bright, practical mind, not devoid of a dash of superstition."[98]

The motif of folk medicine is ridiculed throughout "The Nose." The barber, treating his clients by bloodletting, is, in fact, a terrible drunkard, a possible hint at Russian folk healers' use of vodka for medicinal purposes. The doctor's advice to put the nose in a jar of alcohol is another instance of mockery of unprofessional doctors. In Gogol's time, Dilaktorskaia explains, folk healers treated syphilis with vodka and advised patients to avoid hot bread. In folk medicine, there was also a special recipe that would cure the "bad disease": a flask filled with some potion was to be placed inside bread dough. Once the bread was baked, the flask was removed and used as medication. Dilaktorskaia writes that the episode of the doctor examining Kovalev is an allusion to the healers of the time, their methods of treatment with folk medicine, and a specific way of "scaring away the disease" by striking the patient.

Mockery of doctors' and barbers' unprofessional behavior, as well as of superstitions, were common topics in a folk art called

---

[96] Vladimir Nabokov, *Nikolai Gogol* (New York: New Directions, 1961), 1–2.

[97] They constitute a large part of vol. 9 of Gogol's *Polnoe sobranie sochinenii*.

[98] Quoted in V. Veresaev, *Gogol' v zhizni. Sistematicheskii svod podlinnykh svidetesl'stv sovremennikov* (Moscow: Moskovskii rabochii, 1990), 142.

4. Chronicle of Folk Superstitions

lubok (лубок, plural лубки), Dilaktorskaia writes. *Lubok* posters—popular Russian comics—were used as decoration in houses and inns. They were designed with simple graphics and accompanied by narratives—religious stories and frivolous popular tales. The nose was often a protagonist of these pictures and stories.

Dilaktorskaia's line of argument is continued by Alexandra Pletneva, who suggests that Gogol's "The Nose" contains a reference to a popular *lubok* print called "The Adventure of the Nose and the Frost." This print was issued three times in the first half of the 1830s, with an accompanying text.[99] The protagonist in this story is a nose who is able to run and talk. As in Gogol's text, the nose in this *lubok* has a dual nature—it is a nose, but also an anthropomorphic creature.

Pletneva suggests that Gogol's nineteenth-century readers sensed the connection of the story to this popular print. Since *lubok* was considered low-brow literature, some of these readers might have been shocked by Gogol's appeal to grassroots popular culture. Russian classical literature and popular prints addressed completely different audiences. *Lubok*'s language had its own rules of spelling, morphology, and syntactic structure, which did not correspond to the norms of the literary language of that time; rather, it combined elements of dialects, vernacular Russian, elements of Church Slavonic, and bureaucratic idiom. Pletneva claims that the reason Pushkin found "The Nose" "fantastic, funny, and original" was that he himself had turned to the *lubok* tradition in his poems *The Tale of Tsar Saltan* and *Ruslan and Ludmila*.

A discussion of folk superstitions in "The Nose" would be incomplete without mentioning of the barber Ivan Yakovlevich's famous namesake—Ivan Yakovlevich Koreisha (1783–1861), who was considered a diviner and a blessed man at the time the story

---

[99] Alexandra Pletneva, "Povest' N. V. Gogolia 'Nos' i lubochnaia traditsiia," *Novoe literaturnoe obozrenie* 61 (2003): 152–63.

was written. The son of a priest, Koreisha was educated at the Smolensk Seminary, and then at the Theological Academy.[100] In 1817 his prophecies prevented the wedding of a famous nobleman. As a result of this unfortunate event, in the 1820s Koreisha, who was mentally ill, was placed in a lunatic asylum in Moscow, located in the Preobrazhenka district. He spent the next forty-four years in this hospital. In the early to the mid-1830s, when Gogol worked on "The Nose," dozens of visitors came to see Koreisha daily, believing in his miraculous abilities as a healer and prophet. Koreisha was well known not only in Moscow, but also in Saint Petersburg. In his book published in 1909, the head doctor of the Preobrazhensky Hospital, Nikita Bazhenov (1857–1923), a professor of psychiatry at Moscow University, wrote about his former patient: "His fame as a soothsayer grew and penetrated into all walks of life up to and including the literary and university circles."[101] Because of the rumors circulating in Moscow and Saint Petersburg that Koreisha had the gift of prophecy, many famous contemporaries came to visit him from all over Russia, such as, for example, the academician Fyodor Buslaev.

The name and the image of this strange man was immortalized in Russian literature. Leo Tolstoy mentioned this holy fool in chapter 22 of his novel *Youth* (1857); Alexander Ostrovsky alluded to this figure in two plays—*Balzaminov's Marriage* (1861) and *Enough Stupidity in Every Wise Man* (1868); Mikhail Saltykov-Shchedrin wrote about Koreisha in his novel *History of a Town* (1870); Fyodor Dostoevsky dedicated the entire second chapter in part 5 of his novel *Devils* (1871–1872) to him under the name Semyon Yakovlevich; Nikolai Leskov mentioned Ivan Yakovlevich in his short story "A Little Mistake" (1883). All these writers described the grotesque features of this pseudo-saint. When Koreisha died, his obituary was

---

[100] I draw on N. N. Bazhenov's *Istoriia moskovskogo dollgauza, nyne Moskovskoi gorodskoi Preobrazhenskoi bol'nitsy dlia dushevnobol'nykh* (Moscow: Izdanie Moskovskogo gorodskogo obshchestvennogo upravleniia, 1909), 70–77, and Ivan Pryzhov's "Ivan Iakovlevich," in his *26 moskovskikh prorokov, iurodivykh, dur i durakov: Issledovania* (Moscow: Eksmo, 2008), 81–95.

[101] Bazhenov, *Istoriia Moskovskogo dollgauza*, 74.

4. Chronicle of Folk Superstitions

published not only in Moscow newspapers, but also in the Saint Petersburg newspaper *The Northern Bee*.

Gogol, according to the memoirs of his doctor A. T. Tarasenkov, once attempted to meet with Koreisha. In 1852, three weeks before his death, on a wet, cold, windy, and dark February evening, Gogol took a carriage to a faraway section of Moscow in the district of Sokolniki, where Preobrazhensky Hospital was located. Having arrived, he walked back and forth at the gate, stood for a long time in a snowy field near the hospital, then suddenly returned to his cab and drove back. Tarasenkov assumed that Gogol went to Preobrazhensky Hospital because he wanted to get advice from Ivan Yakovlevich.[102] Nikita Bazhenov is inclined to explain this episode in Gogol's life by the fact that Preobrazhensky Hospital was the only public institution for the mentally ill in Moscow; Gogol knew about it and, sensing a catastrophe threatening his mental well-being, rushed there for help.[103]

After the publication of *The Vita of Ivan Yakovlevich: The Famous Moscow Diviner* (*Zhitie Ivana Iakovlevicha, izvestnogo proroka v Moskve*) by I. G. Pryzhov in 1860, the name Ivan Yakovlevich became officially synonymous with foolishness and the expression "holy fool" (*юродивый*). The idiom "Ivan Yakovlevich," which denoted the concept of a holy fool in a broad sense, was included in M. I. Mikhelson's *Big Explanatory and Phraseological Dictionary* (*Bol'shoi tolkovo-frazeologicheskii slovar'*), published in 1896–1912.

Although Gogol wrote "The Nose" long before Pryzhov's book was published, the possibility of the barber Ivan Yakovlevich's satirical resemblance to Ivan Yakovlevich Koreisha can be seen in several parallels between the two Ivans. The barber bears a physical likeness to the holy fool—an untidy appearance. According to visitors to Preobrazhensky Hospital who came to see Koreisha to discover their fate, "the prophet" was lying in the corner of his

---

[102] A. Tarasenkov, *Poslednie dni zhizni N. V. Gogolia. Zapiski ego sovremennika d-ra A. Tarasenkova*, revised 2nd ed. (Moscow: T-vo skoropechatnia A. A. Levenson, 1902), 17.

[103] See Bazhenov, *Istoriia Moskovskogo*, 74.

room under a dirty blanket with greasy stains. He ate while lying down, inviting visitors to share a meal with him.

His uncleanliness had become proverbial. In a poem on the occasion of Koreisha's death, the poet F. B. Miller wrote under the pseudonym Giatsint Tiul'panov the following lines:

> "Иван Иакович безвременно угас!
>   Угас пророк, достойный лучшей доли!"
> О бедные! мне ваш понятен вопль и сон:
>   Кто будет вас трепать немытой дланью?
> Кто будет мило так дурачить вас, как он,
>   И услаждать ваш слух своею бранью?
> Кто будет вас кормить бурдою с табаком
>   Из грязного, вонючего сосуда,
>   И лакомить подчас засохшим кренделькóм
> Иль кашицей с засаленного блюда?[104]

> "Ivan Iakovlich faded untimely!
>   The prophet worthy of a better destiny has died!"
> O poor people! I understand your cry and delirium:
>   Who will pat you with an unwashed hand?
> Who will fool you gently like him,
>   And sweeten your ear with his abuse?
> Who will feed you balderdash with tobacco
>   From a dirty, stinky vessel
>   And treat you with some dried pretzels
>   Or gruel in a greasy dish?

The barber Ivan Yakovlevich's uncleanliness is described in "The Nose" in a similar way:

> Ivan Yakovlevich, like every decent Russian artisan, was a terrible drunkard. And though he shaved other people's chins every day, his own was eternally unshaven. Ivan Yakovlevich's tailcoat (Ivan Yakovlevich never went around in a frock coat) was piebald, that is, it was black, but all dappled with brownish yellow and gray spots; the collar was shiny,

---

[104] Ivan Pryzhov, "Ivan Iakovlevich," 95.

4. Chronicle of Folk Superstitions

and in place of three buttons there hung only threads. Ivan Yakovlevich was a great cynic, and whenever the collegiate assessor Kovalev said to him while being shaved, "Your hands eternally stink, Ivan Yakovlevich"—Ivan Yakovlevich would reply with a question: "And why should they stink?" to which the collegiate assessor would say, "I don't know, brother, but they stink."[105]

Another affinity between the two Ivans is alcohol. Gogol points out that Ivan Yakovlevich was a drunkard. As strange as it may seem, Ivan Yakovlevich Koreisha was allowed to imbibe vodka with his meals in the hospital. His clients would also bring him large quantities of tobacco, which he was permitted to sniff and chew (tobacco is mentioned many times in "The Nose"). Koreisha was granted these special privileges because the amount of visitation fees his clients paid to the hospital was enormous.

Despite their physical disarray and craving for alcohol, both men acted as healers. In "The Nose" Ivan Yakovlevich performs bloodletting with his fetid hands. He pulls his customers' noses unceremoniously, and his wife suspects that he cut off Kovalev's nose. Ivan Yakovlevich Koreisha was famous, or rather infamous, for his odd methods of treatment. Many respectable ladies and gentlemen revered him as a saint, kissed his hand, prayed, knelt, and touched their forehead to the dirty floor. They would take home packs of sand filled with his urine because it was believed to be therapeutic. Since he was worshiped as a holy fool, the visitors took his "treatments" patiently and tried to endure his stench. In fact, Koreisha's treatment practice was not very different from methods officially used in the asylum: patients were bled with leeches, vomited tartar, and took various kinds of laxatives; burns were also applied to their hands.

Several Russian writers mention the holy fool's lack of articulation and his meaningless verbal utterances. In Dostoevsky's *Devils* the holy fool repeatedly utters the nonexistent word

---

[105] Gogol, "The Nose," 303. The name Ivan Yakovlevich first appears in the version of the story published in *The Contemporary* (here the barber is first called Ivan Fedorovich, then Ivan Yakovlevich).

миловзоры. In Leskov's story his utterances are equally meaningless. In "The Nose" Ivan Yakovlevich is emphatically inarticulate. Thus, when he finds the nose, he says, "By all tokens this incident should be unfeasible: for bread is a baking matter, and a nose is something else entirely. I can't figure it out!"[106]

Holy foolishness (*юродство*) is a paradoxical cultural phenomenon. Mumbling, physically untidy, and impolite with visitors, for many decades Koreisha was worshiped in Russia almost like a saint. Nikita Bazhenov writes, "At first glance, it would seem strange and inexplicable that this man, clearly weak-minded, moreover disgusting because of his uncleanliness, was surrounded by such a halo of popularity that crowds of not only uneducated people, but also more cultured classes flocked to him, as to a prophet."[107] He maintains that to understand this paradox, one must take into account the power of superstitions.

As mentioned in the previous chapter, some scholars suggested that the opening lines of the story contain a parody of *Proskomedia*—the Liturgy of Preparation of the bread for the Eucharist—but none of them raises the question of why the barber assumes the role of a priest in "The Nose." The parallels between the two Ivans allow us to answer this question: by introducing liturgical motifs in "The Nose," by having Ivan Yakovlevich cut the bread, Gogol mocks Russian pseudo-faith and pseudo-saints.

---

[106] Gogol, "The Nose," 302.

[107] Bazhenov, *Istoriia Moskovskogo*, 75.

5
A Case of Castration Anxiety

When in 1835 the editors of *The Moscow Observer* considered the story "dirty" and "vulgar" and refused to publish it, they must have noticed that "The Nose" contained many references to sex. In the story Praskovya Osipovna reprimands her husband for not performing his conjugal duties, using the jargon word *потаскушка* (slut). When Kovalev strolls down the streets of St. Petersburg, he invites female street merchants to his apartment. The police officer admonishes Kovalev saying that "a respectable man would not have his nose torn off, and that there were many Majors in the world whose underclothes were not even in decent condition, and who dragged themselves around to all sorts of improper places."[108] In the window of a shop there is "a lithograph portraying a girl straightening a stocking and a fop with a turned-back waistcoat and a small beard peeping at her from behind a tree."[109]

The first psychoanalytic interpretation of "The Nose" was undertaken by Ivan Yermakov in his *Sketches for an Analysis of the Art of N. V. Gogol* (*Ocherki po analizu tvorchestva N. V. Gogolia*, 1923). Yermakov was a Russian psychiatrist and psychoanalyst, the organizer and head of the Russian Psychoanalytic Society (1922–1925) and of the State Psychoanalytical Institute (1923–1925). In contrast with the critics of the formalist wing who focused on Gogol's use of literary devices, Yermakov saw "The Nose" as a confessional narrative that reflected the writer's feelings, desires, and psyche.

Yermakov's approach was somewhat reminiscent of the psychological trend that prevailed in Gogol studies, the adherents of which believed that Gogol's personality influenced his aesthetics. This psycho-aesthetic approach, as Victor Vinogradov observed in 1925, permeated I. E. Mandel'shtam's *On the Character of Gogol's*

---

[108] Gogol, "The Nose," 315.

[109] Ibid., 322.

Major Kovalev Looking at Himself in the Mirror

5. A Case of Castration Anxiety

Style (1902), Vasily Rozanov's and Innokenty Annensky's essays, A. L. Slonimsky's *The Technique of the Comic in Gogol* (1923), Vasily Gippius's *Gogol* (1924), and Vasily Zenkovsky's publications on religious topics in Gogol's works.[110]

What was new in Yermakov's psychoanalytic reading of "The Nose" was his focus on Gogol's psychological and sexual conflicts going back to his childhood, his fears, sense of guilt, relationships with women, and unresolved emotions. He saw phallic symbolism in the nose and the nose's entry into Kazan cathedral. "The Nose," Yermakov claimed, reflected the writer's complexes, psychoses, and conflicting instincts. Yermakov writes:

> As we have seen, the problem posed in "The Nose" is a sexual one. It throws light on the question of the autonomy of man's sexual activity as symbolized by the separate existence of the nose. . . . Sexual activity asserts its rights, which run counter to the urgings of the ego and the norms of society. The thing that cannot be displayed or talked about without shame and embarrassment—"the nose"—itself evokes a feeling of shame and embarrassment if it is not in its proper place, between the two cheeks. The result is an insoluble problem: it is uncomfortable to have a nose but just as uncomfortable not to have one: the two situations are equally discrediting and disgraceful.[111]

Yermakov's insights into Gogol's psyche were complemented by some rather doubtful linguistic findings. He claimed that the last name Kovalev derives from Kolya—Nikolai Gogol's diminutive name—and thus harks back to his childhood.

Yermakov's *Sketches for an Analysis of the Art of N. V. Gogol* (as well as his *Studies on the Psychology of the Art of A. S. Pushkin* (*Etiudy po psikhologii tvorchestva Pushkina*, 1923) came out in the series "The Psychological and Psychoanalytic Library," of which Yermakov was an editor and the author of prefaces. The series featured the works

---

[110] Vinogradov, *Gogol and the Natural School*.

[111] Ivan Yermakov, "The Nose," in *Gogol from the Twentieth Century: Eleven Essays*, 192.

of Freud, Jung, and other European psychoanalytic scholars. Of thirty-two volumes that were planned, only sixteen were published before the series ended in 1925. In his sketches on Gogol, Yermakov refers to some of these publications, such as Freud's "On the Sexual Theories of Children" (1908) and "On the Transformation of Instinct as Exemplified in Anal Eroticism" (1917), which were published in 1922–23 in M. V. Vul'f's translation.

At that time, psychoanalytic terminology in literary criticism was felt by many as novel and rather inappropriate. In his essay on Gogol published in 1925, Victor Vinogradov briefly commented on Yermakov's pioneering study: "I will not say anything about Prof. Ivan Yermakov's book *Sketches on the Psychology of Gogol's Creativity* because I lack a sense of humor."[112] Although some aspects of Freudian theory had become popular among the Russian cultural elite in the early twentieth century, in terms of theory and practical experience, the psychoanalytic school in Russia was less developed than it was in the West. In the Soviet Russia of the 1930s psychoanalysis fell into disfavor and was labeled ideologically foreign and harmful. In the first *Soviet Literary Encyclopedia* (published in 1929–1939), Yermakov's psychoanalytic approach to literature was the target of devastating criticism. During the next sixty years, his sketches on Gogol, Pushkin, and Dostoevsky were banned in the USSR.

For his time, Yermakov's contribution to Gogol studies was important because it drew attention to some odd or uncomfortable aspects of the story, which had not been examined. Thus, for example, Yermakov pointed out that originally the story bore the title "The Dream" ("Son"), which represents an inversion of the later title "The Nose" ("Nos"), and that Gogol at first attributed all the events in the story to Kovalev's dream but later removed this explanation, thus making the fantastic element seem weird and spooky. The dream motif Yermakov pointed out was further elaborated on in many critical studies.

---

[112] Vinogradov, *Gogol and the Natural School*, 45.

5. A Case of Castration Anxiety

Expanding on the dream motif from a psychoanalytic perspective in the 1960s, the American scholar Peter C. Spycher suggested that the events could have taken place not only in Kovalev's dream, but also in the dream of the barber, who wakes up to find the nose in a loaf of bread. Objecting to Yermakov's arguments about a clash between society's moral code and the amorality of sexuality, Spycher states that Kovalev's dream and the barber's dream are complementary—they form one drama of a sexual problem, because the Major and the barber are "two manifestations of one self." He argues that Kovalev's dream and the barber's dream reflect a third person's dream that comprises the entire story 'The Nose'." This third person is "the author," who chooses such strange plots: "The 'author's' nightmare is Gogol's own," Spycher concludes."[113]

Yermakov was also the first to notice that the events in "The Nose" take place on March 25, the Feast of the Annunciation, thus suggesting some disturbing contrasts and parallels. He writes:

> In "The Nose," the most degrading and disgusting things are associated with animalistic sex, which is appropriate to the spring season, and which contrasts with the pure and lofty Annunciation. Yet both are really the same thing—the sexual—albeit on different levels. Something that in everyday life is usually concealed as being indecent and inadmissible in conversation—sex, impregnation—is openly recognized, celebrated, and talked about as a great event on the Feast of the Annunciation. The fabric of Gogol's art and indeed his very mind is woven from this tendency toward contrast and contradiction.[114]

Yermakov comes up with a bold conclusion: "The story may well be a parody of the Annunciation, in sexual terms. If so, it is a faint echo of Pushkin's mock-epic *The Gabrieliad (Gavriiliada).*"[115] Mikhail

---

[113] Peter Spycher, "N. V. Gogol's 'The Nose': A Satirical Comic Fantasy Born of an Impotence Complex." *Slavic and East European Journal* 7, no. 4 (1963): 370.

[114] Yermakov, "The Nose," 177–78.

[115] Ibid., 179.

Vaiskopf's claim that the beginning of "The Nose" constitutes mockery of the Christian liturgy, as well as L. P. Rassovskaya's juxtaposition of the Annunciation theme in Gogol's "The Nose" and Pushkin's poem *The Gabrieliad*, each representing a religious parody, resonate with Yermakov's earlier reading.[116]

Finally, Yermakov was the first to suggest that the underlying motif of the nose's disappearance was a "bad disease," namely syphilis, which was widespread in Gogol's time: "Symptoms of sickness and death in connection with sex—the fear of contracting syphilis, of getting an infection (first Kovalev has a pimple, then he loses the nose entirely)—can readily be traced in many of Gogol's stories. Both motifs are found in 'The Nose.'"[117] As discussed in chapter 4, "Chronicle of Folk Superstitions," O. G. Dilaktorskaia further elaborated on this topic, as well as on folk superstitions related to this illness.

Despite its ban in Soviet Russia, the Freudian approach became part of the criticism of "The Nose" and was considered legitimate even by those who did not espouse psychoanalytic theories. Vladimir Nabokov, who disliked Freudianism and psychoanalysis, refers to it in his book on Gogol:

> The nose-consciousness resulted at last in the writing of a story, *The Nose*, which is verily a hymn to that organ. A Freudian might suggest that in Gogol's topsy-turvy world human beings are turned upside down (in 1841 Gogol coolly declared that a council of doctors in Paris had found his stomach to be placed upside down) so that the part of the nose is played by some other organ and vice-versa. Whether the "fancy begat the nose or the nose begat the fancy" is inessential. I think it is more reasonable to forget that Gogol's exaggerated concern with noses was based on the fact of his own being abnormally long and to treat Gogol's olfactivism— and even his own nose—as a literary trick allied to the broad

---

[116] See the discussion of this topic in chapter 3, "Mockery of the Demonic and of the Sacred."

[117] Ivan Yermakov, "The Nose," 178.

5. A Case of Castration Anxiety

humor of carnivals in general and to Russian nose-humor in particular.[118]

Caryl Emerson finds that "once Freudian symbolism is accepted as valid, Yermakov's reading of 'The Nose' unfolds in persuasive detail."[119] Ann Shukman aptly calls the story "the supreme sublimation of sexuality," without assigning any derogative meaning to it.[120]

Yet overall, the psychoanalytic approach to "The Nose" is long outdated. In his investigation of the history of psychoanalysis in Russia, Alexander Etkind observes that Yermakov's studies "almost disappeared from scholarly use and are unlikely to return to it."[121] He maintains, "From Yermakov's texts one can often get a feeling of his own fear, inner stiffness and self-censorship: the author is afraid to talk about the integrity about which he wants to write and stops seeing it."[122]

The psychoanalytic perspective stands apart from other approaches considered in the previous chapters, which dealt with various aspects of the story—its language, genre features, satirical angle, religious orientation, and relation to popular beliefs and superstitions. In contrast to these approaches, the psychoanalytic method draws our attention to the author's private life and the caches of his psyche. With Gogol, who had such a complex personality, this task is hardly feasible, however.

---

[118] Vladimir Nabokov, *Nikolai Gogol* (New York: New Directions, 1961), 4.

[119] Caryl Emerson, "Literary Theory in the 1920s: Four Options and a Practicum," in *A History of Russian Literary Theory and Criticism*, ed. Evgeny Dobrenko and Galin Tihanov (Pittsburgh: University of Pittsburgh Press, 2011), 88.

[120] Ann Shukman, "Gogol's 'The Nose' or the Devil in the Works," in *Nikolai Gogol: Text and Context*, ed. Jane Grayson and Faith Wigzell (London: Macmillan, 1989), 78.

[121] Alexander Etkind, *Eros nevozhmozhnogo (Istoriia psikhoanaliza v Rossii)* (Moscow: Gnozis-Progress-Kompleks, 1994), 262.

[122] Ibid. Nonetheless, in 1999, Yermakov's sketches on Russian writers were republished. See I. D. Ermakov, *Psikhoanaliz literatury: Pushkin, Gogol', Dostoevskii* (Moscow: Novoe literaturnoe obozrenie, 1999).

6

An Echo of German Romanticism

The idea that Gogol's art derived from German romanticism has been a subject of controversy since his early poem *Hans Kuechelgarten* (1827)—an imitation of J. H. Voss's *Luise*—was published. After the release of *Arabesques* in 1835, in his review "On Gogol's *Mirgorod*" ("O 'Mirgorode' Gogolia") the literary critic Stepan Shevyrev wrote that in Gogol's works one could sense the fantastic spirit of the fiction of the German romantics E. T. A. Hoffmann and J. L. Tieck. Two decades later, in his landmark essay on Gogol entitled "Sketches of the Gogol Period of Russian Literature" (1853), the radical critic Nikolai Chernyshevsky objected to the idea of German influence on Gogol. He stated that in the mid-1830s, Gogol did not yet know Tieck's name and work. As for Hoffmann, although Gogol was familiar with his name, the two writers did not bear the slightest resemblance to each other: "One invents, independently invents fantastic adventures from purely German life, the other one literally retells Ukrainian legends ('Viy') or popular anecdotes ('The Nose'): what can be similar?"[123]

Chernyshevsky's remark about Hoffmann must have been a reference to the passage in "Nevsky Prospect" in which Gogol introduces comical Russian "doubles" of the German romantics Schiller and Hoffmann:

> Before him sat Schiller—not the Schiller who wrote *Wilhelm Tell* and the *History of the Thirty Years' War*, but the well-known Schiller, the tinsmith of Meshchanskaya Street. Next to Schiller stood Hoffmann—not the Hoffmann, but a rather good cobbler from Ofitserskaya Street, a great friend of Schiller's. Schiller was drunk and sat on a chair stamping his foot and heartedly saying something. All this would not have been so surprising to Pirogov, but what did surprise him was the extremely strange posture of the figures. Schiller was

---

[123] N. G. Chernyshevskii, *Ocherki gogolevskogo perioda* (Moscow: Gos. izdatel'stvo russkoi literatury, 1953), 141.

6. An Echo of German Romanticism

sitting, his rather fat nose stuck out and his head raised, while Hoffmann was holding him by this nose with two fingers and waggling the blade of his cobbler's knife just above the surface of it. Both personages were speaking in German, and therefore Lieutenant Pirogov, whose only German was "*Gut Morgen*," was able to understand nothing of this whole story. Schiller's words, however, consisted of the following:

"I don't want, I have no need of a nose!" he said, waving his arms. "For this one nose I need three pounds of snuff a month."[124]

Notably, Gogol presents this humorous passage in the context of the "nosological" theme: Hoffmann even pulls Schiller's nose, just as the barber pulled Kovalev's nose while shaving him in "The Nose."

In 1921, while considering possible connections of Gogol's "The Nose" to European literature, Victor Vinogradov came to the conclusion that Gogol's grotesque is devoid of any influence; the works of E. T. A. Hoffmann and Laurence Sterne are characterized as "fantastic" and "unnatural grotesque," whereas Gogol's grotesque is "natural" and "naturalistic."[125] Elsewhere, Vinogradov explains in more detail what, in his view, sets Gogol apart from the European romantic tradition. Reviewing articles written in 1920–1922 by the Danish scholar Adolf Stender-Petersen, who juxtaposed Gogol's Ukrainian and Petersburg stories with works by German romantics, Vinogradov notes Gogol's idiosyncratic ability to depict "real life":

> There was no congeniality between Hoffmann and Gogol. They had completely different poetic natures, with diametrically opposite artistic paths. The refined, extravagant Hoffmann was an enthusiast and mystificator, whereas the idealistic dreamer Gogol, through conscious imitation of the poetics of Tieck and Hoffmann, moved toward a bitter acknowledgement of real life, and a cool reproduction of it.

---

[124] Gogol, "Nevsky Prospect," 270.

[125] See Vinogradov, "Naturalisticheskii grotesk," 5–44.

Part Two. Interpretations

> The period of imitation of Hoffmann, embracing the years from 1832 through 1834, is the period of Gogol's lack of freedom and independence. It is a time of formulation of his own personal style while still enchained and struggling to *overcome* [my italics—KB] the poetics of German romanticism, and especially Hoffmann.[126]

Vinogradov wrote this in 1925, before the ideologization of Gogol studies and when the transition from romanticism to realism had already become a common topic in Russian literary studies. In *Young Tolstoy* (*Molodoi Tolstoi*, 1922), Boris Eikhenbaum observes that the main pathos of the young Tolstoy was his denial of romantic patterns, both in style and in genre; that everything in his work was subordinated to the task of destroying romantic poetics.[127] Later, in dogmatic Soviet literary criticism, it became a cliché to view the transition from romanticism to realism as an overcoming of an inferior phase of literary evolution with the goal of reaching a superior stage.

It was common for Soviet scholars to see Pushkin's "overcoming of romanticism" in the poet's transition from the southern narrative poems *The Prisoner of the Caucasus* and *The Fountain of Bakhchisaray* of the early-1820s toward his more mature poetry of the 1830s and "realist" prose. The consensus about Lermontov's transition from romantic feelings and passions in his early narrative poem *Mtsyri* to the realism of his novel *The Hero of Our Time* (1841) was identical. In Russia, romanticism, with its quest for the sublime and the authority of feeling, was primarily associated with Western influences, whereas realism was seen as mainly Russian. The

---

[126] Vinogradov, *Gogol and the Natural School*, 62. Stender-Petersen reads "The Nose" as the parody of a romantic motif (the man without a shadow, the man without a mirror image). See Adolf Stender-Petersen, "Gogol und die deutsche Romantik," *Euphorion* 24 (1922): 291–95. For a recent comparative approach to Gogol and Hoffmann, see A. I. Ivanitskii, "Gogol' i Gofman: Grotesk i ego preodolenie," in *N. V. Gogol' i mirovaia kul'tura: Vtorye gogolevskie chteniia; Sbornik dokladov*, ed. V. P. Vikulova (Moscow: KDU, 2003), 167–80.

[127] Boris Eikhenbaum, *Molodoi Tolstoi* (Petrograd: Izdatel'stvo Z. I. Grzhebina, 1922), 58 and 63.

6. An Echo of German Romanticism

idea of overcoming Western influences thus had an ideological constituent.[128]

In Russian scholarship of the 1930s and 1940s, Gogol was viewed as a realist, satirist, and precursor of socialist realism. A vivid testimony of Gogol's "rehabilitation" can be found in Robert L. Strong's commentary in *The American Slavic and East European Review* of 1955. Strong writes about the Soviet critics' utilitarian approach to Gogol's satire and about the pompous celebration of Gogol's death anniversary in 1952, which served to "reconstruct" a great nineteenth-century writer.[129] This was a new Gogol, "singing of heroic deeds, glorifying the motherland."[130] Of all Soviet scholars, Strong writes, the most dogmatic one was Vladimir Ermilov, who wrote about Gogol's patriotism. At the formal meeting held in the Bolshoi Theater, Ermilov, the principal speaker, declared that Marx, Lenin, and Stalin entertained a high opinion of Gogol and that Chernyshevsky regarded him as the inspiration of critical realism.

Further, Strong expresses his puzzlement about the Soviets' tendentious aim to free the writer from any Western influence:

> Though certainly a very original writer, Gogol was, after all, a professional literary man and could not help being aware of contemporary European trends in literature. Furthermore, despite the fact that Gogol personally seemed to prefer the "classics," such as Homer, Shakespeare, Dante, and Cervantes, definite elements of later writers, particularly the romantics, are to be found in his works. In this connection,

---

[128] A more complex—dialectical—pattern of an intense and ambivalent dialogue with the European tradition is offered and discussed in Priscilla Meyer's *How the Russians Read the French: Lermontov, Dostoevsky, Tolstoy* (Madison: University of Wisconsin Press, 2008).

[129] Robert L. Strong Jr., "The Soviet Interpretation of Gogol," *The American Slavic and East European Review* 14, no. 4 (December 1955): 528–39. After his graduation from the University of Virginia in 1952, Strong worked as a Russian translator at the Library of Congress.

[130] Ibid., 532.

the names of Tieck, Hoffmann, Maturin, DeQuincey, Sterne, and Scott might be mentioned.[131]

To be sure, many Russian scholars would agree with these words but could not express their opinion about Gogol's connections to Western literature freely. In his book on Gogol, the notable scholar Grigory Gukovsky, who in his early career had been affiliated with the formalists, comments about the fundamental difference between the fantastic in Gogol and the fantastic in romantic literature. "For the romantics,—he wrote,—the fantastic is always essentially something higher, more beautiful than the ordinary; for Gogol, the fantastic is the essence of the most ordinary. Thus, for the romantics, the fantastic (the daydream!) is presented as a blessing; for Gogol— as an evil, as the essence of evil."[132] Gukovsky interpreted Gogol's denial of the fantastic principle of German romanticism as his striving toward realism.

Gukovsky's book, published in 1959 posthumously, was written in 1946–1949; consequently, his discussion of Gogol may have been influenced by state ideology. In the spring of 1949, as part of the campaign against "rootless cosmopolitans" at a two-day meeting at Leningrad University, together with Victor Zhirmunsky, Boris Eikhenbaum, and Mark Azadovsky, Gukovsky was accused of "bowing to the West" and dismissed from the Institute of Russian Literature. The "bourgeois aesthetics" and "idealistic concepts" of these scholars were declared "antipatriotic and harmful." Specifically, the scholars were ostracized for their comparative and formalist approach to Russian literature.[133] In July 1949 Gukovsky was arrested. A few months later he died of a heart attack.

Yuri Mann continued Gukovsky's line of critique by arguing that "The Nose" was characterized by the fusion of the fantastic and

---

[131] Ibid., 538.

[132] Gukovskii, *Realizm Gogolia*, 274–75.

[133] P. A. Druzhinin, *Ideologiia i filologiia, Leningrad, 1940 gody, dokumental'noe issledovaniie*, 2 vols. (Moscow: Novoe literaturnoe obozrenie, 2012), vol. 2, 296–300.

6. An Echo of German Romanticism

the real. Mann observed that in Gogol, there is no sharp boundary between everyday reality and another, fantastic reality; that one of the most important attributes of Gogol's grotesque was "the departure from the fantastic" and the combination of the "fantastic style" with a "nonfantastic course of action."[134]

In his book on Gogol published in 1996, Mann elaborates on this idea. He notes that in romantic literature the most common form of mystery is one in which the fantastic is associated with supernatural powers. In this case, the story in question begins with a strange and mysterious occurrence that cannot be explained. As the tension of the mystery increases more and more, the author reveals the will or influence of the bearer of this fantastic power, be it evil or good. Even when the fantastic element is veiled, the process of identification of the unknown power still takes place, occasionally culminating in the discovery of natural causes. Mann reminds us that scholars have associated Gogol's story with Adelbert von Chamisso's *Peter Schlemihl* and E. T. A. Hoffmann's "A New Year's Eve Adventure" — works in which a part of the self gains independence, comes to life, and competes with the former owner.[135]

Mann claims that Gogol removes the bearer of the fantastic (a personified embodiment of surreal power), which creates an impression of a mysterious and bizarre story. Thus, no one is directly responsible for the events occurring in "The Nose." There is no one to pursue, although the persecution still occurs. This lacuna indicates that Gogol's story breaks down the romantic canon. In the very first lines of "The Nose," the reader is faced with a mystery, but clarifications do not follow. Even when the mystery reaches its climax, the author does not offer the reader any clues. In the finale, although the narrator still has an opportunity to provide a motivation for the events, he says only, "Perfect nonsense goes on in the world. Sometimes there is no plausibility at all: suddenly, as if nothing was wrong, that same nose which had driven about in

---

[134] Iu. V. Mann, "Evoliutsiia gogolevskoi fantastiki," in *K istorii russkogo romantizma*, ed. Iu. V. Mann (Moscow: Nauka, 1973), 255.

[135] Mann, *Poetika Gogolia*, 76 and further (chapter 3: "Real'noe i fantasticheskoe").

the rank of state councillor and made such a stir in town is back in place—that is, precisely between the two cheeks of Major Kovalev."[136]

In other words, in Mann's view, "The Nose" reflects Gogol's relationship with the principles of romantic literature and represents a parody of the works of German romantics. As Mann phrases it, in his early works of the Ukrainian cycle Gogol pushes the bearer of the fantastic into the past (into archaic folk culture), whereas in "The Nose" he takes a step further: he completely removes the bearer of the fantastic from the narrative. Using this technique, Gogol parodies not a certain romantic motif or image or one specific work, but the style of the whole phenomenon called German romanticism, with its main opposition of the real versus the fantastic. Hence, in "The Nose" Gogol "settles scores" with the romantic concept of fiction: "Gogol transformed the achievements of romantic fiction, but did not erase them. Removing the bearer of the fantastic, he preserved the fantastic; parodying a romantic mystery, he preserved the mysterious; making 'a form of rumors' the subject of an ironic game, he strengthened the authenticity of the 'incident.'" Mann concludes that Gogol's grotesque emerges out of everyday prosaic foundations, that is, realism. He calls this stage in Gogol's evolution toward realism the "nonfantastic fantastic" (нефантастическая фантастика).[137]

Like Mann, Yuri Lotman considers the fantastic element in Gogol's Petersburg tales an idiosyncratic element of the writer's poetics, but he also connects it with the Petersburg myth and stresses an oral constituent of the Petersburg text of Russian literature:

> Gogol and Dostoevsky based their "Petersburg mythology" on the oral traditions of Petersburg, they canonized it and raised it, along with the tradition of the oral anecdote, to the level of literature.

---

[136] Gogol, "The Nose," 323.

[137] As Mann notes, one of the first scholars to suggest that "The Nose" was a parody of the romantic canon was the Danish Slavist Stender-Petersen. See Mann, *Poetika Gogolia*, 88.

6. An Echo of German Romanticism

All of this mass of "oral literature" from the 1820s and 1830s made Petersburg into a place where the mysterious and fantastic was the norm. The Petersburg tale is like the yuletide ghost story, except that the temporal fantasy is replaced by spatial one.[138]

Several contemporary American scholars emphasize Gogol's German connections, however. Michael Hollquist argues that Gogol's Ukrainian and Petersburg tales are heavily influenced by the German genre of *Kunstmärchen* (fairy tales).[139] In a more recent study of Gogol's German connections, while reading Gogol's "Nevsky Prospect" through Hoffmann's "A New Year's Eve Adventure," Priscilla Meyer argues against the view—common in Russian scholarship—that Gogol moves from romanticism to realism. She reads the eerie ending of "Nevsky Prospect" as Gogol concluding the work "on a sudden note of cosmic terror."[140]

This brings us back to the topic of the previous chapter—the psychoanalytic approach to Gogol and to the Freudian concept of the "uncanny" (*das Unheimliche*), which Yermakov *did not* consider in "The Nose." Interestingly, *Sketches for an Analysis of the Art of N. V. Gogol* was Yermakov's second publication on Gogol. The first one was his afterword to the separate publication of "The Nose" in Moscow in 1921. It is worth noting that in 1919, Freud published his seminal essay *The Uncanny*, in which he explored the intersection of psychoanalysis and aesthetics. In this essay he drew on the work of E. T. A. Hoffmann, whom he referred to as the "unrivalled master of the uncanny in literature."

---

[138] Yuri M. Lotman, "The Symbolism of St. Petersburg," in his *Universe of the Mind: A Semiotic Theory of Culture*, trans. Ann Schukman, introd. Umberto Eco (Bloomington: Indiana University Press, 1990), 197.

[139] Michael Holquist, "'The Devil in Mufti': The *Märchenwelt* in Gogol's Short Stories," *PMLA* 82, no. 5 (October 1967): 352–62.

[140] Priscilla Meyer, "The Fantastic in the Everyday: Gogol's 'Nevsky Prospect' and Hoffmann's 'A New Year's Eve Adventure,'" in *Cold Fusions: Aspects of the German Cultural Presence in Russia*, ed. Gennady Barabtarlo (New York: Berghahn Books, 2000), 71.

Part Two. Interpretations

One of the major characteristics of the uncanny, as had been noted before Freud by Ernst Jentsch, the author of *On the Psychology of the Uncanny* (1906), is the lack of a clear boundary between living flesh and pseudo-alive matter. Freud writes: "E. Jentsch singles out, as an excellent case, 'doubt as to whether an apparently animate object really is alive and, conversely, whether a lifeless object might not perhaps be animate.' In this connection he refers to the impressions made on us by waxwork figures, ingeniously constructed dolls and automata."[141] Freud illustrates this idea with "the seemingly animate doll Olimpia" from Hoffmann's short story "The Sandman" (1816).[142] -

The most striking exposure to the uncanny in Hoffmann's story, Freud maintains, is to the figure of the Sandman, who, according to legend, robs children of their eyes to punish them for not falling asleep at night. Freud explains:

> Psychoanalytic experience reminds us that some children have a terrible fear of damaging or losing their eyes. Many retain this anxiety into adult life and fear no physical injury so much as one to the eye. And there is a common saying that one will "guard something like the apple of one's eye." The study of dreams, fantasies and myths has taught us also that anxiety about one's eyes, the fear of going blind, is quite often a substitute for the fear of castration.[143]

Another example of the uncanny, according to Freud, is the theme of doubles in Hoffmann's novel *The Devil's Elixir* (1815). Doubling is caused specifically by a blurred boundary between two selves: "A person may identify himself with another and so become unsure of his true self; or he may substitute the other's self for his own. The self may thus be duplicated, divided, and interchanged."[144]

---

[141] Sigmund Freud, *The Uncanny*, trans. David McLintock, introd. Hugh Haughton (London: Penguin Classics, 2003), 135.

[142] Ibid., 136.

[143] Ibid., 139.

[144] Ibid., 142.

6. An Echo of German Romanticism

Finally, the superstitious belief in the power of evil intentions and people's ability to harm others with the evil eye or an evil spell is also a feature of the uncanny, argues Freud.

Notably, all these postulates apply to Gogol's "The Nose." The issue of animacy has a prime importance in the story, where the nose is simultaneously a person and an organ of smell. The theme of doubles also underlines the plot of "The Nose": Kovalev's self is duplicated in a nose existing independently (though they are "asymmetrical" doubles: the nose has a higher rank and is better dressed). Kovalev's assumption that the disappearance of his nose was caused by the staff officer's wife Podtochina's evil thoughts and actions also characterizes his feelings as uncanny.[145]

The conclusions Freud and Yermakov reach are basically identical. Freud interprets the fear of losing an eye in Hoffmann's story as symbolic of the fear of castration:

> Severed limbs, a severed head, a hand detached from the arm (as in a fairy tale by Hauff), feet that dance by themselves (as in the novel by A. Schaeffer . . .)—all of these have something highly uncanny about them, especially when they are credited, as in the last instance, with independent activity. We already know that this species of the uncanny stems from its proximity to the castration complex.[146]

Yermakov comes to a similar conclusion about the castration complex in "The Nose": "In trying as best we can to decipher 'The Nose,'" we must say that two things underlie the story: the fear of castration, which goes along with the repressed wish to possess an enormous sex organ; and the desire for unlimited erotic pleasures."[147]

These parallels suggest that Yermakov may have been familiar with Freud's essay, even though it was not published in Russian and was not planned for publication in his series. Given Yermakov's interest in the subject, Freud's analysis of Hoffmann's

---

[145] See chapter 4, "Chronicle of Folk Superstitions."

[146] Freud, *The Uncanny*, 150.

[147] Yermakov, "The Nose," 194.

story may have prompted his decision to interpret "The Nose" from a psychoanalytic perspective.

These parallels are intriguing for yet another reason—the psychoanalytic approach suggests additional ties between Gogol and Hoffmann. The notion of German Romantics' influence on "The Nose," which Nikolai Chernyshevsky in 1856 and Soviet scholars a century later objected to, is now awaiting a revision.

7
Perfect Nonsense

"The Nose" has been viewed as an absurdist work whose events defy interpretations based on reason and logic. This approach is hardly surprising, for the absurd manifests itself on the story's various narrative levels, first of all in the plot—the nose's disappearance, independent existence in the guise of a state councillor, and eventual return to Kovalev's face. The characters' reactions to these events also repudiate common sense. Thus, for example, when the barber finds a nose in his bread, instead of being surprised, he is terrified, whereas his spouse is highly indignant. The doctor gives nonsensical advice to Kovalev, namely, to put his nose "in a jar of alcohol, or, better still, add two tablespoons of aquafortis and warm vinegar."[148]

Kovalev seems to grieve not so much for the loss of his nose as for the inexplicability of this loss. The conclusions he draws sound odd, such as his assumption that it would be better if his nose were cut off in war or in a duel. Kovalev's lament—"There might at least be something instead of a nose, but there's nothing!"—does not lend itself to logic; it is just as preposterous as his intention to marry when he turns "exactly forty-two."[149]

The narrator anticipates that readers will perceive the story as absurd when he remarks at the opening of the third chapter: "Perfect nonsense (чепуха совершенная) goes on in the world."[150] Simon Karlinsky observes that the narrator presents absurd events in "The Nose" in a serious tone: "The most logic-defying piece of writing in Russian literature to this day, 'The Nose' is narrated in a consistently matter-of-fact manner of poker-faced seriousness."[151]

---

[148] Gogol, "The Nose," 321.

[149] Ibid., 306 and 316.

[150] Ibid., 323.

[151] Simon Karlinsky, *The Sexual Labyrinth of Nikolai Gogol* (Chicago: University of Chicago Press, 1976), 129.

The Doctor's Visit

7. Perfect Nonsense

As a result, the narrator's serious tone contributes to the jocular effect of the nonsensical information conveyed to the reader.

Some scholars view the lack of causal relationships in "The Nose" as an idiosyncrasy. Donald Fanger observes that although a number of interpretations of the narrated events exist, none of them is fully persuasive: "Most of these interpretations are plausible, and justified to a point, but each is unconvincing because too much of the text escapes it. Gogol has created a puzzle that many keys may fit, but none open. A trap for the unwary, it represents his most original achievement to date in confronting the question of how to be a writer."[152] Ann Shukman makes a similar point: "As in the case of the other causalities suggested, there is no single, satisfactory focus of motivation in the text as such either on the level of the diegesis or on the level of the narration, a point which is neatly put by Yuri Mann: 'The significance of the events of *The Nose* lies in the fact that they are unprovoked. No one is directly to blame. There is no victimizer, only the victimization. So no devil or demon is present in the text of *The Nose* except on the lips of the characters."[153]

Maintaining this line of argument, Gary Saul Morson elaborates on the lack of cause-and-effect relationships in "The Nose," stressing that not only are the events improbable, they are also unconditioned, unmotivated, and unexplained:

> Let us dwell for a moment on a few of the questions that a good explanation of this story's plot would have to answer: How does Kovalev lose his nose? If the barber cut it off when he shaved Kovalev on Wednesday, then why, as Kovalev asks, was the nose in its proper place on Thursday? Whether or not the barber cut it off, how did the nose get into the barber's roll? Why is there no scar; why is Kovalev's face "as flat as a pancake"? How does the nose grow to human size, and, still more perplexing, how does it become human? Given that it becomes biologically human, how does it become socially human? How does the nose develop a specific identity and

---

[152] Donald Fanger, *The Creation of Nikolai Gogol* (Cambridge, MA: Harvard University Press, 1979), 120.

[153] Shukman, "Gogol's 'The Nose,' or The Devil in the Works," 75.

a history—a rank in the service and a set of acquaintances—
and what happens to the memory of others to make them think
they have known him? Does this perplexing event somehow
manage to alter the past? How does the nose become a nose
again, and, having done so, how does it resume its proper
place on Kovalev's face? In addition to these problems, there
are others of a different kind.[154]

In Russian literary studies the discussion of causality was initiated by Lydia Ginsburg in *On Psychological Prose*—her major contribution to the theory of realism, published in Russian in 1977. For Ginsburg, causal conditionality (*причинная обусловленность*) represents the main characteristic of the nineteenth-century psychological novel, which demonstrates that psychological and historical processes are rooted in the past and linked to the future.[155] She observes that this type of connection first evolved at an early stage of realism in Stendhal's novel *Le rouge et le noir* (*The Red and the Black*, 1830), in which the individual's existence is conditioned by time and social milieu. Further, social conditionality became more and more prominent and was gradually refined in the mature writing of Balzac. At the core of Ginsburg's theory lies her discussion of Leo Tolstoy's psychological analysis of character development as "a dissection of the infinitely differentiated conditionality of behavior."[156] Conditionality in Tolstoy includes various types of influences—besides general historical and social influences, there are the impulses that affect human behavior, coming from both the individual's inner nature and from his/her material surroundings. Ginsburg argues that unlike the writings of Dostoevsky, those of Tolstoy "belong to the explanatory and conditioning branch of nineteenth-century psychologism. . . . What had been merely

---

[154] Gary Saul Morson, "Gogol's Parables of Explanations: Nonsense and Prosaics," in *Essays on Gogol: Logos and the Russian Word*, ed. Susanne Fusso and Priscilla Meyer (Evanston, IL: Northwestern University Press, 1992), 228.

[155] Lydia Ginsburg, *On Psychologial Prose* (Princeton: Princeton University Press, 1991), 221–70.

[156] Ibid., 256.

7. Perfect Nonsense

a tendency in the pre-Tolstoian novel became a conscious principle in Tolstoy's writing, another hypostasis of Tolstoian fluidity. Fluidity presupposes process—a conditional alternation of psychic states."[157]

In his *Narrative and Freedom* (1994) Morson focuses on the idiosyncrasy of conditionality in Dostoevsky. He elaborates on the concept of *sideshadowing* as an anti-determinist principle lying at the base of the narrative structure in Dostoevsky's novels. Unlike foreshadowing, which makes the outcome known in advance and thus predetermined, sideshadowing provides an open sense of possibilities, and thus does not contradict the notion of human freedom and choice among many possibilities.[158]

As for the issue of conditionality in Gogol, Morson argues that here nonsense is occasionally subjected to the laws of logic. Thus, for example, dogs writing letters to each other in "The Diary of a Madman" can be explained as the protagonist's insane imagination. But "The Nose," Morson observes, is absolutely different; here "numerous explanatory systems encounter a series of events that are radically inexplicable. These events simply make no sense whatsoever."[159] The section on "The Nose" in Morson's essay on Gogol is entitled "Pure Anomaly and Absolute Nonsense," thus suggesting that in "The Nose" nonsense is atypical and abnormal.

The lack of causal relationships in "The Nose" places this story apart from both Tolstoy's psychological mode and Dostoevsky's technique of sideshadowing, though it stays somewhat closer to the latter. As Yuri Tynianov pointed out in 1921, Gogol's work had a tremendous impact on Dostoevsky, and "The Nose" was no exception. There is a reference to it in Dostoevsky's short story

---

[157] Ibid., 260–61.

[158] Gary Saul Morson, *Narrative and Freedom: The Shadows of Time* (New Haven: Yale University Press, 1994), 117–72 and 234–64.

[159] Gary Saul Morson, "Gogol's Parables of Explanations," 227.

"Mr. Prokharchin" (1846). In *The Double* (1846) Dostoevsky uses the Gogolian device of creating a mask and the mask's double.[160]

Nevertheless, on the whole, "The Nose" has stronger connections with Russian avant-garde art of the 1920s than with nineteenth-century Russian prose. The musical connection—Dmitry Shostakovich's opera *The Nose* (1928)—will be discussed in the next chapter. As for its literary links, "The Nose" had a direct influence on the Leningrad literary circle OBERIU—an avant-garde collective of poets founded in 1928 by Daniil Kharms and Alexander Vvedensky. Its members' nonsensical verses and absurdist theatrical presentations were criticized in the 1930s, a time of the solemn doctrine of socialist realism, with its cult of realistic art. It may not be accidental that Gogol, Kharms, and Shostakovich were all residents of Petersburg (renamed Petrograd and later Leningrad), the cradle of the Russian absurd. To paraphrase the famous aphorism "All Russian literature came out of Gogol's 'Overcoat'"—ascribed to Dostoevsky but in fact anonymous—one may say that Russian absurdist literature came out of Gogol's "The Nose." As Dmitry Chizhevsky observed,

> There is no cause for surprise that Gogol has been regarded as the founder of a much later tradition—the transsense language of the Russian "Futurists." In fact there has not been a single current in Russian literature since Gogol which has not claimed him—and not without some justification—as its primogenitor. In any event, Gogol was the first Russian writer who was not afraid of linguistic nonsense; it became, in fact, one of his main stays.[161]

The protagonist in Daniil Kharms's prose piece "Ivan Yakovlevich Bobov Woke Up" (1934–1937), written in the years of political repression and mass killings, contains multiple allusions to "The Nose." Its protagonist is the namesake of Gogol's barber,

---

[160] Iurii Tynianov, *Dostoevskii i Gogol' (k teorii parodii)* (Petrograd: Opoiaz, 1921), 6–7.

[161] Dmitry Čiževsky (Dmitry Chizhevsky), "Gogol: Artist and Thinker," *The Annals of the Ukrainian Academy* 2, no. 2 (4) (Summer 1952): 264–65.

7. Perfect Nonsense

Ivan Yakovlevich, whereas his last name alludes to the title of Dostoevsky's story "Bobok" (literally "little bean," but in the context of the story a synonym for "nonsense"), which Mikhail Bakhtin considered a contemporary example of the literary tradition of Menippean satire.[162]

In Kharms's story, Ivan Yakovlevich inherits his namesake's passion for fancy but outdated clothing. If the barber in "The Nose" prefers to wear only tailcoats (which in the 1830s were unsuited to his occupation), the protagonist of Kharms's story is longing for a new pair of striped trousers (which had gone out of fashion more than a decade earlier). Kharms builds up his story with numerous repetitions and exaggerations characteristic of Gogol's prose:

> And Ivan Yakovlevich's old trousers were already so worn out that it became impossible for him to wear them. Ivan Yakovlevich repaired them several times, but eventually it did not help anymore. Ivan Yakovlevich visited all the shops around, and again, not having found striped pants anywhere, he finally decided to buy checkered ones. But checkered trousers were also not available anywhere. Then Ivan Yakovlevich decided to buy gray pants, but he did not find gray ones for himself. Black pants that would match Ivan Yakovlevich's height were not found anywhere either. Then Ivan Yakovlevich decided to buy blue trousers, but while he had been looking for black trousers, the blue ones and the brown ones had disappeared everywhere. And then finally he had nothing to buy but green ones with yellow specks on them. In the store, it seemed to Ivan Yakovlevich that the trousers were not of a very bright color and that the yellow specks did not hurt the eyes at all. But when he got home, Ivan Yakovlevich discovered that one trouser leg was of a noble shade, but the other one was just turquoise with yellow specks glittering on it.[163]

---

[162] Mikhail Bakhtin, *Problems of Dostoevsky's Poetics,* ed. and trans. Caryl Emerson (Minneapolis: University of Minnesota Press, 1984), 144–46.

[163] Daniil Kharms, *Polet v nebesa: Stikhi, proza, dramy, pis'ma* (Leningrad: Sovetskii pisatel', 1988), 320.

Part Two. Interpretations

Striped and checkered trousers were in fashion during the time of NEP (New Economic Policy) in 1921–1924, when Russian fops wore bow ties, soft hats, and boaters, trying to imitate the Americans of the Roaring Twenties, the period of jazz music and expressive dancing. In 1934-1937, when the story was written, this style was associated with bourgeois decadence in the West and thus ideologically and aesthetically inappropriate in the young Soviet state. At the time of Stalin's Great Purge, clothes of this style would definitely attract the unnecessary attention of law enforcement agents. Common sense dictated that sticking out in a crowd, looking different, awkward, and original, was analogous to being explicitly anti-Soviet.

Unlike many law-abiding and cautious Soviet citizens, Kharms preferred to be dressed whimsically and fancifully. He wore leggings and knickerbockers, which were in fashion in the early 1920s in the United States and Britain. He strolled through the streets of Leningrad wearing "fancy hats (a hat or a cap), plaid shorts, knee-high socks, and a chain with rattling keychains, one of which had a skull and crossbones, and he smoked a fantastic-looking pipe."[164] He would appear on the streets wearing "a checkered jacket. His neck was propped up by a snow-white solid collar with a children's silk bow tie. The head of the young man was decorated with a cap with 'donkey ears' made of fabric."[165] Kharms's extravagant clothes were somewhat similar to those of the nose strolling the streets of Petersburg in Gogol's story: "He was in a gold-embroidered uniform with a big standing collar; he had kidskin trousers on; at his side hung a sword. From his plumed hat it could be concluded that he belonged to the rank of state councilor."[166] Kharms loved Gogol's prose and his absurdist style. In a list of his favorite writers,

---

[164] Lada Panova, *Mnimoe sirotstvo: Khlevbnikov i Kharms v kontekste russkogo i evropeiskogo modernizma* (Moscow: Izd. dom Vysshei shkoly ekonomiki, 2017), 38.

[165] A. Mints, "Oberiuty," *Voprosy literatury*, no. 1 (2001): 279.

[166] Gogol, "The Nose," 306.

7. Perfect Nonsense

which he jotted down on November 14, 1937, in his notebook, the first one was Gogol. Like Gogol, Kharms was interested in patristic literature.[167]

Intense fear of being caught for some unknown absurd reason is another feature that connects the two Ivans, one living in Petersburg of the 1830s and the other in Leningrad of the 1930s. Gogol's Ivan Yakovlevich fears being caught by the police for having a nose in his pocket. Kharms's Ivan Yakovlevich, finally wearing a new pair of colorful pants, fears to be seen by others: "When he was wearing the new trousers for the first time, Ivan Yakovlevich came out very carefully. Leaving the entrance hall, he looked first in both directions and, making sure that there was no one nearby, went outside and quickly walked toward his employment office."[168]

There is an odd parallel between the sudden and inexplicable disappearance of the nose from a human face in Gogol's story and the sudden and inexplicable disappearance of people from the face of the earth in Kharms's works. The verb "to disappear" became one of the key phrases in the late 1930s when people disappeared after being arrested unexpectedly in the black of night without warning. Kharms's poem "A man once walked out of his house" ("Iz doma vyshel chelovek," 1937), about a man who stepped out of his house, walked forward, and then suddenly disappeared in a dark forest, is often said to be prophetic. It is said that in the poem, Kharms has predicted his own fate—his arrest in 1941, when he crossed the threshold of his apartment never to come back. This might be a too literal reading of the poem. In the introduction to his collection of translations of works by Kharms, Matvei Yankelevich convincingly calls into question the critical practice of making simplistic

---

[167] On Gogol and Church Fathers see Dmitrii Chizhevskii (Dmitry Chizhevsky), "Neizvestnyi Gogol'," in *Novyi zhurnal* 27 (1951): 142–43. On Kharms's interest in patristics, see Ksana Blank, "Praising the Name: The Religious Theme in Daniil Kharms," in her *Spaces of Creativity: Essays on Russian Literature and the Arts* (Boston: Academic Studies Press, 2017), 106–29. -

[168] Kharms, *Polet v nebesa*, 321.

equivalences between Kharms's art and Stalinist reality.[169] Rather, the major topic of the poem can be understood more broadly, as challenges of human existence and identity.

Appearances and disappearances, being and nonbeing, absence and existence, are themes that connect "The Nose" and another prose piece by Kharms, "The Red-Headed Man" ("Ryzhii chelovek," 1937). Because of its brevity, it can be quoted in full:

> Жил один рыжий человек, у которого не было глаз и ушей. У него не было и волос, так что рыжим его называли условно.
> Говорить он не мог, так как у него не было рта. Носа тоже у него не было.
> У него не было даже рук и ног. И живота у него не было, и спины у него не было, и хребта у него не было, и никаких внутренностей у него не было. Ничего не было! Так что непонятно, о ком идет речь.
> Уж лучше мы о нем не будем больше говорить.[170]

> There was a redheaded man who had no eyes or ears. He didn't have air either, so he was called a redhead arbitrarily.
> He couldn't talk because he had no mouth. He didn't have a nose either.
> He didn't even have arms or legs. He had no stomach, he had no back, no spine, and he didn't have any insides at all. There was nothing!
> So, we don't even know who we're talking about.
> We'd better not talk about him any more.[171]

According to the commentator Anatoly Aleksandrov, on the margin of this piece (the first one in a series in "Incidences" in the *Blue Notebook No 10*), Kharms wrote "versus Kant," apparently referring to Immanuel Kant's concept of "the thing in itself" and forms of

---

[169] Daniil Kharms, *Today I Wrote Nothing: The Selected Writings of Daniil Kharms*, ed. and trans. Matvei Yankelevich (New York: Overlook Duckworth, 2007), 31–32.

[170] Kharms, *Polet v nebesa*, 353.

[171] Translated by Matvei Yankelevich. See Kharms, *Today I Wrote Nothing*, 45.

7. Perfect Nonsense

cognition.[172] Mikhail Iampolski comments on the philosophical underpinning of this miniature text:

> One of Kharms's main themes is the disappearance of objects, the thinning of reality, the achievement of the transcendental. Within the perspective with which Kharms is playing, this type of movement from materiality to ideality is nothing but an inverted creation. God's creation of the world comes from nothing and is described as a phenomenon of "objects." Kharms, as it were, reverses the process; he plays God inversely.[173]

Raising philosophical questions of being, existence, identity, and creation, "The Red-Headed Man" can be interpreted in the context of current medical ethics confronting new philosophical dilemmas regarding physicality. Today, discussions of human organ transplantation, problems of cloning, and the enhancement of human capabilities evolve frequently, as well as the question of what constitutes the core of personal identity. If we look at Major Kovalev from this perspective, we can see him as a human being, rather than a functionary concerned exclusively with his rank. Although Kovalev is a nonentity deserving satirical mockery, his concern may be seen as deeply human when he laments, inarticulately: "Why this misfortune? If I lacked an arm or a leg, it would still be better; if I lacked ears, it would be bad, but still more bearable; but lacking a nose, a man is devil knows what: not a bird, not a citizen—just take and chuck him out the window!"[174] There is some sense in what he says, and the bitterness of these words may be of the same kind as the famous lament of another Gogol character, Akaky Akakievich: "Let me be. Why do you offend me?"[175]

---

[172] Kharms, *Polet v nebesa*, 528–29.

[173] Mikhail Iampolskii, *Bespamiatstvo kak istok (chitaia Kharmsa)* (Moscow: Novoe literaturnoe obozrenie, 1998), 314.

[174] Gogol, "The Nose," 315.

[175] Gogol, "The Overcoat," 397.

Part Two. Interpretations

The question of the absurd in "The Nose" brings us back to the topic previously discussed— Gogol's language game. Idioms seem nonsensical, but in times past they did have meaning. The Russian idiom "to be left with a nose" or the English one "to pull (one's) leg" are not meant to be taken literally. Their meaning cannot be deduced from the sum of their components; it is deduced from the whole phrase rather than from individual words. To grasp the sense of an idiom, one has to learn the meaning of the whole phrase.

Gogol's story resembles an idiom. Its meaning cannot be deduced from the isolated events of the plot—the nose's escape from his owner, his autonomous existence, and his return to the Major's face. None of these events, taken separately, makes sense or sounds plausible. Their meaning is inferred from the story as a whole, though every time, it is different and depends on the perspective one takes.

8
Shostakovich's Opera *The Nose*

In the summer of 1927, twenty-one-year-old Dmitry Shostakovich began working on his first opera, *The Nose*. He completed it in a year. His original plan was that Yevgeni Zamyatin, the author of the novel *We* (1920–1921), would write the libretto, but Zamyatin eventually provided only one scene, that of Kovalev's awakening in Act 3. Thus Shostakovich became the opera's main librettist. He wrote the libretto of Acts 1 and 2 in full and completed the rest of Act 3 with the help of young playwrights Georgy Ionin and Alexander Preis, who at the time were students at the directing department of the Institute of Performing Arts.[176] The authors of the libretto set themselves the task of creating a script in accordance with the laws of musical theater.

In the summer of 1928, soon after the completion of the score, in an interview Shostakovich explained why the idea of writing *The Nose* fascinated him:

> The topic of *The Nose* . . . attracted me with its fantastical, absurd content described by Gogol in strictly realistic tones. I did not deem it necessary to intensify Gogol's satirical text with music of an "ironical" or "parodistic" nature, but, on the contrary, gave it a very serious music accompaniment. The main theatrical effect is created by the contrast between comic action and serious symphonic music; this approach seems all the more justified since Gogol himself describes the comical twists and turns of the subject in a deliberately

---

[176] According to the writer Leonid Panteleev, while still a student, Ionin devoted a lot of time to literature and wrote a novel and an adaptation of Gogol's play *The Order of St. Vladimir, Third Class*. Upon his graduation, he worked at the Theater of Classical Miniatures, where he staged Prosper Mérimée's *The Theatre of Clara Gazul*. Having contracted scarlet fever, he died when he was not yet twenty. Leonid Panteleev, "Gde vy, geroi 'Respubliki Shkid'?" in his *Priotkrytaia dver'* (Leningrad: Sovetskii pisatel', 1980), 189–90. Before Preis graduated from the Institute of Performing arts, he also worked on the libretto for Shostakovich's opera *Lady Macbeth of the Mtsensk District* (together with Shostakovich himself). He died in 1942 at the age of thirty-seven.

serious, uplifted tone. . . . When composing the opera, I was least guided by the notion that opera is primarily a musical genre. In *The Nose*, the elements of action and music are equal. Neither occupies a dominant place. So I tried to create a synthesis of music and theatrical production.[177]

At the premiere, which took place on January 18, 1930, at the Maly Opera Theater in Leningrad (stage director Nikolai Smolich, stage designer Vladimir Dmitriev, conductor Samuil Samosud), the opera galvanized and shocked the audience by its highly innovative modernist spirit. The movie and theater director Grigory Kozintsev recalls his impression of the rehearsal in 1930:

> Gogol's phantasmagoria turned into sound and color. A special figurativeness of the young Russian art, related to both, the most daring experiments in the field of form and urban folklore—signboards of shops and taverns, lubki, music bands on cheap dance floors—burst into the realm of *Aida* and *Il trovatore*. Gogol's grotesque raged: what was a farce here, what was a prophecy?
>
> Incredible orchestral combinations, texts inconceivable for singing ("Why do your hands stink?"—Major Kovalev sang; the romance for the text composed by Smerdyakov was also performed); unusual rhythms (crazy accelerations—beating up of the nose at the police station, with the choir [singing] "Get him! get him! get him!"); mastering everything that before seemed antipoetic, antimusical, vulgar, but was in fact a living intonation, a parody—a struggle with conventionality. Literature has long ago learned to appreciate the nonbookish word, the pictorial power of the real.[178]

Despite the opera's tremendous success, it was greeted with controversy. This was the height of the Cultural Revolution in

---

[177] First published in *Krasnaia gazeta*, July 24, 1928, then reprinted in *Novyi zritel'* 35 (1928). Quoted in Levon Hakobian, "*The Nose*: An Opera; How It Was Composed," in *Dmitri Shostakovich: New Collected Works*, 4th ser.: *Works for Music Theatre*, vol. 50: *The Nose: Full Score*, ed. Viktor Ekimovskii (Moscow: DSCH, 2015), 536.

[178] Grigorii Kozintsev, *Prostranstvo tragedii (Dnevnik rezhissera)* (Leningrad: Iskusstvo, 1983), 222–23.

8. Shostakovich's Opera *The Nose*

Soviet Russia, so critics with an ideological background perceived it as the embodiment of petty bourgeois modernism, foreign to the spirit of the young Soviet music culture of the 1920s. One year later, after being performed sixteen times, the opera was removed from the repertoire. In Soviet Russia it was not revived until 1974, when it was staged by the Moscow Chamber Musical Theater (with music director and conductor Gennady Rozhdestvensky and stage designer Vladimir Talalai, stage director Boris Pokrovsky).[179] At that time Shostakovich was already seriously ill, but he was able to collaborate in this production. A few months later the composer died. The next appearance of *The Nose* on the domestic stage took place in 2004, when the opera was presented by Mariinsky Theater. After that, it was staged in the United States: in 2009 by Opera Boston and in 2010 at the Metropolitan Opera in New York.

Shostakovich created a faithful translation of Gogol's tale into the language of music. The notable Russian musicologist Victor Beljaev termed "The Nose" "the musical equivalent of a great literary work."[180] At the basis of the musical structure of the opera lies the principle of contrasts and oppositions—of the real and the grotesque, comic and serious, degraded and uplifted. All counterparts coexist and interact with each other, all having equal importance; neither text nor music takes over. The contrast between high and low is set in two scenes: one in Kazan Cathedral and the other on the outskirts of Saint Petersburg, where a mob is chasing the nose. The sacred space of the cathedral is expressed with stylization and with symphonic rather than vocal music. Shostakovich characterized it in the following way: "The music in this scene is grandiose and solemn.

---

[179] Pavel Dmitriev recalls the 1974 Pokrovsky production of the opera: "I clearly remember my impressions of this almost monochrome and very integral performance, exceptionally minimalistic in its expressive means, literally chamber, but because of this no less powerful in the effect it exerted on the audience." Pavel Dmitriev, "Tretii nos: V Mariinskom teatre sostoialas' prem'era opery Dmitriia Shostakovicha," *Nevskoe vremia* 70, April 16, 2004, 10.

[180] Quoted in Boris Schwarz, *Music and Musical Life in Soviet Russia, 1917–1970* (London: Barrie and Jenkins, 1972), 71.

Part Two. Interpretations

There is no ethnography of church tunes. The music transmits the very character of the cathedral. In the staging, a satirical discord with the music is necessary."[181] The scene with the crowd on the outskirts of Petersburg in Act 3 is Shostakovich's representation of the city's "low" culture (discussed in chapter 4, "Chronicle of Folk Superstitions").

The various contrasts in the opera are typical of the "Petersburg text of Russian literature." At the time Shostakovich wrote the libretto and the music, there was yet no such term as "Petersburg text," but the tradition already existed, and "The Nose" was already part of it. Levon Hakobian, an expert on Shostakovich, writes that while turning to the Petersburg tradition of Russian literature, the composer reflected both the comic and the cosmic side of things. In Shostakovich's opera, just as in Gogol's story, Petersburg is an enchanted place where surreal, fantastic, and absurd things happen.[182]

---

[181] Reports of D. Shostakovich, postgraduate student at Leningrad State Conservatory, May 1928, MS. Quoted in Alexander Tumanov, "The Correspondence of Literary Text and Musical Phraseology in D. Shostakovich's Opera *The Nose* and Gogol's Fantastic Tale: Textual Changes and Compositional Devices," in *The Force of Vision: Dramas of Desire; Visions of Beauty*, gen. ed. and preface by Earl Miner and Toru Haga, ed. Ziva Ben-Porat, ed. and introd. by Hana Wirth-Nesher, Roseann Runte, and Hans R. Runte (Tokyo: University of Tokyo Press, 1995), vol. 1, 540. Alexander Tumanov points to a curious issue in the libretto of the opera: the reinstatement of Kazan Cathedral, which was in Gogol's text originally, but after the story's first publication, under the pressure of censors, it was replaced with the department store Gostiny Dvor. The original version was reinstated in print almost a century later, in 1928, in the GIZ (State Publishers) edition under the editorship of B. M. Eikhenbaum. The libretto was written in the autumn of 1927, which means that either Shostakovich was familiar with the original version of Gogol's story or he was acquainted with changes made in Eikhenbaum's edition of the text. Tumanov finds both possibilities interesting, especially the latter one, suggesting Shostakovich's personal acquaintance with Eikhenbaum (539–40).

[182] Levon Hakobian (L. O. Akopian), *Dmitrii Shostakovich: Opyt fenomenologii tvorchestva* (Saint Petersburg: Dmitrii Bulanin, 2004), 78. In Russian publications, Hakobian is usually spelled Akopian.

8. Shostakovich's Opera *The Nose*

The phantasmagoric sounds of percussion in interludes and galops re-create the sound of the noisy streets in central Petersburg. The mischievous character of these passages brings to mind the ending of Gogol's "Nevsky Prospect":

> It lies all the time, this Nevsky Prospect, but most of all at the time when night heaves its dense mass upon it and sets off the white and pale yellow walls of the houses, when the whole city turns into a rumbling and brilliance, myriads of carriages tumble from the bridges, postilions shout and bounce on their horses, and the devil himself lights the lamps only so as to show everything not as it really looks.[183]

Shostakovich stressed more than once that it was important to him to maintain the contrast between the comical and the serious, which was characteristic of Gogol's tale. In 1930 he wrote, "Despite all the comical happening on the stage, the music is not comical (*музыка не комикует*). . . . Gogol sets out all the comic incidents in a serious way . . . he doesn't wisecrack."[184] Many scholars take this statement at face value, whereas some perceive the composer's remark as rather deceptive. In Carolyn Roberts Finlay's view:

> Shostakovich was being rather misleading when he wrote that his "music tries not to 'wisecrack.'" On the contrary, his music does so throughout much of the score, beginning with the orchestral "sneeze" which opens the opera, continuing with the deliberately nasal singing used in those parts written for the nose itself, and extending to the musical parodies of Russian romantic opera in the final scenes. Shostakovich's general observations are accurate, however.[185]

---

[183] Gogol, "Nevsky Prospect," 278.

[184] D. Shostakovich, "Pochemu Nos?" *Rabochii i teatr* 3, January 15, 1930, 11.

[185] Carolyn Roberts Finlay, "Operatic Translation and Shostakovich: The Nose," *Comparative Literature* 35, no. 3 (Summer 1983): 198. To be consistent with the system of transliteration used throughout this book, the spelling of Shostakovich's name in this article has been changed.

Various contrasts created and emphasized on the musical plane maintain the atmosphere of the grotesque, whereas the atonal musical texture of some parts of the opera create a sense of absurdity, again characteristic of the story.

In *The Nose* the composer set himself the task of expressing Gogol's artistic language and style. While stating his reasons for writing an opera based on "The Nose," Shostakovich observed that the story was written "in more *vibrant, expressive language* than Gogol's other Petersburg tales and provides many interesting tasks in terms of setting this text to music."[186] Shostakovich maintained that while writing the opera, he had placed an emphasis on the language: "Music in this spectacle does not play a self-sufficient role. The stress is on the presentation of the text."[187]

The opera recreates the *vibrant* and *expressive* language of Gogol's story. Vocal singing alternates and merges with conversational intonations. The recitatives sound unconventional. At the end of a sentence, instead of going down, the intonation often rises. Occasionally, the stress becomes "alogical," that is, falling on unstressed syllables, as, for example, in the phrase *хочется мне горячего хлебца с луком*. This creates an extremely innovative and comical recitative.[188] Musicologist Marina Tcherkashina comments on the use of folk instuments, such as domras and balalaikas, as well as the modern percussion instrument flexatone:

> This combination of academic and non-academic instruments (in a similar manner the story's author combined conventional literary stylistic methods with extra-literary, everyday speech components) contributed to creating a specific timbre coloring. The orchestration is colorful, abounding in exaggeratedly "brazen" timbres, abrupt, muffled, grumbling sounds and effectively intervening tremolos and glissandi. The composer fearlessly discards the academic norms, rejecting the

---

[186] Shostakovich, "Pochemu Nos?" 11.

[187] Ibid.

[188] Alla Bretanitskaia, "O muzykal'noi dramaturgii opery 'Nos,'" *Sovetskaia muzyka* 9 (1974): 50.

8. Shostakovich's Opera *The Nose*

conventional treatment of the orchestra as an ideally coherent and balanced sonic mass akin to an individual musical instrument possessing a rich timbral register.[189]

The composer also emphasizes the oral nature of Gogol's narrative with other devices. While converting the story's prosaic and widely conversational text into music, Shostakovich uses deformations, unnatural registers, and uncommon manners of articulation. Laurel Fay comments: "The vocal writing is declamatory, angular, and requires a wide range of unusual vocal techniques, including the 'pinched' nasal quality with which, appropriately, the 'nose' is expected to sing."[190] The feeling of the grotesque is created by singers in extreme registers, naturalistic imitations (the musical sounds of snoring, sneezing, and shaving), and sudden transitions from simple tonality to atonality and false notes.

In this opera singing coexists with speaking. The expressionistic vocal techniques *Sprechgesang* (Germ. "spoken singing") and *Sprechstimme* (Germ. "spoken voice"), which Arnold Schoenberg used in a number of pieces and Alban Berg in his operas *Wozzeck* and *Lulu*, contribute to the effect of oral narrative. Reed Merrill comments:

> The grotesquely confused events of the plot are contrasted with an equally distorted and strange libretto whose sung and spoken aural effects (Shostakovich's own kind of Shoenbergian "speech-song") are consistently at odds with conventional expectations; the orchestral music creates a third source of conflict and confusion in that it, too, seems antithetical to both the vocal-spoken dialogue and the plot.[191]

---

[189] Marina Tcherkashina, "Gogol and Leskov in Shostakovich's Interpretation," *International Journal of Musicology* 1 (1992): 234.

[190] Laurel Fay, "The Punch in Shostakovich's Nose," in *Russian and Soviet Music: Essays for Boris Schwarz*, ed. Malcolm Hamrick Brown (Ann Arbor: University of Michigan Research Press, 1984), 232.

[191] Reed Merrill, "The Grotesque in Music: Shostakovich's Muse," *Russian Literature Triquaterly* 23 (1990): 304.

Part Two. Interpretations

The use of colloquial language as part of the "low" city culture is marked in the opera just as emphatically. Thus, for example, when the barber finds the nose in the bread and his wife chases him from home, she repeats the word "out!" (вон!) forty-six times. The combination of literary and colloquial styles in the story finds its equivalent in the combination of classical instruments and the Russian folk instruments, which resound in the scene of the dialogue between the barber and the police officer.

Considering the strong connection of the opera to the works of the Russian formalists, musicology professor Alexander Tumanov claims that in the opera the composer is rendering Gogol's technique of *skaz*. Tumanov observes that Shostakovich must have been familiar with Eikhenbaum's essay "How Gogol's 'Overcoat' Is Made" (1919):

> Shostakovich availed himself of the notion of *skaz* in working out the musical and dramatic concept of *The Nose*. The dialogues in the opera alternate with orchestral episodes, which conforms to Eikhenbaum's description of the compositional role of the *skaz* with great accuracy. Shostakovich's opera develops as a "reproductive" *skaz*, both in the form of a lively dialogue and in a form that is purely musical—an orchestral or symphonic *skaz*.[192]

He further notes that the orchestral episodes in the opera are not "objective descriptions of events, but the satirical embodiment of dramatic events in music, where the voice of the author is clearly heard."

Tumanov's observation dovetails with my claim in section "How 'The Nose' is Made" about the presence of *skaz* in Gogol's

---

[192] Alexander Tumanov, "The Correspondence of Literary Text and Musical Phraseology in D. Shostakovich's Opera *The Nose* and Gogol's Fantastic Tale: Textual Changes and Compositional Devices," in Earl Miner (gen. ed. and pref.), Toru Haga (gen. ed. and pref.); Ziva Ben-Porat (ed.), Hana Wirth-Nesher (ed. and introd.), Roseann Runte (ed. and introd.), Hans R. Runte (ed. and introd.), *The Force of Vision: Dramas of Desire; Visions of Beauty* (Tokyo: University of Tokyo Press, 1995), 1:536-37.

8. Shostakovich's Opera *The Nose*

"The Nose." Yet it must be noted again that although the chances that Shostakovich was familiar with Eikhenbaum's essay on Gogol's "Overcoat" are very high, as mentioned earlier, in this essay Eikhenbaum does not discuss the issue of *skaz* in "The Nose."

Mirroring the story's tripartite structure, the opera is composed of three acts (ten scenes). Librettos often simplify the plots of literary works on which the operas are based, but this is not the case with Shostakovich's *The Nose*. Indeed, some episodes are omitted, such as Kovalev's two trips to the pastry shop, his first glimpse of the nose outside Kazan Cathedral, and his visit to the police commissioner, who reproaches him for not being a decent person. On the other hand, in contrast to the limited number of characters appearing in Gogol's story, the libretto has seventy-eight solo singing roles, nine spoken roles, a chorus, and an orchestra. *The Nose* includes several dynamic mass scenes, which follow operatic tradition. The opera culminates in Act 3, Scene 7, which takes place in the suburbs of Petersburg, at the post station (for changing horses), when the nose attempts to escape to Riga and the residents of the city are trying to catch him. A crowd of people is chasing the nose, among them police officers, travelers—men, women, and children—students, a woman selling bagels; all are shouting *Так его! Так его! Так его!* (Take him! Take him! Take him!).

Further additions in the opera are borrowings from other literary works. The libretto contains quotes from Gogol's own works, such as "The Fair at Sorochintsy," "May Night," "Christmas Eve," "Old-World Landowners," "The Tale of How Ivan Ivanovich Quarreled with Ivan Nikiforovich," *Taras Bulba*, and *The Marriage*.[193] The most notable are quotes from Gogol's play *The Marriage*, inserted in the episode with Podtochina's daughter, whom Kovalev courts but does not intend to marry. This character is mentioned in the story but does not make an appearance; in the opera, however, Podtochina's daughter does appear on the stage, in Scene 8 when the mother receives a letter from Kovalev.

---

[193] A. Bretanitskaia, *"Nos" D. D. Shostakovicha* (Moscow: Muzyka, 1983), 17.

Part Two. Interpretations

The most grotesque addition occurs in Act 3, when ten police officers, sitting in an ambush near the post station and waiting for the nose, sing lyrically, in Reed Merrill's words, "a strangely crude and incomprehensibly grotesque song whose reference and context are equally mysterious:

> Like a dog, with his tail between his legs,
> Like Cain fidgeting around
> He made tobacco run from "his nose."[194]

The lyrics of this song are taken from an epigraph to chapter 8 of Gogol's *The Fair at Sorochyntsi*. They are lines from I. P. Kotliarevsky's heroic-comic poem *Aeneid* (1791), written in Ukrainian:

> Поджав хвист, мов собака,
> Мов Каин затрусывсь увесь;
> Из носа потекла табака.[195]

Torn from their original context, in the opera these words from a humorous eighteenth-century poem sound nonsensical and extremely funny. They are made into a song performed by a chorus of police officers, which renders it even more absurd. This insertion in the libretto maintains the absurdist style of Gogol's tale.

It is well known that Shostakovich had an excellent sense of humor. His correspondence with friends sparkles with jokes, puns, and wordplay. His colleague Georgy Ionin, who was not yet twenty when he worked on the text of the libretto, also had a sharp sense of humor.[196] Talented and witty, the authors of the libretto must have used this passage out of youthful playfulness,

---

[194] Reed Merrill, "The Grotesque in Music: Shostakovich's Muse," *Russian Literature Triquarterly* 23 (1990): 311.

[195] N. V. Gogol', "Sorochinskaia iarmarka," in *Polnoe sobranie sochinenii*, vol. 1, ed. V. L. Komarovich (1937), 127.

[196] His translating skills and abilities (he spoke four foreign languages) and his jocular character are recorded by Leonid Panteleev and Grigory Belykh. See G. Belykh and L. Panteleev, *Respublika ShKID* (Leningrad: Sovetskii pisatel', 1960).

8. Shostakovich's Opera *The Nose*

because its awkwardness matched the spirit of Gogol's wordplay in "The Nose."

Of particular interest is a quote from Dostoevsky's *The Brothers Karamazov*. In Act 2, Scene 6, the servant Ivan, lying on a couch, is singing Smerdiakov's song. Caryl Emerson comments that this literary borrowing is suggestive in light of Yuri Tynianov's theory of parody in his essay on Gogol and Dostoevsky:

> Here, then, is one example of literary montage: three prose texts not so much juxtaposed side by side as glinting through one another: 1836–1881–1928. The first and third are parodic grotesque, the second grimly serious. But the final entry in any sequence always comes with the prior contexts (in effect, whole other worlds) attached to it. In this accretion of contexts and world lies the essence of Russian literary tradition, where not infrequently—as Tynianov wrote in 1921, apropos of Dostoevsky's parody of Gogol—a parodied tragedy becomes a comedy, and a parodied comedy takes on the potential for tragedy.[197]

The lyrics of the song composed by Smerdyakov pretending to reflect romantic and religious feelings are intentionally bad. A good example of Dostoevsky's humor, the couplet from Smerdyakov's song deserves to be quoted: Непобедимой силой привержен я к милой. / Господи, помилуй ее и меня! / Царская корона – была б моя милая здорова! / Господи, помилуй ее и меня! ("By invincible power I am committed to my sweetheart. / God have mercy on her and on me! / The king's crown—I wish my sweetheart to be healthy! / God have mercy on her and on me!").

In the episode of the servant Ivan's singing Smerdyakov's song, the folk instrument balalaika contrasts with the song's refrain Господи помилуй ("God have mercy"), traditionally chanted in the Russian Orthodox liturgy. The words of the prayer are comically modified: the traditional "have mercy on me" is changed into

---

[197] Caryl Emerson, "Shostakovich and the Russian Literary Tradition," in *Shostakovich and His World*, ed. Laurel Fey (Princeton: Princeton University Press, 2004), 193.

the sentimental "have mercy on her and me." The lofty stylistic register contrasts with the lowly one (wishes of good health for the sweetheart expressed in colloquial language). The insertion of Smerdyakov's song is notable for yet another reason—it mimics Gogol's wordplay with idiomatic expressions, as discussed in section "How 'The Nose' is Made." In the libretto, the servant Ivan's song of Smerdyakov is preceded by Shostakovich's stage directions: "Kovalev's apartment. Ivan lies on the couch in the front, spits at the ceiling and plays the balalaika." As mentioned earlier, the Russian idiom "to spit at the ceiling" literally means "to spend time doing nothing." Shostakovich expresses the idiom musically: The servant is playing the balalaika and singing a silly song, thus "spending time doing nothing."

It is also notable that by applying lines from Dostoevsky's novel written in 1879-1880 to Gogol's 1830s story, young Shostakovich creatively transgressed time boundaries, just as the composer did it in his late vocal cycle *Four Verses of Captain Lebyadkin* (opus 146), set to the poems of a minor character in Dostoevsky's novel *Devils*.[198]

While translating Gogol's story into the language of music, Shostakovich interpreted it in the spirit of the 1920s—a time of special interest in Gogol literary studies, a time of avant-garde artistic experiments, and a time of cinematographic fragmentation. The spirit of the opera is tightly connected with the general cultural atmosphere of the era.

Some musicologists observed that "The Nose" was influenced by Vsevolod Meyerhold's artistic style, especially regarding Shostakovich's melding of theater drama and music. The connection is not accidental. Shostakovich was familiar with Meyerhold's experimental approach to staging, including his production of Gogol's *The Inspector General* in 1926. In 1927 this play was performed in Leningrad, where Shostakovich saw it in the same year he began working on *The Nose*. A big part of the work on the opera was carried out in 1928, when Shostakovich lived in Meyerhold's

---

[198] Ksana Blank, "Captain Lebyadkin's Poetry in Shostakovich and Dostovsky," in *Spaces of Creativity*, 130–52.

8. Shostakovich's Opera *The Nose*

Moscow apartment and worked as a pianist and head of the music department at Meyerhold State Theatre. The composer hoped that Meyerhold would also stage *The Nose*. Before he returned to Leningrad, where he eventually wrote Act 3, Shostakovich gave the score of Acts 1 and 2 to Meyerhold.[199] Shostakovich affirmed Meyerhold's influence, especially the impact of the staging of Gogol's *Inspector General*'s on *The Nose*: "No doubt about it, he had a creative influence on me. Somehow, I even began to compose music in a different way. I wanted to resemble Meyerhold in some way.... I was fascinated and infected by Meyerhold's eternal desire to move forward, constantly seeking and saying a new word."[200]

Other critics drew links between *The Nose* and the Western operatic tradition, especially Alban Berg's opera *Wozzeck*. Like Berg's opera, based on Georg Büchner's stage play written in 1836, Shostakovich's *The Nose* is based on a story written in the 1830s. Both operas begin with a shaving scene, both have an episode with a doctor, and both narrate the protagonist's misfortunes. Again, the parallels are not accidental. In June 1926 *Wozzeck* was premiered in Leningrad. Shostakovich attended the performance. Some musicologists stressed differences in the styles of the two operas, referring to Shostakovich's use of parody absent in Berg's opera.[201]

Sexual overtones in *The Nose* bring to mind Ivan Yermakov's Freudian approach to the story in his *Sketches for an Analysis of Gogol's Work* (1923). In the spirit of Yermakov's interpretation of the story, in the opera Kovalev is a lover of the fair sex. The role of Podtochina's daughter, a new character whom Kovalev courts, is expanded based on Gogol's play *The Marriage*. The servant, Ivan, is singing Smerdyakov's song about his sweetheart. In Act 3 the police

---

[199] For an account of Meyerhold's influence on Shostakovich, see L. Bubennikova, "Meierkhol'd i Shostakovich (Iz istorii sozdaniia opery 'Nos')," *Sovetskaia muzyka* 3 (March 1973): 43.

[200] D. Shostakovich, "Iz vospominanii: K 100-letiiu so dnia rozhdeniia Vs. E. Meierkhol'da," *Sovetskaia muzyka* 3 (1974): 55.

[201] Alla Bretanitskaia, "O muzykal'noi dramaturgii opery 'Nos,'" *Sovetskaia muzyka* 9 (1974): 49.

officers, with frivolous overtones, address the merchant woman selling bagels, which made the Soviet opera critic V. M. Bogdanov-Berezovsky remark angrily, "It is simply a sexual episode which the author plays up for the sake of his own personal satisfaction ... a dangerous tendency toward rude naturalism and physiology in Shostakovich's music."[202] Finally, the opera ends with Kovalev shrieking *Рас-красоточка!* ("Beauty-cutie!") — a licentious invitation to the female street merchant selling shirtfronts.

It has also been noted that the spirit of *The Nose* is consonant with the absurdist spirit of the OBERIU (Union of Real Art) circle. The young Shostakovich shared the audaciousness of the OBERIU poets and had personal relationships with some of them. In 1930 he was planning to write an opera titled *Karas'* based on Nikolai Oleinikov's lyrics. Commenting on Shostakovich's music in *The Nose*, the music scholar Tamara Levaia observes: "In the prose of the classic writer, he saw an absurd image of society in which the shadow of mass psychosis and the threat of the disappearance of the individual have already become distinguishable."[203] In Levaia's view, the combination of comic and serious elements in the opera creates a connection with "the poetics of the absurd, which brought him closer to the underground poets, and above all to Daniil Kharms."[204]

---

[202] V. M. Bogdanov-Berezovsky, *Sovetskaia opera* (Leningrad: Izdanie Leningradskogo otdeleniia VTO, 1940), 121.

[203] Tamara Levaia, "Neobarokko i absurd (eshche raz ob opere 'Nos' Shostakovicha)," in *Etot mnogoobraznyi mir muzyki: Sbornik statei k 80-letiiu M. G. Aranovskogo*, ed. Z. A. Imamutdinova, A. A. Baeva, and N. O. Vlasova (Moscow: Gos. institut iskusstvoznaniia, 2010), 390–91. Levaia observes that Kharms's miniatures have a symphonic quality: continual transformations of the plot emphasize the idea of the incomprehensibility and infinite irrationality of being. Another musical form Kharms used is, according to Levaia, a Baroque polyphony, as, for example, Kharms's *Incidences* (*Sluchai*). On Shostakovich and OBERIU see also Ksana Blank, "Shostakovich, Dostoevsky, Lebyadkin, and OBERIU," in *Liber amicorum Liudmile Kovnatskoi*, ed. Lidia Ader and Olga Manulkina (St. Petersburg: BiblioRossika, 2016), 345–48.

[204] Levaia, "Neobarokko i absurd," 387.

8. Shostakovich's Opera *The Nose*

Levon Hakobian remarks that the opera introduces a theme of "pursuit, humiliation and beating of the weak by the strong" characteristic of the late 1920s, when it was written. Several characters in the opera are assigned the role of victim, chased by police officers or a crowd of people. This theme is absent in the text of Gogol's tale, but it is implicitly present in the works of the OBERIU poets Kharms, Oleinikov, and Vvedensky.[205]

The avant-garde spirit of the 1920s did not come across in the production that was premiered in Saint Petersburg's Mariinsky Theatre on April 10, 2004 (with music director and conductor Valery Gergiev, director Yuri Alexandrov, production designer Zinovy Margolin). It seemed excessively eclectic and full of special effects, with a metal construction resembling Tatlin's tower lying flat on the stage, clouds of smoke emerging from below the stage, which must have symbolized Petersburg fog, and, at the end, Khozrev-Mirza dressed in an outfit made of Burberry fabric, marching through the stage on a plush camel.[206]

The spirit of the 1920s was successfully presented at the Metropolitan Opera by the South African artist William Kentridge, which premiered on March 5, 2010. The art historian Maria Gough argues that Kentridge's "extreme visualization of this remarkably experimental work brought to the fore a new reading or inflection of it, one having to do less with its indisputably satirical register and more with its thematization of metamorphosis and, more broadly, social transformation."[207] Kentridge reconnected *The Nose* with the aesthetics of the Russian and Soviet avant-garde, drawing inspiration for the visual counterpart from the works of artists Liubov Popova, Kazimir Malevich, Vladimir Tatlin, Gustavs Klucis, Varvara Stepanova, Alexander Rodchenko, and especially El Lissitsky.[208]

---

[205] Hakobian, "*The Nose*: An Opera; How it Was Composed," 538.

[206] I saw this performance at the Mariinsky Theatre in July 2004.

[207] Maria Gough, "Kentridge's Nose," *October* 134 (Fall 2014): 4.

[208] Ibid., 9. Aside from the staging of the opera, Kentridge recorded his vision

Part Two. Interpretations

Creating audacious artistic ties with Gogol's other works, with Dostoevsky's *Brothers Karamazov*, written at the end of the nineteenth century, with the OBERIU circle and the Russian formalists of the 1920s, Shostakovich's opera places Gogol's "The Nose" into the context of Russian culture. To complete our discussion of Gogol's short story, a few words must be said about the connections of "The Nose" to European modernism.

---

of the nose's private life in a portfolio of thirty etchings that he conceived between 2006 and 2009. These were published in book form under the title *William Kentridge Nose* (Johannesburg: David Krut, 2010).

9
A Play with Reality: "The Nose," Kafka, and Dalí

Besides its connections with the twentieth-century Russian avant-garde, "The Nose" has ties with European modernism, particularly with the works of Franz Kafka, and specifically with his novella *The Metamorphosis* (1915). "The Nose" and *The Metamorphosis* open with the protagonists' awakening and their discovery of a supernatural phenomenon. Analyzing the affinities between Gogol and Kafka, Victor Erlich, an eminent authority on Russian modernism, comments that "Gogol's nonsense narrative lacks the quality of an existential disaster. Yet it shares with the grimmer story of Kafka the discrepancy between its 'realistic' mode of presentation and the utterly incredible central event."[209] This combination, as well as the motif of metamorphosis featured in both stories, creates "a testimony to the 'surrealist' topsy-turvy nature of their unique worlds."[210]

Although Kafka was familiar with Gogol's work, there is no evidence that *The Metamorphosis* was inspired by "The Nose." Polish literary critic Roman Karst notes that Gogol's name in Kafka's letters and diaries appears only sparsely. Although Kafka read *Dead Souls* and *The Inspector General*, this was after he had written *The Metamorphosis*.[211] Karst observes: "Whether Kafka was familiar with the whole of Gogol and the extent to which he was enchanted by the Russian's magic can scarcely be determined; moreover, these are not the most important questions. Some similarities between the two stemming from accident or simply from literary existence are deceptively great. Both are surrounded by mystery, although

---

[209] Victor Erlich, "Gogol and Kafka: Note on 'Realism' and 'Surrealism,'" in *For Roman Jakobson*, ed. Morris Halle et al. (The Hague: Mouton, 1956), 102.

[210] Ibid., 104.

[211] Roman Karst, "The Reality of the Absurd and the Absurdity of the Real: Kafka and Gogol," *Mosaic: An Interdisciplinary Critical Journal* 9, no. 1: *Literature and Ideas* (Fall 1975): 68.

innumerable books and essays have been written about them; both had a predilection to destroy everything which they had written; both had a tragic life and died young, in their forties."[212]

Some scholars point to the striking parallels between the death of Gogol and of the fictional character in Kafka's *A Hunger Artist* (published in 1922), as well as between the two artists' attitudes toward their art.[213] They suggest the possibility that Kafka had known about the last days of Gogol's life, his fasting and death, from Dmitry Merezhkovsky's book *Gogol, His Work, Life, and Religion* (translated into German in 1911), as well as from the psychiatrist N. N. Bazhenov's report containing an account of Gogol's illness and tragic death, published in 1902.

Analyzing the writers' use of the grotesque, Roman Struc suggests that the similarities in theme and motif between "The Nose" and *The Metapmorphosis* can be traced to Hoffmann, whom Gogol and Kafka both knew well, which throws additional light on the connection of "The Nose" to European literature, as discussed in chapter 6, "An Echo of German Romanticism."[214]

In his juxtaposition of "The Nose" and *The Metamorphosis*, Yuri Mann stresses that in neither work do we find a personified cause for the fantastic events (some kind of evil spirit). Mann writes: "Something incredible and unforeseen interferes with the everyday and trivial routine of things. The reaction of the characters is built on the contrast of extraordinary and the trivial."[215] The transformation has no rationale, but the characters do not mind the absence of causality; they do not seem to be surprised. Their concerns are

---

[212] Ibid.

[213] Leland Fetzer and Richard H. Lawson, "Den Tod zur Schau gestellt: Gogol und Kafkas' Hungerkünstler," *Modern Austian Literature* 11, no. 1 (1978): 167–77.

[214] Roman Struc, "Categories of the Grotesque: Gogol and Kafka," in *Franz Kafka: His Place in World Literature; Proceedings of the Comparative Literature Symposium*, ed. Wolodymyr T. Zyla (Lubbock: Texas Tech University, 1971), 135.

[215] Iurii Mann, "Vstrecha v labirinte (Frants Kafka i Nikolai Gogol')," *Voprosy literatury* 2 (1999): 173.

9. A Play with Reality: "The Nose," Kafka, and Dalí

purely pragmatic. Gregory Samsa is worried that his boss will be angry because of his absence. Major Kovalev is concerned that he will be unable to visit his female acquaintances. The major thrust of Yuri Mann's books on Gogol, as previously mentioned—the combination of real and fantastic features in Gogol—is equally relevant to Kafka, in whose works absurdity and reality form a single whole.

In Yuri Mann's view, the connections between "The Nose" and *The Metamorphosis* prove that Gogol anticipated modernist aesthetics. He writes: "Gogol's emergence into the forefront of world culture in the twentieth century, especially in the second half of it, the perception of him as an unusually relevant artist who anticipated the tendencies of irrationality and absurdism in contemporary art— it was this event that put forward the relationship between the two names as a historical and literary issue."[216]

The coexistence of the real and the fantastic (incongruous, dreamlike) in Gogol's prose invites other juxtapositions with the modernist artists, not only in literature but also in visual arts.

Surrealism, a cultural movement that started in the twentieth century, has been mentioned in Gogol studies, though briefly. Thus, for example, Dmitry Chizhevsky observed that if there had been a surrealist movement in Russia, it would have considered Gogol its predecessor.[217] In Simon Karlinsky's *The Sexual Labyrinth of Nikolai Gogol*, the word "surrealism" is part of the title of the chapter on "The Nose." Karlinsky notes that "Together with Lewis Carroll, both Gogol and Lautréamont belong in the select company of authentic nineteenth-century surrealists in literature."[218] The critic concludes that Gogol's "vision of the surreal within the ordinary" is "beyond compare."[219] Neil Cornwell ends his essay on the absurd in Gogol with a discussion of Gogol's surrealist technique. Cornwell

---

[216] Ibid., 163.

[217] Chizhevskii, "Neizvestnyi Gogol," 127.

[218] Karlinsky, *The Sexual Labyrinth of Nikolai Gogol*, 124.

[219] Ibid., 130.

discusses some parallels and affinities, in art and real life, between Gogol and Antonin Artaud, a French surrealist and absurdist and the founder of the Theatre of Cruelty.[220]

Indeed, Gogol's surrealist technique is prominent in his portrayal of grotesque and monstrous creatures, which often look terrifying, comical, and sometimes obscene, in a mix of the real and the imaginary, the natural and the supernatural. This fusion of dream and reality permeates the "strange and disturbing world" of Gogol's prose in general, and "The Nose" in particular.

In my claim that Gogol's artistic method is a precursor of surrealism, I will adopt the definition of the term "surrealism" that an expert on contemporary Spanish literature, Paul Ilie, gives in his book *The Surrealist Mode in Spanish Literature*:

> There are several criteria for determining whether a work is surrealistic. Probably the most infallible is the subjective effect it has upon the observer, the feeling that he is in the presence of a strange, disturbing world. This is invariably the impact made by the paintings of De Chirico, Ernst, Dalí, Tanguy, and Magritte. The odd sensations of uncanniness, incongruity, and absurdity are all part of the aesthetic experience of surrealism. A more objective criterion, however, is the technique of irrationality involving a new type of illogic based on free association. Here, traditional forms of meaning are replaced by the unrestricted juxtaposition of words, ideas, and images. These haphazard relationships produce a reality that is no longer bound by the laws of logic, causality, or syntax. The result is a work of art filled with unusual encounters, dissimilar planes of reality, and psychological dissociations of many kinds. Whether these results are due to pure psychic automatism or to a deliberate and rational attempt to create an incongruous or grotesque world, the aesthetic consequences are the same. That is, surrealism projects the forms of distortion and the emotions of alienation. This is often accomplished by the artistic use of dream states and hallucinations, the adaptation of Freudian psychoanalysis to art, and the exploitation of occultism and the supernatural.

---

[220] Neil Cornwell, "The Absurd in Gogol and Gogol Criticism," *Essays in Poetics: The Journal of the British Neo-Formalist Circle* 29, no. 9 (Autumn 2004): 8.

9. A Play with Reality: "The Nose," Kafka, and Dalí

But more often, the artist uses these elements in conjunction with other, more conscious techniques. Consequently, a work of art may be surrealistic only in part, and yet be just as interesting to us for its contribution to the aesthetics of the surrealist mode.[221]

Gogol's affinity with surrealist artists who came a few decades after his death is especially obvious when Gogol's "The Nose" is juxtaposed with the work of the surrealist artist Salvador Dalí.[222] The prime example of this connection is the device of the grotesque fragmentation of the body that both artists use.

Dalí's adherence to the fragmentation technique manifests itself throughout his artistic career. Severed parts of the body—fingers, hands, breasts—first appear in his canvases in 1927–28, when the artist gradually turned to surrealism. In these paintings one can see faces without noses (*The Sick Child / Self-Portrait in Cadaqués*, circa 1923) and without mouths (*The Lugubrious Game*, 1929; *The Enigma of My Desire*, 1929; and *The Great Masturbator*, 1929).[223] In his later career Dalí depicts severed hands (*Feather Equilibrium* 1947), isolated lips and eyes (a drawing for *Spellbound*, 1945), mustaches (*Dalí's Mustache*, 1950), and feet (*Original Sin*, 1941). He portrays Vladimir Lenin with an elongated bare buttock (*The Enigma of William Tell*, 1933).[224]

---

[221] Paul Ilie, *The Surrealist Mode in Spanish Literature: An Interpretation of Basic Trends from Post-Romanticism to the Spanish Vanguard* (Ann Arbor: University of Michigan Press, 1968), 5.

[222] This part of the chapter is based on my (unpublished) paper "Conquest of the Irrational: Reading Gogol along with Salvador Dalí," presented at the AATSEEL conference, December 1998, San Francisco.

[223] Very similar images permeate Dalí's early poetic experiments, such as, for example, a poem dedicated to Lydia of Cadaqués, a young woman Dalí admired: "A quiet ear over a small upright wisp of smoke indicating a shower of ants over the sea. / Near the cold boulder there lies an eyelash. / A torn piece of flesh signaling bad weather. / There are six breasts lost inside a square water" (1927). See *The Collected Writings of Salvador Dalí*, ed. and trans. Haim Finkelstein (Cambridge: Cambridge University Press, 1998), 27.

[224] Isolated body parts appear, though less often, in other surrealists' paintings— semiabstract works by Joan Miró, paintings by Max Ernst and René Magritte.

Part Two. Interpretations

Commenting on surrealists' "tearing apart and scattering of the human body," the art historian Jacqueline Chenieux-Gendron gives it the label "Dionysiac."[225] Haim Finkelstein explains Dalí's fascination with the technique of fragmentation in psychoanalytical terms, claiming that this device originates in Jacques Lacan's concept of *corps morcelé* ("fragmented body") and his theory of the "mirror stage":

> In Lacan's formulation, in this stage, occurring from the age of six months, the infant, seeing its own image in the mirror, attains a perception of the totality of its body and becomes conscious of itself as a unified entity. In the first six months of life, the infant has no sense of being an individual and perceives itself as being in pieces. Seeing itself in the mirror, the infant contrasts the wholeness of this specular image with his own sense of "fragmented body."[226]

Dalí was personally acquainted with Lacan; they exchanged ideas and influenced each other.[227] He was intrigued by Lacan's idea of

---

[225] Jacqueline Chenieux-Gendron, *Surrealism*, trans. Vivian Folkenflik (New York: Columbia University Press, 1990), 5.

[226] Haim Finkelstein, *Salvador Dalí's Art and Writing, 1927–1942: The Metamorphosis of Narcissus* (Cambridge: Cambridge University Press, 1996), 235.

[227] The way Dalí describes their first encounter, in his autobiographical book *The Secret Life of Salvador Dalí* (1942), is relevant to the theme of "nosology":

> At six o'clock sharp—the appointed time of our meeting—the doorbell rang. I hurriedly put away my copper, Jacques Lacan entered, and we immediately launched into a highly technical discussion. . . . We conversed for two hours in a constant dialectical tumult. He left with the promise that we would keep in constant touch with each other and meet periodically. After he had gone I paced up and down my studio, trying to reconstruct the course of our conversation and to weigh more objectively the points on which our rare disagreements might have a real significance. But I grew increasingly puzzled over the rather alarming manner in which the young psychiatrist had scrutinized my face from time to time. It was almost as if the germ of a strange, curious smile would then pierce through his expression.
>
> Was he intently studying the convulsive effects upon my facial morphology of the ideas that stirred in my soul?

9. A Play with Reality: "The Nose," Kafka, and Dalí

"fragmented body." In his *50 Secrets of Magic Craftsmanship*, Dalí makes a comment on Van Gogh cutting off his ear:

> Van Gogh was mad, and unconditionally, generously and gratuitously cut off his left ear with the blade of a razor. I am not mad either [*sic!*], yet I would be perfectly capable of allowing my left hand to be cut off, but this under the most interesting circumstances imaginable: on condition, namely, hat I might, for ten minutes, be able to observe Vermeer of Delft seated before his easel as he was painting.[228]

The psychoanalytic twist of "The Nose" was already discussed in chapter 5, "A Case of Castration Anxiety," but it can now be mentioned that Lacan's ideas of the "mirror stage complex" and the *corps morcelé* are relevant to "The Nose" and to Gogol's original intention to title the story "The Dream" ("Son"), as they throw light on the role of the mirror in the story. Kovalev is constantly looking at himself in the mirror (he does it seven times, mostly upon wakening). According to Lacan, the self-image of *corps morcelé* manifests itself mostly in dreams, thus inducing feelings of dismemberment and mutilation.[229] In the morning, Kovalev checks his appearance in the mirror and finds that his nose is lacking.

> I found the answer to the enigma when I presently went to wash my hands (this, incidentally, is the moment when one usually sees every kind of question with the greatest lucidity). But this time the answer was given me by my image in the mirror. I had forgotten to remove the square of white paper from the tip of my nose! For two hours I had discussed questions of the most transcendental nature in the most precise, objective and grave tone of voice without being aware of the disconcerting adornment of my nose. What cynic could consciously have played this role through to the end?

See Salvador Dalí, *The Secret Life of Salvador Dalí* (1942; repr., New York: Dover Publications, 1993), 18.

[228] Salvador Dalí, *50 Secrets of Magic Craftsmanship*, trans. Haakon M. Chevalier (New York: Dial Press, 1948), 13.

[229] Jacques Lacan, *Écrits: A Selection*, trans. Alan Sheridan (New York: Norton, 1977), 4.

Part Two. Interpretations

While in "The Nose" fragmentation of the body is the central event of the plot, in Gogol's other works body parts and pieces of garments also lead an independent existence: they detach from their owners and occasionally disappear. Mustaches, whiskers, sleeves, hats, and boots stroll about Petersburg at the beginning of the story "Nevsky Prospect." People with missing features come into view in Gogol's Ukrainian cycle: Ivan Nikiforovich's eyes "disappear completely between his bushy eyebrows and plump cheeks" ("Two Ivans," 1834). In *Dead Souls*, "Manilov's joy was so pronounced that his nose and lips were all that remained of his face—his eyes disappeared entirely."[230] Another character in the novel, Nozdryov, constantly cheating at cards, occasionally returns home without one of his pitch-black side whiskers, which eventually grows back.[231] In *Dead Souls* there is also the following portrait: "The light and shadows were so intermingled now that the very objects seemed fused. The black and white barrier assumed a nebulous color; the sentinel's whiskers seemed to grow out of his forehead above his eyes and he did not appear to have a nose at all."[232]

Like Gogol, Dalí experimented with the misplacement of a fragmented body part. His painting *Dematerialization near the Nose of Nero* (1947) shows a marble bust of Nero with the nose chopped off from his face and placed on his neck. In Dalí's plaster cast of a classical bust, *Tête otorhinologique de Vénus* (1964/1970), the positions of the nose and ear on Venus are swapped.

The events in "The Nose"—the detachment of the nose from the face of Major Kovalev and the nose's independent existence under the guise of a state councillor—may be viewed as surreal. It has been often claimed that the nose transforms into a state councillor,

---

[230] Nicolai V. Gogol, *Dead Souls*, trans. George Reavey, introd. George Gibian (New York: W. W. Norton, 1971), 166–67.

[231] Ibid., 80. In Ilya Kutik's apt definition, "Nozdrev—Nostrilor, who *is* a walking nose." Ilya Kutik, *Writing as Exorcism: The Personal Codes of Pushkin, Lermontov, and Gogol* (Evanston, IL: Northwestern University Press, 2005), 69.

[232] Gogol, *Dead Souls*, 155.

9. A Play with Reality: "The Nose," Kafka, and Dalí

and later the state councillor transforms back into the nose.[233] In fact, we, as readers of "The Nose," do not see any transformations. The most amazing aspect of Gogol's story is that the nose *is* a state councillor and the state councillor *is* a nose.

Dalí uses a similar method when he introduces double images representing two different objects at once. In some of his works, "humanized" noses appear as parts of double images. Thus on the cover illustration for *Sunset* magazine (1947), a woman's nose, placed upside down, *simultaneously* represents a man in uniform, with the woman's eyes standing in for the epaulettes on the man's uniform. In Dalí's painting *Great Paranoiac* (1936), the nose is composed of a man's torso. On the painting *The Image Disappears* (1938), the nose is formed by a woman's body. Noses figure in Dalí's other kinds of projects, such as interiors. From a photograph of the actress Mae West, an icon of the 1920s, he designed a surrealist apartment, with pieces of furniture made in the form of her nose, lips, and eyes (1934–35). Dalí viewed multiple images as paranoiac and developed his theory of paranoia in several of his theoretical works.[234]

Although it is likely that Dalí was familiar with Gogol's story, this issue is of secondary importance.[235] The affinity between

---

[233] See, for example, Annenskii, "Problema Gogolevskogo iumora," 8–10, and Shukman, "Gogol's 'The Nose' or the Devil in the Works," 64.

[234] Haim Finkelstein comments on Dalí's *Oui 1: La revolution paranoiaque-critique*: "The object seen in external reality undergoes a change of meaning or context without any physical modification (this would constitute a hallucination), the new context being a function of some obsessive idea that, as Dalí would have it, is mostly erotic in nature. The paranoiac process may continue on and on, 'the number of images limited only by the mind's degree of paranoiac capacity.'" Finkelstein, *Salvador Dalí's Art and Writing*, 190.

[235] Dalí's wife, Gala (Elena Ivanovna Diakonova), who was of Russian descent, grew up surrounded by books, and her collection of Russian classics was preserved in her library as the most valuable treasure. See an article by Estrella de Diego, curator of the Dalí exhibition in Barcelona held in the summer of 2018, entitled "Gala: Ni musa ni esposa," *El País Semanal*, June 27, 2018, https://elpais.com/elpais/2018/06/21/eps/1529594991_371039.html, accessed September 15, 2019. In her youth, she was friendly with Anastasia Tsvetaeva, the younger sister of the Russian poet Marina Tsvetaeva, whom Gala had met through Anastasia. An avid reader, she introduced her first husband,

Part Two. Interpretations

Gogol's and Dalí's artistic styles may result from a similarity in their personalities and temperaments, aptly formulated by S. I. Resniansky and B. N. Chikin:

> The personalities of both of them organically corresponded to the nature and content of their work; their personality, spirituality, determined their "metaphysical" aspirations, and their worldview and faith formed their personal attitudes and behavior. Here we find a wide range of common points: a constant, "ontological" feeling of loneliness; estrangement from others and from oneself, self-estrangement; numerous oddities in their behavior and lifestyle that attracted the attention of others and bothered them; obvious deviations from the "norm" in their psyche, forcing others to explicitly and implicitly consider them "crazy"; in the view of others, rejection and misunderstanding prevailed; both were wanderers in life and in their "souls"; the faith of both was strong, but not orthodox, often seeming "heretical," contrary to the generally accepted canons and principles established by the church and religion; in their creativity both preferred the same artistic methods and techniques: hyperbolization, exaggeration, grotesque, "bold" analogies and metaphors, estranged humor, uncertainty, duality, "immoderate" fantasy, chaotic mixture of details and trifles, of reality and fiction, focusing on the terrible, incomprehensible, "exceptional,"

Paul Éluard, to contemporary Russian literature. After she married him in 1917, Gala and Éluard worked together on the translation of Alexander's Blok play *Balaganchik* (*The Puppet Show*). In his autobiography, Dalí writes that during his long sessions of painting, Gala read to him aloud. Dalí, *The Secret Life of Salvador Dalí*, 248n1. For Dalí, Gala was more than a muse and a wife. Many of his paintings of her, signed Gala Salvador Dalí, demonstrate that she was his colleague. She contributed to his 1942 autobiography and other written works. Meilan Solly observes, "Through the influence she wielded over Salvador and their circle of artist friends—as well as the surrealist texts and objects she produced herself—Gala had an enormous impact on the development of avant-garde art." See Meilan Solly, "Why Gala Dalí—Muse, Model and Artist—Was More Than Just Salvador's Wife," *Smithsonian. Com*, July 30, 2018, https://www.smithsonianmag.com/smart-news/why-gala-dalimuse-model-and-artistwas-more-just-salvadors-wife-180969776/, accessed September 15, 2019. See also Raphael Minder, "Dalí's Wife Was More Than Model and Muse," *New York Times*, July 30, 2018, section C, 1.

9. A Play with Reality: "The Nose," Kafka, and Dalí

on "breaks" and ugliness of reality, on the illogical, absurdity of being, etc.[236]

Despite (or because of) their religious instincts, both artists had demonic visions, which led them to experiment with reality.[237] Like romantics and symbolists, surrealists used hallucinatory descriptions, but unlike their predecessors, they objected to obscurity and vagueness of vision. In his search for ways to conquer the irrational, Dalí turned to photography and documentaries—two major sources of concise and concrete details. According to him, the images on his surrealistic canvases were borrowed from the reality of the external world only to become "illustration and proof" of the reality of his own mind.[238] That explains why isolated objects on his canvases look perfectly realistic, or as it is sometimes said, "photorealistic."[239]

Gogol's nightmares are rendered with equally realistic concreteness: the nose wears a "gold-embroidered uniform with a big standing collar," "kidskin trousers," and a "plumed hat," he carries a sword on his side. The authenticity of life in Petersburg in the story raises no doubts. The topography is true to reality: the action takes place on Voznesensky and Nevsky prospects, Konyushennaya Street, Kazan Cathedral, Tauride Garden, Police and Anichkov bridges.

Yet this reality is also a figment of Gogol's imagination. As the writer admitted, the morbid phantasms depicted in *Dead Souls* originated in his own hallucinations: "As for inventing nightmares, I have not invented any either; these nightmares weigh on my soul:

---

[236] S. I. Resnianskii and B. N. Chikin, "Dali i Gogol'," in *Mertsaniie tainy, sbornik esse* (Moscow: Unity, 2009), 83.

[237] Hallucinations had the most destructive effect on the two artists' psyches, who suffered similar fates: Gogol starved himself to death, and Dalí attempted to achieve immortality by dehydrating himself, so that during his last seven years he had to be fed liquids through a tube.

[238] Dalí, *Oui 1*, 15.

[239] Consider, for example, his *Basket of Bread* (1945).

what was in my soul is what issued forth from it."[240] "The Nose" was written by an author who was simultaneously a realist and a mystic, a great paranoiac and a skillful craftsman. "God has given me a many-sided nature," Gogol wrote in *Selected Passages from Correspondence with Friends*.[241]

As discussed in chapter 7, "Perfect Nonsense," the narrative in "The Nose" does not obey the laws of causation inherent in the nineteenth-century psychological novel. Fragmentation of the human body and other unconditioned events taking place in the story (the appearance of the nose in the barber's bread and the nose's autonomous existence in the guise of a state councillor) do not find analogues in Gogol's other works either. In "Nevsky Prospect," sideburns, mustaches, hats, dresses, scarves, and ladies' sleeves walk along the main thoroughfare of the city, but these objects are rather metonymies, whereas the nose is not a metonymy of a person; he is a person. He speaks and acts as a real being, he jumps out of the carriage, he frowns, he prays, and attempts to go to Riga. Such actions are inexplicable from a positivist perspective, common in mid-nineteenth century literature.

As we have seen in the last few chapters, "The Nose" stands much closer to the aesthetics of the 1920s and 1930s—the absurdism of Daniil Kharms and the avant-garde music of Dmitry Shostakovich. Parallels also exist between "The Nose" and the works of European modernist artists—Franz Kafka and Salvador Dalí. During the years of modernism, the artists' perception of the objective world changed, resulting in a new vision of reality. They moved away from objectivity, but without completely abandoning the realistic method of representation, which creates an unstable, fragmented, absurd, and cacophonic picture of the world. Gogol anticipated this new perception of the world and expressed its spirit in his story "The Nose."

---

[240] Gogol, *Selected Passages from Correspondence with Friends*, 108.

[241] Ibid., 104.

Instead of a Conclusion

It would be hard if not impossible to find another story in world literature which would be simultaneously (or consecutively) interpreted as a joke, farce, anecdote, social satire, psychoanalytic inquiry, religious pursuit, anticlerical sentiment, mirror of folk superstitions, and pure nonsense. It would be hard to find another story that has been viewed as a tribute to romanticism, realism, and absurdism, as well as a precursor of surrealism and socialist realism; that has been said to have affinities with the paintings of Bosch, Bruegel, and Dalí. A story that is very different from all other works by the same author but that has strong connections with the works of poets, artists, and composers who lived a hundred years after it was written.

Although I find some of these interpretations more interesting than others, I tried to present them impartially. While I see their logic and feel the intuition in all of them, my own conviction remains the same as it was at the beginning—at the core of this story's weirdest and oddest plot lies Gogol's masterful language game.

Selected Bibliography

Annenskii, Innokentii. "O formakh fantasticheskogo u Gogolia." In *Kniga otrazhenii*, edited by N. T. Ashimbaeva, 207–15. "Literaturnye pamiatniki series." Moscow: Nauka, 1979.

———. "Problema Gogolevskogo iumora." In *Kniga otrazhenii*, edited by N. T. Ashimbaeva, 7–20. "Literaturnye pamiatniki series." Moscow: Nauka, 1979.

Bakhtin, M. M. "Dopolneniia." In M. Bakhtin, *Sobranie sochinenii*, vol. 2, edited by S. G. Bocharov and L. S. Melikhova, 412–27. Moscow: Russkie slovari, 2000.

———. *Problems of Dostoevsky's Poetics*. Edited and translated by Caryl Emerson. Minneapolis: University of Minnesota Press, 1984.

———. "Rable i Gogol' (Iskusstvo slova i narodnaia smekhovaia kul'tura). In M. Bakhtin, *Sobranie sochinenii*, vol. 4, book 2, edited by I. L. Popova, 517–22. Moscow: Iazyki slavianskikh kul'tur, 2010.

Bazhenov, N. N. *Istoriia Moskovskogo dollgauza, nyne Moskovskoi gorodskoi Preobrazhenskoi bol'nitsy dlia dushevnobol'nykh*. Moscow: Izdanie Moskovskogo gorodskogo obshchestvennogo upravleniia, 1909.

Belinskii, V. G. "From an essay 'O russkoi povesti i povestiakh g. Gogolia.'" In *Gogol' v russkoi kritike, antologiia*, edited by S. G. Bocharov, 16–36. Moscow: Fortuna EL, 2008.

———. *Polnoe sobranie sochinenii*. Edited by B. I. Bursov. 13 vols. Moscow: Izdatel'stvo AN SSSR, 1955.

Bel'trame, Franka. "K voprosu o paradoksal'nosti bogoiskaniia v povesti Gogolia 'Nos.'" In *Gogol' kak iavleniie mirovoi literatury*, edited by Iu. V. Mann et al., 168–77. Moscow: IMLI RAN, 2003.

Bely, Andrey. "Gogol'." In *Gogol' v russkoi kritike: Antologiia*, edited by S. G. Bocharov, 264–277. Moscow: Fortuna EL, 2008.

Belykh, G., and L. Panteleev. *Respublika ShKID*. Leningrad: Sovetskii pisatel', 1960.

Berdyaev, Nikolai. *Dukhi russkoi revoliutsii*. Moscow: T8 RUGRAM, 2018.

Birikh, et al., eds. *Slovar' russkoi frazeologii: Istoriko-etimologicheskii spravochnik*. Saint Petersburg: Folio-Press, 1998.

Selected Bibliography

Blank, Ksana. "Captain Lebyadkin's Poetry in Shostakovich and Dostoevsky." In Ksana Blank, *Spaces of Creativity: Essays on Russian Literature and the Arts*, 130–152. Boston: Academic Studies Press, 2017.

———. "Po zakoldovannym mestam Gogolia." *Novoe literaturnoe obozrenie* 11 (1995): 177–180.

———. "Praising the Name: The Religious Theme in Daniil Kharms." In Ksana Blank, *Spaces of Creativity: Essays on Russian Literature and the Arts,* 106–29. Boston: Academic Studies Press, 2017.

———. "Shostakovich, Dostoevsky, Lebyadkin, and OBERIU." In *Liber amicorum Liudmile Kovnatskoi,* edited by Lidia Ader and Olga Manulkina, 345–48. Saint Petersburg: BiblioRossika, 2016.

Bocharov, S. G. "Around 'The Nose.'" In *Essays on Gogol: Logos and the Russian Word*, edited by Susanne Fusso and Priscilla Meyer, 34–54. Evanston, IL: Northwestern University Press, 1992.

Bowman, Herbert E. "The Nose." *The Slavonic and East European Review* 31, no. 76 (December 1952): 204–11.

Bretanitskaia, Alla. *"Nos" D. D. Shostakovicha*. Moscow: Muzyka, 1983.

———. "O muzykal'noi dramaturgii opery 'Nos.'" *Sovetskaia muzyka* 9 (1974): 47–53.

Brodsky, Joseph. "Nobel Lecture." In *From Nobel Lectures: Literature, 1981–1990*, translated by Barry Rubin and edited by Sture Allén, 106–14. Singapore: World Scientific Publishing, 1993.

Bubennikova, L. "Meierkhol'd i Shostakovich (Iz istorii sozdaniia opery 'Nos')." *Sovetskaia muzyka* 3 (March 1973): 43–47.

Buks, Nora. "Locus-poeticus: Salon de coiffure v russkoi kul'ture nachala XX veka." *Slavic Almanac: The South African Journal for Slavic, Central and Eastern European Studies* 10, no. 1 (2004): 2–23.

Chenieux-Gendron, Jaqueline. *Surrealism*. Translated by Vivian Folkenflik. New York: Columbia University Press, 1990.

Chernyshevskii, N. G. "Ocherki gogolevskogo perioda russkoi literatury." In N. Chernyshevskii, *Polnoe sobranie sochinenii*, edited by V. Ia. Kirpotin, vol. 3. Moscow: OGIZ GIKHL, 1947.

Chizhevsky, Dmitry. "About Gogol's 'Overcoat." In *Gogol from the Twentieth Century. Eleven Essays*, edited by Robert A. Maguire, 293–322. Princeton: Princeton University Press, 1974.

———. (Dmitry Čiževsky). "Gogol: Artist and Thinker." *The Annals of the Ukrainian Academy* 2, no. 2 (4) (Summer 1952): 261–279.

———. (Dmitrii Chizhevskii). "Neizvestnyi Gogol'." In *Novyi zhurnal* 27 (1951): 126–157.

Cornell, John F. "Anatomy of a Scandal: Self-Dismemberment in the Gospel of Matthew and in Gogol's 'The Nose.'" *Literature and Theology: An International Journal of Religion, Theory, and Culture* (L&T) 16, no. 3 (September 2002): 270–90.

Cornwell, Neil. "The Absurd in Gogol and Gogol Criticism." *Essays in Poetics: The Journal of the British Neo-Formalist Circle* 29, no. 9 (Autumn 2004): 1–16.

Dalí, Salvador. *The Collected Writings of Salvador Dalí*. Edited and translated by Haim Finkelstein. Cambridge: Cambridge University Press, 1998.

———. *50 Secrets of Magic Craftsmanship*. Translated by Haakon M. Chevalier. New York: Dial Press, 1948.

———. *Oui 1: La revolution paranoiaque-critique*. Paris: Editions Denoel/Gonthier, 1971.

———. *The Secret Life of Salvador Dalí*. Translated by Haakon M. Chevalier. Reprinted ed. New York: Dover Publications, 1993. Original ed., 1942.

Demidenko, Iuliia. *Restorany, traktiry, chainy: Iz istorii obschestvennogo pitaniia v Peterburge XVIII nachala XX veka*. Moscow: Tsentralpoligraf, 2011.

Descharnes, Robert, and Gilles Neret. *Salvador Dalí*. 2 vols. Cologne: Benedikt Taschen, 1994.

Dilaktorskaia, O. G. "Fantasticheskoe v povesti N. V. Gogolia 'Nos.'" *Russkaia literatura* 1 (1984): 153–65.

———. "Khudozhestvennyi mir peterburgskikh povestei N. V. Gogolia." In N. V. Gogol', *Peterburgskie povesti*, edited by O. G. Dilaktorskaia, 207–57. "Literaturnye pamiatniki" series. Saint Petersburg: Nauka, 1995.

Dmitriev, Pavel. "Tretii nos: V Mariinskom teatre sostoialas' prem'era opery Dmitriia Shostakovicha." *Nevskoe vremia* 70: (April 16, 2004), 10.

Dostoevskii, Fedor. "Dvoinik." In F. Dostoevskii, *Polnoe sobranie sochinenii*, vol. 1. Leningrad: Nauka, 1972.

Druzhinin, P. A. *Ideologiia i filologiia: Leningrad, 1940 gody, dokumental'noe issledovaniie*. 2 vols. Moscow: Novoe literaturnoe obozrenie, 2012.

Eikhenbaum, B. M. "How 'The Overcoat' Is Made." In *Gogol from the Twentieth Century, Eleven Essays*, edited by Robert A. Maguire, 267–92. Princeton: Princeton University Press, 1974.

———. "Illiuziia skaza." In B. Eikhenbaum, *Skvoz' literaturu: Sbornik statei*, 152–56. Leningrad: Academia, 1924.

———. "Kak sdelana 'Shinel'" Gogolia." In B. Eikhenbaum, *Skvoz' literaturu: Sbornik statei*, 171–195. Leningrad: Academia, 1924.

———. *Molodoi Tolstoi*. Saint Petersburg: Izdatel'stvo Z. I. Grzhebina, 1922.

Emerson, Caryl. "Coming to Terms with Bakhtin's Carnival: Ancient, Modern, sub Specie Aeternitatis." In *Bakhtin and the Classics*, edited by R. Bracht Branham, 5–26. Evanston, IL: Northwestern University Press, 2002.

———. "Literary Theory in the 1920s: Four Options and a Practicum." In *A History of Russian Literary Theory and* Criticism, edited by Evgeny Dobrenko and Galin Tihanov, 64–89. Pittsburgh: University of Pittsburgh Press, 2011.

———. "Shostakovich and the Russian Literary Tradition." In *Shostakovich and His World*, edited by Laurel Fey, 183–227. Princeton: Princeton University Press, 2004.

Erlich, Victor. "Gogol and Kafka: Note on 'Realism' and 'Surrealism.'" In *For Roman Jakobson*, edited by Morris Halle et al., 100–108, The Hague: Mouton and Co., 1956.

Ermilov, V. *N. V. Gogol'*. Moscow: Sovetskii pisatel', 1952.

Etkind, Alexander. *Eros nevozhmozhnogo (Istoriia psikhoanaliza v Rossii)*. Moscow: Gnozis-Progress-Kompleks, 1994.

Evdokimov, Paul. *Gogol et Dostoïevsky ou la descente aux enfers*. Paris: Desclée de Brouwer, 1961.

Evdokimova, Svetlana. "Gorod zemnoi i grad nebesnyi: Peterburg v po-vesti Gogolia 'Nos.'" In *Peterburgskaia tema i "Peterburgskii tekst" v russkoi literature XVIII-XX vekov*, edited by V. M. Markovich, 43-54. St. Petersburg: Izdatel'stvo S.-Peterburgskogo universiteta, 2002.

Fanger, Donald. *The Creation of Nikolai Gogol*. Cambridge, MA: Harvard University Press, 1979.

Fay, Laurel. "The Punch in Shostakovich's Nose." In *Russian and Soviet Music: Essays for Boris Schwarz*, edited by Malcolm Hamrick Brown, 229–243. Ann Arbor, MI: University of Michigan Research Press, 1984.

Fetzer, Leland, and Lawson, Richard H. "Den Tod zur Schau gestellt: Gogol und Kafkas' Hungerkünstler." *Modern Austian Literature* 11, no. 1 (1978): 167–77.

Selected Bibliography

Finkelshtein, Haim. *Salvador Dalí's Art and Writing, 1927–1942*. Cambridge: Cambridge University Press, 1996.

Finlay, Carolyn Roberts. "Operatic Translation and Shostakovich: The Nose." *Comparative Literature* 35, no. 3 (Summer 1983): 195–214.

Freud, Sigmund. *The Uncanny*. Translated by David McLintock, introduction by Hugh Haughton. London: Penguin Classics, 2003.

Ginsburg, Lydia. *On Psychologial Prose*. Translated and edited by Judson Rosengrant. Princeton: Princeton University Press, 1991.

Gippius, V. V. "Tvorcheskii put' Gogolia." In *Ot Pushkina do Bloka*, edited by G. M. Fridlender, 46–200. Moscow: Nauka, 1966.

Gogol, Nikolai (Nikolai Gogol'). "Avtorskaia ispoved'." In N. Gogol', *Polnoe sobranie sochinenii*, vol. 8: *Stat'i*, edited by N. L. Meshcheriakov, 432–67. Moscow: Izd-vo AN SSSR, 1952.

———. *The Collected Tales of Nikolai Gogol*. Translated by Richard Pevear and Larissa Volokhonsky. New York: Pantheon Books, 1998.

———. *Dead Souls*. Translated by George Reavey, with an introduction by George Gibian. New York: Norton, 1971.

———. "Leaving the Theater after the Presentation of a New Comedy." Translated by Isabel Heaman. In N. Gogol, *Hanz Kuechelgarten, Leaving the Theater, and Other Works*, edited by Ronald Meyer, 63–91. Ann Arbor, MI: Ardis, 1990.

——— (Nikolai Gogol'). "Materialy dlia slovaria russkogo iazyka." In N. Gogol', *Polnoe sobranie sochinenii*, vol. 9: *Nabroski, Konspekty, Plany, Zapisnye knizhki,* edited by N. F. Bel'chikov, 439–85. Moscow: Izd-vo AN SSSR, 1952.

——— (Nikolai Gogol'). "Pis'ma, 1820–1835." In N. Gogol', *Polnoe sobranie sochinenii*, vol. 10, edited by N. L. Meshcheriakov, commentaries by N. L. Stepanov. Moscow: Izd-vo AN SSSR, 1940.

——— (Nikolai Gogol'). "Povesti." In N. Gogol', *Polnoe sobranie sochinenii*, vol. 3, edited by V. L. Komarovich, 5–260. Moscow: Izd-vo AN SSSR, 1938.

———. *Selected Passages from Correspondence with Friends*. Translated by Jesse Zeldin. Nashville: Vanderbilt University Press, 1969.

———. "Taras Bulba." In *Village Evenings near Dikanka and Mirgorod*. Translated by Christopher English. New York: Oxford University Press, 1994.

Goncharov, S. A. *Tvorchestvo Gogolia v religiozno-misticheskom kontekste*. Saint Petersburg: Izd-vo RGPU im. A. I. Gertsena, 1997.

Selected Bibliography

Gorny, Sergei. *Sankt-Peterburg (Videniia)*. Edited by A. M. Konechnyi. Saint Petersburg: Giperion, 2000.

Gough, Maria. "Kentridge's Nose." *October* 134 (Fall 2014): 3–27.

Griboedov, A. S. *Gore ot uma: Komediia v chetyrekh deistviiakh v stikhakh*. Moscow: Detskaia literatura, 1967.

Grigor'ev, Apollon. *Literaturnaia kritika*. Moscow: Khudozhestvennaia literatura, 1967.

Gukovskii, G. A. *Realizm Gogolia*. Leningrad: Gosudarstvennoe izdatel'stvo khudozhestvennoi literatury, 1959.

Hakobian, Levon (L. O. Akopian). *Dmitrii Shostakovich: Opyt fenomenologii tvorchestva*. Saint Petersburg: Dmitrii Bulanin, 2004.

———. "*The Nose*: An Opera; How it Was Composed." In *Dmitri Shostakovich: New Collected Works*, 4th ser.: *Works for Music Theatre*, vol. 50: *The Nose*, full score, edited by Viktor Ekimovskii, 535–40. Moscow: DSCH, 2015.

Hodgart, Matthew. *Satire: Origins and Principles*. With a new introduction by Brian A. Connery. New Brunswick, NJ: Transaction Publishers, 2010.

Holquist, Michael. "'The Devil in Mufti': The *Märchenwelt* in Gogol's Short Stories." *PMLA* 82, no. 5 (October 1967): 352–62.

———. "The Tyranny of Difference: Gogol and the Sacred." In *Cold Fusions: Aspects of the German Cultural Presence in Russia*, edited by Gennady Barabtarlo, 62–73. New York: Berghahn Books, 2000.

Iakovlev, V. V., ed. *Deviatnadtsatyi vek*. Vol. 2, book. 5 of *Tri veka Sankt-Peterburga: Entsiklopediia*. Saint Petersburg: Fakul'tet filologii i iskusstv SPbGU, 2006.

Iampolskii, Mikhail. *Bespamiatstvo kak istok (chitaia Kharmsa)*. Moscow: Novoe literaturnoe obozrenie, 1998.

Illie, Paul. *The Surrealist Mode in Spanish Literature: An Interpretation of Basic Trends from Post-Romanticism to the Spanish Vanguard*. Ann Arbor, MI: University of Michigan Press, 1968.

Ivanits, Linda. *Russian Folk Belief*. With a foreword by Felix J. Oinas. Armonk, NY: M. E. Sharpe, 1989.

Ivanitskii, A. I. "Gogol' i Gofman: Grotesk i ego preodolenie." In *N. V. Gogol' i mirovaia kul'tura: Vtorye gogolevskie chteniia; Sbornik dokladov*, edited by V. P. Vikulova, 167–80. Moscow: KDU, 2003.

Karlinsky, Simon. *The Sexual Labyrinth of Nikolai Gogol*. Cambridge, MA: Harvard University Press, 1976.

Selected Bibliography

Karst, Roman. "The Reality of the Absurd and the Absurdity of the Real: Kafka and Gogol." *Mosaic: An Interdisciplinary Critical Journal* 9, no. 1: *Literature and Ideas* (Fall 1975): 67–81.

Kayser, Wolfgang. *The Grotesque in Art and Literature*. Translated by Ulrich Weisstein. Reprinted ed. New York: McGraw-Hill, 1963. Original ed., 1957.

Kharms, Daniil. *Polet v nebesa: Stikhi, proza, dramy, pis'ma*. Leningrad: Sovetskii pisatel', 1988.

———. *Today I Wrote Nothing: The Selected Writings of Daniil Kharms*. Edited and translated by Matvei Yankelevich. New York: Overlook Duckworth, 2007.

Konechnyi A. A., et al., eds. *Byt Pushkinskogo Petersburga: Opyt entsiklopedicheskogo slovaria*. 2 vols. Saint Petersburg: Izd. Ivana Limbakha, 2003.

Kozhina, M. N., ed. *Stilisticheskii entsiklopedicheskii slovar' russkogo iazyka*. Moscow: Nauka, 2003.

Kozintsev, Grigorii. *Prostranstvo tragedii (Dnevnik rezhissera)*. Leningrad: Iskusstvo, 1983.

Kutik, Ilya. *Writing as Exorcism: The Personal Codes of Pushkin, Lermontov, and Gogol*. Evanston, IL: Northwestern University Press, 2005.

Lacan, Jacques. *Ecrits: A Selection*. Translated by Alan Sheridan. New York: Norton, 1977.

Levaia, T. N. "Neobarokko i absurd (eshche raz ob opere 'Nos' Shostakovicha)." In *Etot mnogoobraznyi mir muzyki: Sbornik statei k 80-letiiu M. G. Aranovskogo*, edited by Z. A. Imamutdinova, A. A. Baeva, and N. O. Vlasova, 387–91. Moscow: Gos. institut iskusstvoznaniia, 2010.

Lotman, Yuri (Iurii Lotman). "Gogol' i sootnesenie smekhovoi kul'tury s komicheskim i ser'eznym v russkoi natsional'noi traditsii." *Materialy Pervogo vsesoiuznogo simpoziuma po vtorichnym modeliruiushchim sistemam* 5 (1974): 131–133.

———. "The Symbolism of St Petersburg." In *Universe of the Mind: A Semiotic Theory of Culture*, translated by Ann Shukman, introduction by Umberto Eco, 191–202. Bloomington: Indiana University Press, 1990.

Lubensky, Sophia. *Russian-English Dictionary of Idioms*. New York: Random House, 1995.

Selected Bibliography

Maguire, Robert A. *Exploring Gogol*. Stanford: Stanford University Press, 1994.
Makogonenko, G. P. *Pushkin i Gogol'*. Leningrad: Sovetskii pisatel', 1985.
Mandel'shtam, I. E. *O kharaktere gogolevskogo stilia: Glava iz istorii russkogo literaturnogo iazyka*. Gel'singfors: Novaia tip. Guvudstadsbladet, 1902.
Mann, Iu. V. "Evoliutsiia gogolevskoi fantastiki." In *K istorii russkogo romantizma*, edited by Iu. V. Mann, 219–58. Moscow: Nauka, 1973.
———. *Poetika Gogolia: Variatsii k teme*. Moscow: Coda, 1996.
———. "Vstrecha v labirinte (Frants Kafka i Nikolai Gogol')." *Voprosy literatury* 2 (1999): 162–186.
Markovich, V. M. *Peterburgskie povesti N. V. Gogolia*. Leningrad: Khudozhestvennaia literatura, 1989.
Mashkinskii, S., ed. *Gogol' v vospominaniiakh sovremennikov*. Seriia literaturnykh memuarov. Moscow: Gosudarstvennoe izdatel'stvo khudozhestvennoi literatury, 1952.
McCarthy, Michael. *Spoken Language and Applied Linguistics*. Cambridge: Cambridge University Press, 1998.
Merezhkovsky, Dmitry. "Gogol and the Devil." In *Gogol from the Twentieth Century. Eleven Essays*, selected, edited, translated, and introduced by Robert A. Maguire. Princeton: Princeton University Press, 1995.
Merrill, Reed. "The Grotesque in Music: Shostakovich's Muse." *Russian Literature Triquarterly* 23 (1990): 303–14.
Meyer, Priscilla. "The Fantastic in the Everyday: Gogol's 'Nevsky Prospect' and Hoffmann's 'A New Year's Eve Adventure.'" In *Cold Fusions: Aspects of the German Cultural Presence in Russia*, edited by Gennady Barabtarlo, 62–73. New York: Berghahn Books, 2000.
———. *How the Russians Read the French: Lermontov, Dostoevsky, Tolstoy*. Madison: University of Wisconsin Press, 2008.
Mints, A. "Oberiuty." *Voprosy literatury* 1 (2001): 227–94.
Mochulskii, Konstantin. *Dukhovnyi put' Gogolia*. Paris: YMCA-Press, 1976.
Moon, R. "Textual Aspects of Fixed Expressions in Learners' Dictionaries." In *Vocabulary and Applied Linguistics*, edited by P. J. Armaud and H. Béjoint, 13–27. Basingstoke, UK: Macmillan, 1992.
Morson, Gary Saul. "Gogol's Parables of Explanations: Nonsense and Prosaics." In *Essays on Gogol: Logos and the Russian Word*, edited by Susanne Fusso and Priscilla Meyer, 209–239. Evanston, IL: Northwestern University Press, 1992.

Selected Bibliography

———. *Narrative and Freedom: The Shadows of Time.* New Haven: Yale University Press, 1994.

Nabokov, Vladimir. *Nikolai Gogol.* New York: New Directions, 1961.

Obolensky, A. "Gogol and Hieronymous Bosch: A Comparative Essay." Edited by Nadja Jernakoff. In *Transactions of the Association of the Russian-American Scholars in the USA*, 115–32. New York: Association of Russian-American Scholars in USA, 1984.

Panova, Lada. *Mnimoe sirotstvo: Khlevbnikov i Kharms v kontekste russkogo i evropeiskogo modernizma.* Moscow: Izd. dom Vysshei shkoly ekonomiki, 2017.

Panteleev, Leonid. "Gde vy, geroi 'Respubliki Shkid'?" In L. Panteleev, *Priotkrytaia dver'*, 187–92. Leningrad: Sovetskii pisatel', 1980.

Pletneva, Alexandra. "Povest' N. V. Gogolia 'Nos' i lubochnaia traditsiia." *Novoe literaturnoe obozrenie* 61 (2003): 152–63.

Popova, I. L. "'Rable i Gogol' kak nauchnyi siuzhet M. M. Bakhtina." *Izvestiia RAN, seriia literatury i iazyka* 68, no. 6 (2009): 12–18.

Propp, Vladimir. *On the Comic and Laughter.* Edited and translated by Jean-Patrick Debbèche and Paul Perron. Toronto: University of Toronto Press, 2009.

———. "Priroda komicheskogo u Gogolia," edited by V. I. Eremina. *Russkaia literatura* 1 (1988): 27–43.

Pryzhov, Ivan. "Ivan Iakovlevich." In I. Pryzhov, *26 moskovskikh prorokov, iurodivykh, dur i durakov: Issledovania*, 81–95. Moscow: Eksmo, 2008.

Pushkin, Alexander. *Eugene Onegin.* A new translation by James E. Falen. Oxford: Oxford University Press, 2009.

———. *Stikhotvoreniia, 1817–1825. Litseiskie stikhotvoreniia v pozdneishikh redaktsiiakh.* Edited by M. A. Tsiavlovskii et al. Vol. 2, book 1 of *Polnoe sobranie sochinenii v 16 tomakh.* Moscow: Izdatel'stvo AN SSSR, 1937–1959.

Rassovskaia, L. P. "Koschunstvennye proizvedeniia Pushkina i Gogolia ('Gavriiliada' i 'Nos')." *Vestnik SamGU*, special issue (2003): 32–44.

Redfern, Walter. *Clichés and Coinages.* Oxford: Basil Blackwell, 1989.

Resnianskii, S. I., and B. N. Chikin. "Dali i Gogol'." In *Mertsaniie tainy, sbornik esse*, 74–87. Moscow: Unity, 2009.

Reyfman, Irina. *How Russia Learned to Write: Literature and the Imperial Table of Ranks.* Wisconsin: The University of Wisconsin Press, 2016.

Selected Bibliography

Rozanov, V. V. "Genii formy." In *Gogol' v russkoi kritike: antologiia*, edited by S. G. Bocharov, 233–41. Moscow: Fortuna, 2008.

———. "Iz 'Uedinennogo' and 'Opavshikh list'ev.'" In *Gogol' v russkoi kritike: Antologiia*, edited by S. G. Bocharov, 304–13. Moscow: Fortuna, 2008.

Sannikov, V. Z. *Russkii iazyk v zerkale iazykovoi igry*. Moscow: Iazyki russkoi kul'tury, 1999.

Schwarz, Boris. *Music and Musical Life in Soviet Russia, 1917–1970*. London: Barrie and Jenkins, 1972.

Scollins, Kathleen. *Acts of Logos in Pushkin and Gogol: Petersburg Texts and Subtexts*. Boston: Academic Studies Press, 2017.

Seifrid, Thomas. "Suspicion toward Narrative: The Nose and the Problem of Autonomy in Gogol's 'Nos.'" *The Russian Review* 52, no. 3 (July 1993): 382–96.

Shostakovich, D. "Iz vospominanii: K 100-letiiu so dnia rozhdeniia Vs. E. Meierkhol'da." *Sovetskaia muzyka* 3 (1974): 54–55.

———. "Pochemu 'Nos'?" *Rabochii i teatr* 3 (January 15, 1930): 11.

Shukman, Ann. "Gogol's 'The Nose,' or The Devil in the Works." In *Nikolai Gogol: Text and Context*, edited by Jane Grayson and Faith Wigzell, 64–82. London: Macmillan, 1989.

Sicher, Efraim. "Dialogization and Laughter in the Dark, or How Gogol's Nose Was Made: Parody and Literary Evolution in Bachtin's Theory of the Novel." *Russian Literature* 28 (1990): 211–34.

Slonimsky, Alexander. "The Technique of the Comic in Gogol." In *Gogol from the Twentieth Century. Eleven Essays*, selected, edited, translated, and introduced by Robert A. Maguire, 323–74. Princeton: Princeton University Press, 1974.

Spycher, Peter. "N. V. Gogol's 'The Nose': A Satirical Comic Fantasy Born of an Impotence Complex." *Slavic and East European Journal* 7, no. 4 (1963): 361–74.

Stasov, V. V. "Gogol' v vospriiatii russkoi molodezhi 30–40-kh gg." In *N. V. Gogol' v vospominaniiakh sovremennikov*, edited by S. I. Mashinskii, 396–403. Moscow: Gosudarstvennoe izdatel'stvo khudozhestvennoi literatury, 1952.

Stender-Petersen, Adolf. "Gogol und die deutsche Romantik." *Euphorion* 24 (1922): 291–95.

Strakšiene, Margarita. "Analysis of Idiom Translation Strategies from English into Lithuanian." *Studies about Languages* 14 (2009): 13–19.

———. "Analysis of Idiom Translation Strategies from English into Russian." *Studies about Languages* 17 (2010): 29–33.
Strong Jr., Robert L. "The Soviet Interpretation of Gogol." *The American Slavic and East European Review* 14, no. 4 (December 1955): 528–39.
Struc, Roman. "Categories of the Grotesque: Gogol and Kafka." In *Franz Kafka: His Place in World Literature: Proceedings of the Comparative Literature Symposium*, edited by Wolodymyr T. Zyla, 135-56. Lubbock: Texas Tech University, 1971.
Svetlov, S. F. *Peterburgskaia zhizn' v kontse XIX stoletiia.* "Zabytyi Peterburg" series. Saint Petersburg: Giperion, 1998.
Tarasenkov, A. *Poslednie dni zhizni N. V. Gogolia: Zapiski ego sovremennika d-ra A. Tarasenkova.* Revised 2nd ed. Moscow: T-vo skoropechatnia A. A. Levenson, 1902.
Tcherkashina, Marina. "Gogol and Leskov in Shostakovich's Interpretation." *International Journal of Musicology* 1 (1992): 229–44.
Timenchik, Roman. "Ruki bradobreia." In R. Timenchik, *Chto vdrug: Stat'i o russkoi literature proshlogo veka*, 516–49. Moscow: Mosty kul'tury, 2017.
Toporov, V. N. *Peterburgskii tekst russkoi literatury: Izbrannye trudy.* Saint Petersburg: Iskusstvo-SPb, 2003.
Tumanov, Alexander. "The Correspondence of Literary Text and Musical Phraseology in D. Shostakovich's Opera *The Nose* and Gogol's Fantastic Tale: Textual Changes and Compositional Devices." In *The Force of Vision: Dramas of Desire; Visions of Beauty*, general editors and preface by Earl Miner and Toru Haga, edited by Ziva Ben-Porat, edited and with an introduction by Hana Wirth-Nesher, Roseann Runte, and Hans R. Runte, 534–43. Tokyo: University of Tokyo Press, 1995.
Tynianov, Iurii. *Dostoevskii i Gogol' (k teorii parodii).* Petrograd: Opoiaz, 1921.
———. "Literaturnoe segodnia." In Iu. Tynianov, *Poetika; Istoriia literatury; Kino*, 150–66. Moscow: Nauka, 1977.
Ul'ianov, N. "Arabesk ili apokalipsis?" *Novyi zhurnal* 57 (1959): 116–31.
Uspenskii, B. A. "Vremia v Gogolevskom 'Nose' ('Nos' glazami etnografa)." In B. Uspenskii, *Istoriko-filologicheskie ocherki*, 49–68. Moscow: Iazyki slavianskoi kul'tury, 2004.
Vaiskopf, Mikhail. "Nos v Kazanskom sobore: O genezise religioznoi temy u Gogolia." In M. Vaiskopf, *Ptitsa-troika i kolesnitsa dushi: Raboty, 1978–2003*, 164–85. Moscow: Novoe literaturnoe obozrenie, 2003.

Selected Bibliography

———. *Siuzhet Gogolia. Morfologiia; Ideologiia; Kontekst.* Moscow: Radiks, 1993.

Veresaev, V. *Gogol' v zhizni. Sistematicheskii svod podlinnykh svideles'stv sovremennikov.* Moscow: Moskovskii rabochii, 1990.

Vinogradov, V. V. "Etiudy o stile Gogolia." In V. Vinogradov, *Poetika russkoi literatury: Izbrannye trudy*, 228–66. Moscow: Nauka, 1976.

———. *Gogol and the Natural School.* Translated by Debra K. Erickson and Ray Parrott. Introduction by Debra K. Erikson. Ann Arbor, MI: Ardis, 1987.

———. "Iazyk Gogolia." In *Iazyk i stil' russkikh pisatelei: Ot Karamzina do Gogolia*, edited by D. S. Likhachev and A. P. Chudakov, 271–30. Moscow: Nauka, 1990.

———. "Iazyk Gogolia i ego znachenie v istorii russkogo iazyka." In *Iazyk i stil' russkikh pisatelei: Ot Gogolia do Akhmatovoi; Izbrannye trudy*, edited by A. P. Chudakov, 54–96. Moscow: Nauka, 2003.

———. "Naturalisticheskii grotesk: Siuzhet i kompozitsiia povesti Gogolia 'Nos.'" In V. Vinogradov, *Poetika russkoi litetaruty: Izbrannye trudy*, 5–44. Moscow: Nauka, 1976.

———. *Ocherki po istorii russkogo literaturnogo iazyka XVII–XIX vv.* Moscow: Gos. uchebno-ped. izd-vo, 1934.

———. "Problema skaza v stilistike." In V. Vinogradov, *O iazyke khudozhestvennoi prozy*, 42–55. Moscow: Nauka, 1980.

———. "Shkola sentimental'nogo naturalizma." In V. Vinogradov, *Poetika russkoi literatury, Izbrannye trudy*, 141–87. Moscow: Nauka, 1976.

Wittgenstein, Ludwig. *Philosophical Investigations.* Translated by G. E. M. Anscombe, P. M. S. Hacker, and Joachim Schulte. Revised 4th ed. by P. M. S. Hacker and Joachim Schulge. Oxford: Wiley-Blackwell, 2009.

Yermakov, Ivan. "The Nose." In *Gogol from the Twentieth Century. Eleven Essays*, selected, edited, translated, and introduced by Robert A. Maguire, 155–98. Princeton: Princeton University Press, 1974.

Zen'kovskii, V. N. *N. V. Gogol'.* Paris: YMCA-Press, 1961.

Index

A

absurd, the, 57, 59, 69, 77, 123, 179, 184, 187, 190-191, 194, 200, 204, 209, 218
absurdity, 8, 67, 71, 74, 78, 91-92, 112, 117, 196, 209-210, 217, see also nonsense
anecdote, 101, 104, 113-114, 116-119, 146, 168, 174, 219, see also joke, laughter
Annenkov, P. V., 154
Annensky, Innokenty, 117, 123, 163
Annunciation, Feast of, 51, 68, 70, 136, 139-140, 142-150, 152, 165-166
apocalyptic vision, 136
Artaud, Antonin, 210
Ascension, 140-141, 147
avant-garde, 53n5, 184, 202, 205, 216n235, 218

B

Bakhtin, Mikhail, 98-99, 102, 121-123, 136, 185
Balzac, Honoré de, 182
Bazhenov, Nikita, 156-157, 160
Belinsky, Vissarion, 9, 96-97, 114, 125-127, 132
Beltrame, Franca, 142-143
Bely, Andrey, 7n1, 10, 96-97, 107-108
Berdyaev, Nikolai, 134
Berg, Alban, 197, 203
  Wozzeck, 197, 203
Bestuzhev-Marlinsky, Alexander, 56
Bocharov, Sergei, 139
Bogdanov-Berezovsky, V. M., 204
Bosch, Hieronymous, 135-136, 138, 219
Brik, Osip, 121
Bruegel the Elder, Pieter, 135
Bulgarin, Faddei, 72, 96

C

calendar (Gregorian and Julian), 82, 149
castration anxiety, 10, 161

Chamisso, Adelbert von, 173
Chernyshevsky, Nikolai, 9, 116, 168, 171, 178
Chizhevsky, Dmitry, 142n72, 184, 209
causal conditionality, 182
Contemporary, The, (Sovremennik), 9n4, 51n2, 112, 114, 150n87, 159n105
Cornell, John F., 143
Christianity, 141, 146 see also Orthodox Church

D

Dal', Vladimir, 60
Dalí, Salvador, 135n54, 210-219
devil, 8, 71, 88, 92-94, 106, 113, 130, 133, 135-138, 146, 153, 157, 160, 167, 181, 189, 195, see also evil spirits
Dilaktorskaia, O. G., 71, 75, 77-78, 151-155, 166
Dobrolyubov, Nikolai, 9
Dostoevsky, Fyodor, 62, 106, 107n52, 138, 156, 164, 174, 182-184, 201
  The Double, 63, 184
  The Gambler, 62

E

Eikhenbaum, Boris, 98-99, 120, 123, 170, 172, 194n181, 198-199
Éluard, Paul, 216n236
Emerson, Caryl, 123, 167, 201
Erlich, Victor, 207
Etkind, Alexander, 167
Evdokimov, Paul, 134, 138-139, 146
evil spirits, 134-135, 137, 151, 153, see also devil

F

face, 10, 59, 61-62, 68-69, 77, 89, 91, 96, 131, 133, 139, 144-145, 149, 179, 181-182, 187, 190, 195, 212, 214
Fanger, Donald, 97n32, 109, 181
fantastic, the, 10, 70, 80, 107, 112, 116, 122, 124, 127, 129, 132, 138, 147,

Index

152, 155, 164, 168-169, 172-175, 194, 208-209
Fay, Laurel, 197
Florensky, Pavel, 139
folk superstitions, 156, 166, 219
formalists, *see* Russian formalist school
Freud, Sigmund, 164, 175-177, *see also* Yermakov

G

Gala (Elena Ivanovna Diakonova), 215n235
Ginsburg, Lydia, 182
Gippius, Vasily, 127-128, 131, 163
Goethe, Johann Wolfgang von, 71
Gogol, Nikolai
   Characters in "The Nose"
      Ivan Yakovlevich, 54, 58-62, 83, 88, 102, 105, 155-160, 184-185, 187
      Kovalev, Platon Kuzmich, Major, 8, 10, 52, 55, 58, 60, 63, 65-70, 72-77, 79, 82-84, 88-92, 95, 100-101, 103-106, 114, 117, 126, 128-132, 134, 140-145, 149, 151-154, 159, 161-166, 169, 174, 177, 179, 181-182, 189, 191-192, 199, 202-204, 209, 213-214
      Podtochina, Praskovya Osipovna, 56, 75, 79, 88, 95, 105, 130-131, 152, 161
   Arabesques, 96, 116, 168
   Dead Souls, 7, 62, 96, 106n51, 108-109, 112, 115-116, 125, 128, 207, 214, 217
   Evenings on a Farm near Dikanka, 82n32, 96, 115
   Inspector General, The, 106n51, 109, 115-116, 121n21, 125, 127-128, 207
   Marriage, The, 92n12, 199, 203
   Meditations on the Divine Liturgy, 140
   Mirgorod, 82n32, 116, 121, 168
   Nevsky Prospect, 8, 67, 80-81, 120, 131-132, 168, 175, 195, 214, 218
   The Notes of a Madman, 8
   The Overcoat, 7, 81, 98-99, 120n21, 142n72, 184, 199
   The Petersburg Tales, 67, 80, 92n12, 97n32, 101, 107n52, 122, 142, 149, 151, 174-175, 196
   Selected Passages from Correspondence with Friends, 125, 218
   Taras Bulba, 82, 121, 199
Goncharov, S. A., 142
Griboedov, Alexander, 60, 81
   Woe from Wit, 60
Grigoryev, Apollon, 9-10
grotesque, the, 115, 121-123, 128, 129, 135-136, 157, 169, 173-174, 192-193, 196-197, 200-201, 208, 210-211, 216
Gukovsky, Grigory, 128, 172

H

Hakobian (Akopian), Levon, 194, 205
Hoffmann, E. T. A., 168-170, 173, 172, 175-178, 208
Holquist, Michael, 146

I

Iampolski, Mikhail, 189
idiomatic expressions, 8-9, 61, 82, 86, 91, 99, 103-104, 172, 202, *see also* phraseological units
Ilie, Paul, 210
Incarnation, 51, 144-145
Ionin, Georgy, 191, 200

J

Jakobson, Roman, 121
Jentsch, Ernst, 176
joke, 10, 85, 91, 110, 112-113, 137, 146-147, 200, 219, *see also* anecdote, laughter
Jung, Carl Gustav, 164

K

Kafka, Franz, 207-209, 218
   The Metamorphosis, 207-209
Karlinsky, Simon, 179, 209
Karst, Roman, 207
Kharms, Daniil, 184-189, 204-205, 218
Koreisha, Ivan Yakovlevich, 155-160
Kotliarevsky, I. P., 200
Kozintsev, Grigory, 192

Index

L

Lacan, Jacques, 212-213
language game, 9, 85-86, 91-92, 97, 104, 123, 190, 219
laughter, 112-119, 121-123, 133-136, *see also* joke, anecdote
Leskov, Nikolai, 98, 156, 160
Lissitsky, El, 205
Lotman, Yuri, 106, 123, 174

M

Makogonenko, Georgy, 129
Malevich, Kazimir, 205
Mandelshtam, Osip, 53
Mandel'shtam, I. E., 117-118, 161
Mann, Yuri, 123, 129, 134, 172-174, 181, 208-209
Markovich, Vladimir, 97n32, 101
McCarthy, Michael, 104
Merezhkovsky, Dmitry, 133-134, 208
Merrill, Reed, 197, 200
Mesmer, A. F., 79
Meyerhold, Vsevolod, 202-203
Miller, F. B., 158
Mochulsky, Konstantin, 138, 146
Morson, Gary Saul, 181, 183
Moscow, 70, 114, 121, 151n90, 156-157, 175, 193, 203
    Preobrazhensky Hospital, 156-158
Moscow Observer, The, 9n4, 113-114, 150n87, 161

N

Nabokov, Vladimir, 108, 117, 153, 166
nonsense, 10, 102, 107, 173, 179, 183-185, 207, 218-219, *see also* absurd, absurdity
Northern Bee, The, 9n4, 72, 84, 127, 157

O

Obolensky, Alexander, 134, 138
Oleinikov, Nikolai, 204-205
Orthodox Church, 51, 69, 113, 141, *see also* Christianity
Ostrovsky, Alexander, 156

P

Peter the Great, 65, 79, 145
Petersburg, *see* St. Petersburg
Petersburg text of Russian literature, 106, 107n52, 150, 174, 194

phraseological units, 95, *see also* idiomatic expressions
Pletneva, Alexandra, 155
Popova, Liubov, 205
Preis, Alexander, 191
Propp, Vladimir, 120, 121n21, 123
Pushkin, Alexander, 9n4, 61, 80, 84, 94, 106-107, 109, 112-114, 116, 118, 124, 137, 144, 150n87, 164-166, 170
    Eugene Onegin, 94
    The Bronze Horseman, 61
    The Gabrieliad, 144, 165-166

R

Rabelais, François, 121, 135-136
Rassovskaya, L. P., 144, 166
realism, 122, 170-172, 174-175, 182, 184, 207n210, 219
Redfern, Walter, 8, 103
Remizov, Alexey, 98
Rodchenko, Alexander, 205
romanticism, 7, 121n21, 122, 137, 168, 170, 172, 174-175, 219
Rozanov, Vasily, 108, 163
Russian Formalist school, 10, 97-99, 104, 120, 121n21, 128, 161, 172, 198, 206, *see also* skaz

S

sacred space, 142, 147, 193
sacred time, 142, *see also* Annunciation
Saltykov-Shchedrin, Mikhail, 156
satire, 8, 10, 114, 124-125, 127, 130-132, 144, 146, 171, 185, 219
Schiller, Johann Christoph Friedrich, 168
Scollins, Kathleen, 145
Shklovsky, Viktor, 103
Shostakovich, Dmitry, 184, 191, 193-204, 206, 218
    The Nose, 184, 191-193, 196, 198-199, 202-205
Shukman, Ann, 167, 181
skaz, 9, 86, 97-100, 102, 120n21, 198-199, *see also* Russian Formalist school
Slonimsky, Alexander, 120, 121n21, 123, 163
socialist realism, 171, 184, 219
Stasov, V. V., 93

Index

Stendhal (Marie-Henri Beyle), 182
Stender-Petersen, Adolf, 169, 170, 174
Sterne, Laurence, 119, 122, 169, 172
Strong, Robert L., 171
St. Petersburg (Saint Petersburg, Petersburg), 7, 9, 51-53, 57, 59, 66-72, 80-82, 93, 100-101, 106, 107n52, 128, 132, 144-147, 149-150, 156-157, 161, 169, 174-175, 184, 186-187, 193-194, 199, 205, 214, 217
    Admiralty, 59
    Anichkov Bridge, 217
    Catherine Canal, 58
    English embankment, 59
    Fontanka River, 52, 58, 80
    Gostiny Dvor, 9n4, 194n181
    Kazan Cathedral, 9n4, 65, 90, 128, 130, 136, 139, 142-143, 146, 153, 163, 193, 194n182, 199, 217
    Konyushennaya Street, 101, 132, 217
    Kunstkamera, 78
    Moika River, 52, 58, 80
    Neva River, 58-59, 62
    Nevsky Prospect, 8, 53, 60, 80-81, 101, 130, 132, 145, 147, 195, 217
    Police Bridge, 217
    Sadovaya Street, 58, 66, 145
    St. Isaac's Bridge, 58-59, 62, 75, 102
    Tauride Garden, 132, 217
    Voznesensky Prospect, 52, 58, 140, 147, 217
surrealism, 207n210, 209-211, 219

T

Table of Ranks, 65
Tatlin, Vladimir, 205
Tcherkashina, Marina, 196
Tieck, J. L., 168-169, 172
Tolstoy, Leo, 54, 156, 170, 182-183
    Youth, 156
    War and Peace, 54
Toporov, V. N., 106
Tsvetaeva, Anastasia, 215n235
Tsvetaeva, Marina, 215n235
Turgenev, Ivan, 63, 77

Tynianov, Yuri, 98, 120-121, 123, 183, 201

U

Ulyanov, Nikolai, 134-139
uncanny, the, 134, 175-177
Uspensky, Boris, 123, 149-150

V

Vaiskopf, Mikhail, 139-144, 166
Van Gogh, Vincent Willem, 213
Vinogradov, Victor, 7n1, 98-100, 107, 118-120, 161, 164, 169-170
Vyazemsky, Petr, 80, 94
Vvedensky, Alexander, 184, 205

W

Wittgenstein, Ludwig, 85

Y

Yermakov, Ivan, 161, 163-167, 175, 177, 203, *see also* Freud

Z

Zamyatin, Yevgeni, 191
Zhirmunsky, Victor, 172
Zenkovsky, Vasily, 117, 134, 137, 163

Acknowledgements

I would like to thank the editorial team of Academic Studies Press for their work on every stage of the production of this book. My special thanks go to the Acquisitions Associate Ekaterina Yanduganova and Production Editor Kira Nemirovsky. Additionally, I thank Dalia Geffen for her careful copyediting of this book's manuscript.

Two anonymous readers appointed by ASP gave me confidence to proceed with the book's publication. Their insightful comments were extremely valuable. I appreciate their taking time to read my manuscript and give me feedback.

I would like to thank Julia Belomlinsky for her skillful artwork that she produced in 2018 specifically for this book – six illustrations of the scenes from Nikolai Gogol's story "The Nose."

I would also like to thank Nikita Eliseev of The National Library of Russia, Saint Petersburg and Rakhil Kane of Saint Petersburg State Theater Library for their guidance in my library research.

I am thankful to many Princeton undergraduates who read "The Nose" in my courses and enjoyed Gogol's wordplay and his verbal humor. Many years ago, their interest in Gogol's artistic language provided motivation for me to embark on this project.

Finally, I am grateful to my family: my mother Lucy and my daughter Julia for their patience and care, my grandsons Leopold, Kostas and Felix for their life-giving energy, and to my husband Gregory for his love and support.

www.ingramcontent.com/pod-product-compliance
Lightning Source LLC
Chambersburg PA
CBHW070349240426
43671CB00013BA/2444